CHILD ABUSE AND NEGLECT

REFERENCE BOOKS ON FAMILY ISSUES
(VOL. 15)

GARLAND REFERENCE LIBRARY
OF SOCIAL SCIENCE
(VOL. 423)

Reference Books
On Family Issues

CHILD ABUSE AND NEGLECT
An Information and Reference Guide

Timothy J. Iverson
Marilyn Segal

GARLAND PUBLISHING, INC. • NEW YORK & LONDON
1990

Library of Congress Cataloging-in-Publication Data

Iverson, Timothy J., 1959–
   Child abuse and neglect: an information and reference guide /
Timothy J. Iverson, Marilyn Segal.
      p. cm. — (Reference books on family issues; vol. 15)
(Garland reference library of social science; vol. 423)
   Includes bibliographical references.
   ISBN 0–8240–7776–8 (alk. paper); 0–8153–0468–4 (pbk. alk. paper)
   1. Child abuse—United States. 2. Abused children—Services for—
United States. 3. Child abuse—United States—Prevention.
4. Social work with children—United States. I. Segal, Marilyn M.
II. Title. III. Series: Reference books on family issues; v. 15.
IV. Series: Garland reference library of social science; v. 423.
HV741.I94   1990
362.7'6'0973—dc20   89–71495
                                                                  CIP

Printed on acid-free, 250-year-life paper
Manufactured in the United States of America

To

Travis and Shawn

Contents

Preface

The plight of abused and neglected children has received unprecedented attention during the past thirty years. Policies, programs, and initiatives have sprung up all over the country. Media attention has brought a dramatic increase in awareness of the problems of child physical and sexual abuse. Yet the problem is simply not being solved.

Children continue to be maltreated at alarming rates, and many of our programming efforts are understaffed, underfunded, and inefficient. Although all states mandate reporting of suspected child abuse and neglect, many cases go unreported. Investigations are often conducted by individuals who are undertrained and overburdened. There is often inadequate follow-up to prevent repeated episodes of maltreatment and the measures taken to improve long-term family functioning are rarely sufficient.

The reasons behind our inadequate response to the problems of child abuse and neglect are complex. While the importance of protecting children is recognized, many individuals are uncomfortable invading the privacy of the family. Furthermore, many types of maltreatment are not qualitatively different from "normal" childrearing practices; they are only more extreme. When society condones spanking, occasional bruises are tolerable. When parents must work but child care is not accessible, leaving children alone for a few hours can easily appear justified. When a society values and rewards aggressiveness, monetary and physical strength, and individualism to such a degree that humanitarian considerations become secondary, prioritizing children's needs is impossible. When the inevitable occurs, however, and a child is injured, these behaviors suddenly become maltreatment.

We are currently at a crossroads. Children are beginning to be viewed as our nation's greatest asset, and there is little doubt that the quality of children's early environment greatly impacts the individuals they are to become. We have yet, however, to act upon this knowledge. We have passed laws, engaged in public awareness campaigns, initiated a variety of programs, and accumulated a vast literature on the importance of preventing abuse and neglect, but we have not mounted a serious, unified effort to assure that our children are provided for in the optimal way.

The goals of this book are threefold. In the first two chapters, the problems of child abuse and neglect are placed in the context of an evolving society. Historical issues are explored, and current theories and definitions are discussed in reference to our current childrearing standards. In addition, the critical importance of expanding and improving our research methodology in regard to maltreatment is discussed. Understanding the social context of maltreatment and the procedures for studying this phenomenon provides the foundation for managing the complex problems of child abuse and neglect.

The second goal of the book is to provide an overview of the characteristics of maltreated children and their families. Chapters 3 and 4 address these issues and are organized according to the factors promoting maladaptive parenting and the ways children's development manifests the effects of such parenting. These chapters were organized by characteristics rather than by type of maltreatment in an effort to provide a format conducive to identifying risk factors of maladaptive parent-child interactions, rather than focusing on discrete factors which can be labeled physically abusive, neglectful, etc.

The final goal of this book is to serve as a resource to the helping professions. Chapter 5 familiarizes the reader with the current reporting and intervention procedures in cases of maltreatment, and Chapter 6 and the appendices provide information on prevention and resources available for additional information. In addition, the references cited throughout the text were selected to provide the reader with a broad base of additional literature to consult for more detailed information on specific areas of interest.

It is hoped that these three goals will converge to provide the reader with a broad-based understanding of abuse and neglect in our society and provide sufficient information for the reader to work effectively within the system to promote adaptive parenting and prevent future cases of maltreatment.

Without the contribution of several individuals, this book would not have been possible. The resource information can be largely attributed to Sandy Peterson and Claire Campbell, both of whom spent countless hours compiling the information and assuring its accuracy. Suzan L. Tanner, Aharona Surowitz, and Noreen Weber were paramount in providing supporting information from both the child abuse literature and interviews with individuals involved in the field. A special thanks is extended to Pat Neibel, director of the Broward County Child Protection Team, for the time she took to provide information and photographs relevant to identifying maltreatment. Finally, the many hours spent editing and preparing the manuscript were largely the role of LaVonne Iverson, and her tireless perseverance is very much appreciated.

Child Abuse and Neglect

Chapter 1

Perspectives on Child Maltreatment

"Child abuse cannot occur in the absence of social values consistent with the acceptance of interpersonal violence."

"Although values certainly contribute to the potential for abuse, the characteristics of the perpetrators should be of primary interest in explaining maltreatment. Social or situational explanations simply do not account for the fact that some people mistreat their children and others do not."

"Everybody has their breaking point. Even the most psychologically healthy individual can mistreat his or her child if subjected to sufficient stress."

"We can stop the hitting, the sexual acts, the deprivation, but we cannot teach parents to love their kids. This emotional cavity represents a fundamental character flaw in all maltreating parents."

Child abuse and neglect can be approached from many perspectives. Whereas everyone agrees that child maltreatment is an unfortunate, sometimes horrifying fact of modern existence, viewpoints diverge considerably in regard to how the problem can be best understood and most effectively addressed. Like the proverbial blind men describing the elephant, however, perspectives which differ considerably at first glance are actually complementary aspects of a complex, multifaceted phenomenon.

Just as various theoretical and definitional perspectives contribute to our understanding of maltreatment, historical and cultural issues add pieces to the puzzle. Historical perspectives illustrate how maltreatment has evolved into a high priority social issue and provide insight into the relationship among different causal explanations for child abuse and neglect. Theoretical perspectives, in turn, provide insight into the various factors contributing to the occurrence of maltreatment and offer schemes for conceptually organizing this information. Definitional issues, especially culturally based biases in defining maltreatment, depict the normative attitudes which determine how individuals and society respond to concerns about childrearing. Awareness of these various pieces of the puzzle provides the basic foundation for understanding the perpetuation of maltreatment in a presumably enlightened society.

The goals of this chapter are to explore the origins, evolution, and current status of child abuse and neglect in modern society and present an overview of the theoretical models that have been used to explain the dynamics of child maltreatment. After discussing the prevalence of the problem of child abuse, the evolution of maltreatment as a major social issue is explored through a historical review of childrearing practices and the changing concepts of what constitutes unacceptable treatment of children.   Subsequently, child abuse models are examined, and a framework for organizing these models in accordance with their etiological focus is provided. The final section examines definitions of child maltreatment as a reflection of the value system of a society and as a barometer of society's concern for the health and welfare of children.

The Prevalence of Maltreatment

Child abuse and neglect have become priority issues at national, state, and local levels during the past two decades. As a result, an enormous amount of information is now available about child maltreatment. Several national agencies exist which are devoted to studying and increasing public awareness of issues surrounding child abuse and neglect and several major universities have produced a huge body of research about the causes, effects, and treatment of child abuse and neglect. Yet the problem is simply not being solved.

The American Humane Association (1986) estimated that over 1.7 million reports of child abuse or neglect were filed in the United States in 1984. Over half of the children for whom data were available were victims of physical neglect (55%), while approximately 25% suffered some form of physical injury. Approximately 13% and 11% were victims of sexual and emotional abuse, respectively, and about 10% of the victims suffered other forms of maltreatment.

The 1.7 million reports documented by the AHA represent a 158% increase in the number of cases reported in 1976. The extent to which this increase reflects an increase in the actual incidence of child maltreatment or an increase in public awareness and action is unclear. The explosion of interest and attention suggests that an increase in public awareness is at least in part responsible for the rise in reporting. Regardless of the reason, the steady increase in reports suggests that there is still a significant number of children who continue to be mistreated. In fact, estimates of the number of children who are maltreated each year range as high as 6.5 million for physical abuse alone (Straus & Kantor, 1987, p. 49).

The number of children abused and neglected each year, even by conservative estimates, is staggering. At first glance, it seems paradoxical that a society which is expanding rapidly in technology, communications, and awareness of human rights can simultaneously have a child maltreatment problem of such proportions. Yet, upon closer examination, it appears that these forces which "enlighten" a society also tend to heighten awareness to the plights of that society. The following overview of child abuse and neglect through the ages will illustrate the social evolution of maltreatment and provide insight into the development of our modern perspectives.

Historical Perspectives

Ancient times

Child maltreatment, as we define it today, was at one time permissible behavior. In ancient times, children were brought into the world to serve and carry on the family line. Infants were solely their parents' possessions and had no rights of their own (Radbill, 1980). Consequently, the fate of a child depended entirely upon the needs and desires of the parent. Such a family structure was very conducive to maltreatment.

Historically children could be killed by their parents until they were granted the right to live, usually through some early ritual (Radbill, 1980). Doing away with unwanted infants was apparently not uncommon and certainly was considered within the boundaries of acceptable social behavior. Early philosophers clearly supported infanticide in cases where children were illegitimate or for some reason were unlikely to contribute to the good of society. Such reasons included physical deformities, mental deficiencies, or behavior suggesting the child may be "unnatural" or "abnormal." Similarly, physicians as early as the second century A.D. considered infanticide a legitimate, even desirable, option for children who were born at risk for later physical or behavioral problems (Lynch, 1985). Destroying children who were bound to be a burden on society was viewed as promoting the general welfare of society.

Historically, even after children were granted the right to live, there was no assurance that they would be appropriately or adequately cared for. Children had very little "use" until they were old enough to physically aid their parents in the home and in the workplace, and the worth of these young children was largely dependent upon their potential utility in this capacity. Children who were mentally or physically handicapped were less likely to contribute to the family, and consequently these children were particularly prone to being abused and neglected.

Ancient society also promoted maltreatment through its child labor practices with young children being subjected to harsh and demanding working conditions. For example, children as young as six years old were used as cheap labor, beaten, purposely malnourished, and subjected to unhealthy conditions, all in the name of employment (Radbill, 1980). Interestingly, child labor continues to be an issue in our society, particularly in agriculture. Legislation regulating the use of children on farms has been passed as recently as 1977.

Physical abuse and neglect, by our current definitions, were tolerated historically because these behaviors were often consistent with the needs of parents and society. Sexual abuse of children, other than incest, was tolerated for much the same reason. Historically, children were "loaned to guests" or hired out for sexual use (Radbill, 1980). Children were easy targets for the lusts and perversions of adults simply because they were expected to be obedient. Incest, on the other hand, even in ancient times was viewed as taboo (Radbill, 1980). Victims of incest were often shunned and subjected to abusive treatment. The philosopher, Plato, believed that children conceived incestuously "if they cannot prevent its birth, [be disposed of] on the understanding that no such child can be reared" (translated by Cornford, 1975). From early times to the present, incest has been viewed as qualitatively different, somehow more deviant, than other forms of maltreatment.

When we assume an historical perspective, maltreatment in ancient times appears to be more of a societal phenomena than a function of deviant individuals. Physical abuse, neglect, and, to some degree, sexual abuse were considered to be socially acceptable behavior. Given the needs and structure of ancient society, maltreatment was, from their perspective, adaptive behavior. Over time, with changes in social, economic and political realities, the norms and attitudes about the treatment of children have also changed.

The Renaissance

The Renaissance, from approximately 1300-1700 A.D., was a period of dramatic change in social values and attitudes. The pursuit of learning, exploration, and individualism were hallmarks of this period. Social changes involved the emerging recognition of certain inherent rights for individuals regardless of who they were. In conjunction with these changes, people started to recognize that children had rights and that the mistreatments being tolerated may be an infringement of these rights. By the fifteenth and sixteenth centuries, writers and philosophers began recognizing the need to demonstrate compassion toward the weak, and during the seventeenth century both the child within the family and the family within society were gaining increasing status (Radbill, 1980).

These social changes were creating a milieu in which child maltreatment would be viewed as less and less within the limits of acceptable social behavior and increasingly attributed to unkindness or deviancy on the part of the perpetrator. These changes in attitudes represent the historical roots of today's theoretical debates over whether child maltreatment should continue to be thought of as a societal problem or whether it is caused by individual character flaws or inadequacies.

Modern times

Although attitudes towards children had been changing throughout the Renaissance, the nineteenth century brought the first real social reforms for the protection of children. References to the inappropriateness of inflicting physical injury on children were beginning to emerge in the medical literature by the early 1800's (Lynch, 1985). In America, a law providing for the care of neglected children had appeared in the mid-1700's (Folks, 1902), and the mid-1800's brought unprecedented publicity to the plight of maltreated children.

The publicity of the mid-1800's was initiated by the often-cited case of Mary Ellen, a severely abused child whose plight received national publicity in 1874. The New York Times followed the case, in part because of the political notoriety of Henry Bergh, then president of the Society for the Prevention of Cruelty to Animals (SPCA). With the help of Mr. Bergh, Mary Ellen's case went to court and her stepmother was found guilty of assault and battery (Williams, 1983). In addition to "saving" little Mary Ellen, this case and its resulting publicity was instrumental in the development of the Society for the Prevention of Cruelty to Children (SPCC), a group which was to provide both child advocacy and child protection. The SPCC was very active for several years subsequent to its creation and the rights of children continued to become more explicit and wide-reaching during this time.

The nineteenth-century outcry for the protection of children began to diminish in the early twentieth century. National attention was diverted to more immediate crises such as World War I, and, consequently, financial support for the SPCC agencies was considerably diminished (Williams, 1983). Despite the social reforms which had occurred during the late 1800's, child welfare and protective services for children remained dismal. Children's rights had been formally recognized but action directly addressing maltreatment was brief and this action diminished as the sensationalism died away.

The early 1900's saw little improvement in the protection of children. The Social Security Act of 1930 mandated child welfare services for neglected, dependent children (DeFrancis, 1973, p. 303), but in the absence of a public outcry such as that which occurred during the late 1800's, the actions taken were grossly inadequate compared to what we today presume to have been the magnitude of the problem.

The current wave

The early 1960's brought the current wave of interest in child maltreatment. Since the publication of Henry Kempe's landmark article on a symptom cluster indicative of physical abuse (Kempe et al., 1962), legislation for protecting children has flourished, and many professions have become involved in protecting and treating maltreated children. The literature relevant to child maltreatment from the fields of medicine, psychology and social work would now fill volumes. This recent rediscovery of the problem of child maltreatment again paralleled broader social movements, such as the civil rights movements, which critically re-examined the social values and morals of the time, particularly the treatment of minorities. Within the context of such a social re-evaluation, the maltreatment of children again became the source of public outcry.

The sensationalism which has surrounded child abuse and neglect for the past few decades is now again beginning to diminish. Social attitudes, however, appear to be changing for the better, fueled by the widespread legislation for protecting children and our ever-expanding knowledge about child development. Child maltreatment, at least as it is characterized by severe physical abuse, neglect, and sexual abuse, is clearly no longer considered to be within the norms of acceptable social behavior in our society.

True attitudinal changes within a society, however, are slow to occur. Whereas severe cases of maltreatment are now clearly deviant in reference to our social norms, many accepted behaviors and childrearing practices share common denominators with maltreatment. Spanking, as long as it does not cause bruises, is currently accepted in our society. Similarly, children are frequently threatened and coerced to get them to behave. Power, individualism, and privacy remain exceptionally highly regarded values in our society. These "values," when carried too far, are entirely consistent with the dynamics of abuse.

From a social-historical perspective, then, it appears we are at a juncture. Child abuse and neglect are considered unacceptable in our society, but many of the social forces which give rise to maltreatment are still very much a part of our social structure. Looking toward the future, continuing efforts are needed to promote healthy childrearing practices and reduce maltreatment. As the sensationalism of the past decades dies away, complacency about maltreatment is a growing danger.

Section summary

Historical perspectives depict maltreatment as a social problem related to societal values and attitudes. Many behaviors which we now consider abusive or neglectful were historically within the parameters of acceptable social behavior. As individual rights and the social responsibility to uphold these rights have increased, the manner in which children are treated has come under social scrutiny. Maltreatment has come to be viewed as socially unacceptable or deviant behavior, but many of the underlying social values consistent with maltreatment have persisted. Childrearing practices which overcome these potentially harmful forces must be strived for continually.

The evolution of maltreatment into a social problem has given rise to several theoretical and definitional issues. In reference to theory, debate continues over whether maltreatment continues to be a function of the social values and attitudes which permit maltreatment within certain limits, or specific etiological factors which increase risk and directly precipitate maltreatment. In regard to definitions, differences abound regarding the acceptable limits of parental authority and behavior. For example, if it is socially acceptable to spank a child, what factors distinguish physical discipline from abuse? Similarly, the role that cultural beliefs and traditions play in determining appropriate parental behavior frequently leads to differences in opinion about what constitutes maltreatment. Because the historical evolution of maltreatment as a social phenomenon has given rise to the theoretical and definitional issues with which we now struggle, these issues can best be understood within the context of their historical roots.

History and Theory

The evolution of maltreatment as a social phenomenon outlined in the preceding section provides a practical way to conceptually organize the various etiological theories of child maltreatment. Current theoretical perspectives, although diverse, tend to address three general issues. These issues involve 1) sociocultural attitudes conducive to maltreatment, 2) individual characteristics of the perpetrators, and 3) environmental factors or stressors which contribute to the maltreatment of children. Current models of child abuse and neglect emphasize these three etiological factors to different degrees and in different ways. Before presenting the major models of maltreatment, let us use the historical perspectives to better understand how the primary etiological factors interrelate.

The stages of social change

The historical evolution of maltreatment as a social phenomenon can be arbitrarily divided into three stages, representing *historical acceptance, tentative prohibition,* and (one hopes) *prohibition.* These stages, as they relate to the sociocultural, individual, and environmental etiological factors, are summarized in Table 1-1.

TABLE 1-1

The etiology of maltreatment through the ages

Period	Stage	Etiological Factors		
		Individual	Social	Environmental
Ancient times through the Middle Ages	*Acceptance:* Maltreatment, except incest, was within the limits of acceptable behavior. In some cases, socially promoted.	NA since the behavior was not viewed as deviant.	Social attitudes and values consistent with maltreatment allowed it to exist as an unchallenged aspect of society.	Absence of stress was not necessarily a protective factor, but presence of stress probably exacerbated maltreatment.
The Renaissance through the present	*Tentative Prohibition:* Children's rights recognized, efforts to protect children in severe cases emerge, but many social values remain consistent with maltreatment.	Perpetrator begin to be seen as socially deviant, sources of pathology sought.	Social attitudes become increasingly incompatible with maltreatment. This begins with most severe cases. As social awareness increases, the tolerance for maltreatment decreases.	Environmental stress most likely to cause maltreatment at this stage. Social expectations are quickly changing and stress may cause regression to more familiar or primitive behaviors. Absence of stress is a protective factor.
Future	*Prohibition:* Children's rights fully recognized, social values consistent with providing necessary actions to promote child development.	Perpetrators are viewed as deviant in terms of social norms. Individual factors become the primary cause of maltreatment.	Social values and attitudes are incompatible with maltreatment. Maltreatment not attributed to social conditions.	Environmental stress unlikely to cause maltreatment in "normal" individuals, as fundamental attitudes are not consistent with maltreatment. Will interact with dysfunctional individual characteristics to produce maltreatment.

As depicted in Table 1-1, sociocultural attitudes were historically responsible for the perpetration of maltreatment (stage 1). Because maltreatment in early times was within the boundaries of acceptable social behavior, individual characteristics of perpetrators were not an issue.

As social values narrowed (stage 2), maltreatment became increasingly perceived as outside the limits of acceptable social behavior. Consequently, the perpetrators of maltreatment came to be seen as increasingly socially deviant, and the characteristics setting them apart from nonperpetrators became of interest. This social prohibition of maltreatment was and continues to be tentative, however, because values and behavior patterns consistent with maltreatment continue to dominate our social structure.

The extent to which these underlying social values contribute to dysfunctional parent-child relations decreases as social values change, and different segments of society differ in the rate in which these changes are internalized. If social values continue to evolve in this manner, Stage 3 (*prohibition*) will eventually result. Ideally, if Stage 3 were ever achieved, social values and attitudes would be entirely incompatible with abuse and neglect, and maltreatment would be entirely a function of individual problems leading to deviant social behavior.

The relationship among sociocultural, individual, and environmental etiological factors can be illustrated in any social domain involving rapidly evolving social norms and values. Similar progressions from social acceptance to prohibition are currently evident with, for example, smoking, sexual behaviors and civil rights. As more is learned about the health hazards of smoking, for example, increasing social limits are being established while at the same time social forces remain evident which actually promote smoking.

Current etiological factors

Etiological factors at our current social stage, *tentative prohibition*, reflect changing social expectations, the consequent trend for maltreatment to be considered socially deviant, and conditions which cause individuals to behave in a manner inconsistent with these social expectations. These conditions include 1) differences in experience with evolving sociocultural expectations, 2) intrapersonal characteristics which lead to behavior which is dysfunctional by current community standards, and 3) environmental factors leading to stress and a consequent regression to more familiar or primitive behavior patterns, patterns which are becoming socially unacceptable. This set of conditions and the contribution they make to maltreatment are summarized in Table 1-2.

The etiological factors in Table 1-2 are all currently operative. They contribute to maltreatment in different ways, differentially affect various segments of the population, and imply different strategies for the prevention and treatment of child abuse and neglect. Within this context, various models of maltreatment can be utilized in a complementary manner, each contributing unique and important information. By keeping in mind the evolutionary process behind the etiological factors, the models presented below can be organized in an integrative manner and be subsequently researched and utilized in a comprehensive context.

TABLE 1-2
Etiological processes during the stage of tentative prohibition

Etiological Factors	Examples/Sources	Causative Process	Interventions
Differences in experience	Isolation, culturally specific practices	Parenting behaviors are based on norms or beliefs subscribed by the perpetrators, but not accepted by the larger society.	Education, parent teaching, outreach
Environmental stress	Difficult child, family problems, occupational stress	Precipitates or exacerbates regressive behavior, including maltreatment. If pervasive, may cause exhaustion and helplessness or "giving up."	Social programs or crisis counseling to reduce stress. Teaching more adaptive coping behaviors.
Intrapersonal factors	Cognitive deficits, personality traits, interpersonal deficits	Characteristics interfere with learning, coping with stress, and the capacity for healthy parent-child relationships.	Therapy/counseling, supervision

TABLE 1-3
Major models of maltreatment

Model	Type of Maltreatment	Etiological Emphasis			Citations
		Individual Pathology	Social Conditions	Environmental Conditions	
Individual-psychological	PA, SA, N	yes	no	somewhat	Kempe et al, 1968 Steele & Pollack, 1968, 1974; Groth & Birnbaum, 1978 (SA) Polansky, 1981 (N)
Social learning	PA	no	yes	yes	Straus, Gelles, & Steinmetz, 1980; Gelles, 1983
Social	PA	no	yes	yes	Gil, 1970
Ecological	PA, N	yes	yes	yes	Bronfenbrenner, 1979 Garbarino, 1977 Garbarino & Gilliam, 1980
Transactional	PA, N, SA	yes	yes	yes	Cicchetti & Rizley, 1981
Four-factor model of sexual abuse	SA	yes	yes	yes	Finkelhor, 1986 Finkelhor & Browne, 1985 Browne & Finkelhor, 1986
The stages of sexual abuse	SA	NA			Sgroi, Blick, & Porter, 1982

Models of Child Abuse and Neglect

The above section described how the sociocultural, individual, and environmental etiological factors can all play concurrent roles in maintaining child abuse and neglect. The theories to be discussed in this section elaborate on these factors and explore the specific mechanisms by which the factors operate to precipitate and maintain abusive environments. Table 1-3 summarizes the primary emphases of the models to be discussed, and provides references for further reading. The skeletons of these theories are presented in the following pages. Most of the models to be discussed are either generic or address physical abuse and neglect. Finkelhor and Sgroi's models and the individual-psychological model are applicable to sexual abuse, but very little writing, either empirical or conceptual, exists for emotional abuse.

The Individual-Psychological Model

Physical abuse

Early studies on child abuse (Kempe, et al., 1962; Galdston, 1965; Steele and Pollock, 1968) portrayed the causes of abuse as arising primarily from the perpetrators' psychological problems. The "psychopathological model" of child abuse postulates that the parent who abuses suffers from a psychological pathology or sickness that accounts for maltreating a child. Individual-psychological theories are primarily explanatory, rather than conceptual, in nature. In other words, this model proposes variables which predispose certain individuals to abuse or neglect rather than organizing these variables within a descriptive conceptual framework.

Several characteristics have been hypothesized to distinguish maltreating parents from nonmaltreating parents. Early authors described perpetrators of physical abuse with a variety of characteristics, including impulsivity, immaturity, depression (Steele and Pollock, 1968; Kempe et al., 1962; Bennie and Sclare, 1969), and poor emotional control and inadequacy (Bennie and Sclare, 1969). In addition, perpetrators were thought to be self-centered, hypersensitive, and quick to react with poorly controlled aggression (Kempe et al., 1962), to have pervasive anger (Zalba, 1971), and to be dependent, egocentric, narcissistic, demanding, and insecure (Steele and Pollock, 1968). The individual/psychological model, which concentrates on "kinds of people" theories, has defined child abuse as qualitatively deviant from normal caregiver-child relationships.

Sexual abuse

Discussions of sexual abuse most commonly invoke the individual-psychological model. This is not surprising in view of the traditional belief that sexual abuse is somehow different, more deviant, than other forms of maltreatment. Perpetrators of sexual abuse have been described as emotionally immature, having low self-esteem, and being generally ineffective in their interpersonal relationships (Hammer & Glueck, 1957; Groth & Birnbaum, 1978; Loss & Glancy, 1983). Panton (1978) portrays sexually abusive adults as anxious, inadequate individuals who feel insecure in their associations with others and who expect rejection and failure in adult heterosexual advances. Groth (1982) characterizes sexually abusive fathers as either fixated or regressed, depending upon their primary sexual orientation and level of sociosexual development. In psychodynamic theories that rely on Oedipal dynamics, sexual abusers are described as having intense conflicts about their mothers that make it difficult or impossible for them to relate to adult women (e.g., Hammer & Glueck, 1957).

Neglect

Neglect, although more typically viewed as a function of adverse environmental conditions, has also been conceptualized as resulting from the character deficits of neglectful parents. Although ecological factors are not discounted, Polansky and his colleagues (Polansky et al., 1981; Polansky et al., 1985) view neglect as resulting largely from mothers' personality deficits, such as "*infantilism*" and "*apathy-futility*". Polansky et al. (1985) suggest that the loneliness and isolation characteristic of neglectful mothers may be largely a result of these personality characteristics. For example, neglectful mothers are discussed as being less able to utilize available support systems rather than actually lacking access to these support systems.

It is clear from the above descriptions that the individual-psychological model of maltreatment is primarily concerned with characteristics which make perpetrators of maltreatment different from nonperpetrators. Sociocultural and environmental factors receive little attention in theories of this nature. Consequently, this perspective leads to interventions which focus on changing the perpetrators. By remediating the psychopathology of the perpetrators, treatment is meant to increase the ability of the adult to interact with others in an appropriate, adaptive, manner.

Individual-psychological theories of maltreatment have been subjected to more empirical testing than other theories of maltreatment. Chapter 3 discusses the research on maltreating parents in more detail. Briefly, many studies are available which compare abusive parents to either nonabusive parents or to standardization samples, and a significant number of these studies do demonstrate elevated levels of personality dysfunction or maladaptive interpersonal behavior in the maltreatment samples. However, many nonabusive parents also exhibit these characteristics, and there is sufficient variability in the research to indicate that the individual-psychological model cannot, in itself, adequately describe the phenomenon of child maltreatment.

The Social Learning Model

Social learning theories of human behavior typically involve three components. First, individuals learn certain behavior patterns from prior experience with these behaviors. Second, specific social conditions exist which encourage the use of these previously learned behaviors. Finally, an individual engages in specific behaviors because of the contingencies (rewards or punishments) that these behaviors produce. Social learning theory has been primarily discussed in terms of physical abuse and focuses on prior exposure to violence, social conditions which encourage violence in certain situations, and the rewards and punishments associated with violence toward other family members.

Physical abuse

Straus, Gelles, and Steinmetz (1980) and Gelles (1983) discuss models of physical abuse from a social learning perspective. Straus and Gelles (1980) discuss the importance of the family to the early learning of violent behavior and point out that violence in the family is commonplace in our society. The emotional and moral meaning of violence is also learned in the family, and Straus et al. (1980) postulate that there are three lessons unintentionally learned by children that have grown up in violent families. These lessons are those who love you the most are also those who hit you, there is a moral rightness in hitting other members of the same family, and violence is permissible when other things don't work. These lessons are seen as the link between love and violence which is so much a part of human experience.

Gelles' (1983) exchange/social control theory, which provides a model for all family violence, is based on theories of exchange and social control. Exchange theory involves the assumptions that human interaction is guided by the pursuit of rewards and the avoidance of punishments or costs and that there is an expectation of reciprocity in exchanging rewards (Gelles and Straus, 1979). When rewards are not reciprocally exchanged, increased anger, resentment, conflict, and violence may result. Social control theory postulates that family violence occurs in the absence of social controls which would bond people to the social order and negatively sanction family members for acts of violence. The contributions of such values as individualism and privacy to the potential for physical abuse are emphasized by this theory.

Gelles (1983) discusses three aspects of social control theory relevant to family violence. First, family members are more likely to use violence in the home when they perceive that the costs of being violent are less than the rewards. Second, the absence of effective social controls over family relations decreases the costs of one family member being violent toward another. Third, certain social and family structures, such as sex-role stereotypes, serve to reduce social control in family relations, and, therefore, reduce the costs and/or increase the rewards of being violent.

Sexual abuse

Although a formal social learning theory of sexual abuse has not been proposed, there has been discussion about causative factors of sexual abuse consistent with social learning theory. Many perpetrators of sexual abuse appear to have been subjected to early sexual contact with adults (Gebhard et al., 1965; Groth & Burgess, 1979; Langevin et al., 1985) and it has been suggested that these early sexual experiences may condition children such that, when they become adults, they find children sexually arousing (Wenet, Clark, & Hunner, 1981). Finkelhor (1986) discusses several possible explanations for the relationship between a history of sexual assault and later perpetration. Explanations consistent with social learning theory include modeling and having internalized parent-child sexual activity as part of an individual's behavioral repertoire through participation in, and possibly having been reinforced for, adult-child sexual contact.

The strengths of social learning theory are that it addresses the manner in which socially sanctioned violence is passed from one generation to the next within families and it looks at the contingencies which may be associated with specific acts of maltreatment. In addition, it explores the ways in which violence may be socially prohibited on one level but sanctioned on another. Consequently, social learning theories are very useful for conceptualizing the contingencies which maintain maltreatment in a given family structure.

The Social Model

Social theories of maltreatment, such as that of Gil (1970), focus on the sociocultural and environmental factors which interact to create a cultural milieu conducive to maltreatment. Theories of social causation assume that, given the appropriate set of social and environmental conditions, anyone can become abusive or neglectful toward their children. Because of this assumption, along with the fact that intervention from a social perspective would focus on changing social conditions rather than individuals, social theories are often seen as being in direct opposition to individual-psychological theories (e.g., Giovanonni & Becerra, 1979).

Gil's theory describes violence toward children as the product of a complex multidimensional process, involving two general organizational components. The first component, labeled "levels of manifestation," is a framework in which different types of abuse and neglect can be conceptualized. The second component, labeled "levels of causation," organizes social and environmental etiological factors according to generality.

Gil (1970) discusses three interrelated levels of manifestation of child abuse. The first is the interpersonal level. This level refers to maltreatment in the home and in childcare settings and is the level on which maltreatment is most commonly discussed. The second level is the institutional level, which refers to the policies and practices of a broad array of childcare, educational, welfare, and correctional institutions and agencies. The accepted use of corporal punishment in the school system, for example, would represent this level of manifestation. The third level of manifestation is the societal level, where the interplay of values and social, economic, and political institutions and processes shape the social policies by which the rights and lives of all children are determined. An example of the third level of manifestation is the traditional lack of legislative emphasis on social programs for young children.

Gil's levels of causation organize factors related to the etiology of maltreatment. The first level of causation involves the dominant social philosophy and value premises of a society, its social, economic, and political institutions, and the quality of human relations to which these institutions, philosophies, and values give rise. In other words, for maltreatment to occur, the most general values of society must be fundamentally consistent with behavior of this nature. The second level of causation involves the social definition of children's rights and the extent to which a society sanctions the use of violence, particularly in the childrearing context. The third level of causation involves environmental factors, such as the stress and frustration resulting from poverty, which may trigger abusive acts. These levels are not independent but exert their influence through multiple interactions with each other (Gil, 1975).

A strength of the social model is that it presents maltreatment as a problem maintained by fundamental social institutions and policies. Consequently, the model is extremely useful for identifying, describing, and directing social policy. The major drawbacks of this model are twofold. First, the generality of the propositions makes it difficult to confirm or disconfirm the theories through empirical testing. Second, the individual differences in response to similar social and environmental circumstances are not directly addressed.

The Ecological Model

The ecological perspective of human development was most fully developed by Urie Bronfenbrenner (1977, 1979), who conceived that an individual develops within a network of environmental systems, each of which are nested inside the next. The intimate relationships between the child and the parents cannot be understood without understanding how the conditions surrounding the family (community, culture, national events) affect the interaction between child and parent. In part, the ecological model provides a framework for organizing the many propositions espoused by the previously discussed theories.

Using the ecological framework of Bronfenbrenner, Garbarino (1977; Garbarino & Gilliam, 1980) presents a systems approach to sociocultural risk. The four systems, the microsystem, mesosystem, exosystem, and macrosystem place the causes and types of maltreatment on a continuum of individual to social cultural contexts.

Garbarino's first system is the microsystem. The microsystem refers to the immediate setting in which the individual experiences and creates reality. The product of a healthy microsystem is a child who successfully deals with more complex, wider spheres of reality. Such a child learns to have self-respect, self-confidence, and to be socially and intellectually competent. Child maltreatment is thought to directly interfere with these developmental tasks.

The next level is termed the mesosystem. The systems on this level involve the relationships between the different social spheres, such as home and school, in which the developing individual experiences reality. The number and the quality of connections between the child's microsystem and mesosystem provides a measure of the mesosystem's strength. Weak links between these systems, such as the only common bond between home and school being the child's participation in both, could be a source of sociocultural risk. Social isolation, or the absence of links at the mesosystem level, is commonly identified as a contributing factor in maltreatment (e.g., Garbarino, 1977; Polansky et al., 1985).

The quality of a child's mesosystems are governed by exosystems where the child himself does not participate but where events occur which have a direct bearing on the adults who interact with the child. These situations include centers of power (such as school boards and planning commissions) and parents' workplaces (which regulate hours worked or job transfers). In exosystems, risk comes about in two ways. First, the parents or other significant adults can be affected in a way that impoverishes their behavior in the child's microsystem. For example, long working hours, traveling, or job stress can adversely affect family life. Second, risk occurs when decisions are made which adversely affect the child directly, such as the school board suspending extracurricular activities or a planning commission commercializing a neighborhood park.

Micro-, meso-, and exosystems are set within the broad ideological and institutional patterns of a particular culture (macrosystems). Risk at the macrosystem level occurs when an ideology or cultural alignment threatens to impoverish children's microsystems and mesosystems or sets exosystems against them. Any social pattern (such as sexism or racism) or societal event that impoverishes the ability and willingness of adults to care for children and for children to learn from adults is a source of developmental risk (Garbarino, 1977).

Garbarino (1977) goes on to describe two processes which lead to abusive behavior. The first process involves the psychopathological assault, either physical, emotional, or sexual, by the parent. Abuse of this nature is seen as resulting from the individual pathology of the parent. The second etiological process is based upon our culture's support of the use of physical punishment and control. For a pattern of maltreatment to occur within families there must be cultural justification for the use of force against children and a generally held belief that children are the property of parents. At this level, the central issue of maltreatment is the misuse of power by adults.

Both the primary advantage and disadvantage of the ecological theory are its breadth. By including a variety of etiological factors at various societal levels, the ecological theory is probably the most comprehensive theory of maltreatment. Because of its complexity and the generality of many of its assumptions, however, it does not lend itself to validation through empirical testing. Like theories of social causation, ecological theories are most useful in broadly conceptualizing maltreatment and directing social policy.

The Transactional Model

Transactional theory is derived largely from the ecological perspective. It focuses on child development in the context of the parent-child relationship and the sociocultural and environmental factors which promote or disrupt this relationship. Cicchetti and Rizley (1981) present a framework for conceptualizing maltreatment which organizes individual, sociocultural, and environmental factors according to whether they increase or decrease the likelihood of maltreatment and according to whether they are temporary or lasting. These factors are respectively labeled potentiating factors, compensatory factors, transient factors, and enduring factors.

Potentiating factors, or factors which increase the likelihood of maltreatment, include sociocultural, individual, and environmental factors, and are grouped according to whether they are transient or enduring. Examples of transient potentiating factors include job loss, divorce, or stress resulting from other environmental factors. Enduring potentiating factors include personality characteristics associated with maltreating parents, social values consistent with maltreatment, and environmental factors such as poverty (Cicchetti & Rizley, 1981).

Compensatory factors decrease the likelihood of maltreatment and also include a variety of factors grouped according to whether they are transient or enduring. Examples of transient compensatory factors include a good job, the availability of social support, and other environmental factors which decrease stress in the family. Enduring compensatory factors include positive personality attributes, good social skills, high intelligence, and other factors contributing to an individual's ability to function adaptively (Cicchetti & Rizley, 1981).

In addition to the above organizational framework, transactional theory highlights parent-child developmental forces. Healthy child development involves adaptive behavioral organization in reference to developmentally salient tasks (Aber & Cicchetti, 1984). For example, a primary research focus of transactional theorists is the study of how maltreatment affects parent-child attachments in the second year of life. By disrupting such attachments, maltreatment is thought to cause the child to be developmentally at risk.

Research support for the transactional perspective has primarily focused on the developmental sequelae of maltreatment. There is ample evidence that maltreatment disrupts the socioemotional functioning of young children (this research is discussed in more detail in Chapter 4), but the long-term implications of this early disruption have not yet been fully delineated.

A unique strength of the transactional theory is its emphasis on factors which decrease the likelihood of maltreatment as well as factors contributing to maltreatment. The inclusion of these compensatory factors allows for the conceptualization and development of active prevention efforts, both with maltreating parents and the child victims.

The Four-Factor Model of Sexual Abuse

The four-factor model of sexual abuse is based on factors which Finkelhor (1986) proposes to organize the available research on why adults sexually abuse children. It is currently the only comprehensive effort to conceptualize what is known about the etiology of sexual abuse. The four factors identified by Finkelhor are emotional congruence, sexual arousal, blockage, and disinhibition. The characteristics discussed are primarily, although not exclusively, aligned with the individual-psychological perspective insofar as they focus on the manner in which sexual abusers differ from nonabusers.

Emotional congruence refers to the apparent "fit" between the emotional needs of adult sexual abusers and the characteristics of children. This congruence may occur because of immaturity, poor self-esteem, or a sense of social inadequacy on the part of the perpetrators. For example, because of a poor sense of social efficacy, perpetrators may gain a false sense of power, respect, or control from sexual behavior with children.

The second factor addresses the issue of becoming sexually aroused by children. Finkelhor (1986) reviews evidence that some sexual abusers show increased physiological arousal to children, and discusses possible mechanisms by which this may occur. For example, sexual arousal may be conditioned by the abuser's experiences as a child or the perpetrator may have been exposed to pornography or others' sexual activities with children, which lead to heightened arousal in similar situations. The processes by which such conditioning may occur are consistent with the propositions of social learning theory discussed earlier.

The third factor discussed by Finkelhor is blockage, which refers to the apparent inability of some sexual abusers to obtain sexual gratification from more socially appropriate sexual activities such as adult heterosexual relationships. Psychodynamic theories, for example, assume that unresolved oedipal conflicts interfere with the ability of an adult male to adaptively relate to adult women. Other possible sources of blockage involve marital stress, traumatic sexual experiences, and exposure to excessively restrictive norms about certain sexual activities such as masturbation.

The final factor discussed by Finkelhor is disinhibition, or the lack of responsiveness on the part of the sexual abuser to the conventional social prohibitions which serve as deterrents. Normal inhibitions may be lacking in individuals with disorders of impulse control, or impulse control may be reduced when an individual is under stress or under the influence of alcohol. Finkelhor (1980) suggests that living with stepchildren may also reduce inhibitions because of either different norms or different exposure to the child at an early age.

Finkelhor's (1986) four-factor model provides a useful conceptualization of the causes of sexual abuse. Although the model was derived largely from empirical data, the validity and relative importance of the factors have not yet been systematically studied in a prospective manner. Still, the model provides a much needed framework for better organizing and understanding what is currently known about sexual abuse.

The Stages of Sexual Abuse

One additional model of sexual abuse, discussed by Sgroi, Blick, and Porter (1982), addresses the stages of sexual abuse. It is not a true etiological model, but does trace the progression of parent-child sexual activity. The stages proposed by Sgroi et al. involve 1) engagement, 2) sexual interaction, 3) secrecy, 4) disclosure, and 5) suppression.

The engagement phase involves the circumstances which allow the abuse to occur. These circumstances include the perpetrator having access and opportunity to molest and the inducements provided by the perpetrator.

The sexual interaction phase involves a progression from less invasive to more invasive sexual activity. For example, early activity may involve stimulating contact through clothing or nudity with no contact, with subsequent activities progressing to masturbation, sexual intercourse, or other highly invasive contacts.

The third phase discussed by Sgroi et al. is secrecy, which allows the perpetrator to avoid accountability and perpetuate the abuse. Secrecy may be maintained by rewards or threats or because the victim values the relationship with the perpetrator and enjoys the special attention he or she is receiving.

Disclosure, the fourth phase, can be either accidental or purposeful. Accidental disclosure occurs, for example, when the abuse is observed by someone, when the child is injured, or when the child acts out sexually. Purposeful disclosure may occur when the child desires to end the abusive relationship or get revenge on the perpetrator.

Finally, the phase of suppression often follows disclosure. Efforts to "forget" the abuse or deny the implications may occur. In addition, the perpetrator may try to undermine the credibility of the victim in an effort to avoid responsibility.

These five stages provide a useful conceptualization for understanding the behaviors of perpetrators and victims. Because this model does not discuss etiological factors, its primary application is in identifying and intervening in cases of sexual abuse rather than identifying causative or preventative measures.

Section summary

The theoretical perspectives reviewed above indicate that maltreatment of children is a multifaceted phenomenon. A single instance of abuse provides a host of embedded questions. What are the characteristics of the individuals directly involved in the abuse incident? What are the accepted societal attitudes, values, and norms? What were the specific environmental factors operating at the time of the incident? Answers to these questions are complex, but the available models of maltreatment, if considered in an integrative fashion, provide useful clues as to where the answers will be found.

Models of maltreatment are in their infancy. Although many possible etiological factors have been proposed, little is known about how these various factors interact with each other. Theories set forth to explain maltreatment are faulted for different reasons. Theories that do not take into account the complexities and interactions of factors associated with abuse are faulted for being naive. Theories that do take into account the complexities are faulted because they cannot be falsified. Further, most theories are primarily concerned with physical abuse and to some degree with neglect and sexual abuse. Emotional abuse has received little attention in the theoretical literature. Yet, the above models provide a starting point, and represent a significant step toward understanding maltreatment.

The historical and theoretical perspectives discussed to this point have been primarily based upon biases consistent with Western philosophies of childrearing. Definitional issues, however, cannot be discussed without some appreciation for cultural differences in what may or may not be considered desirable childrearing practices. The following discussion of cultural perspectives of child maltreatment highlights the importance of cultural relativity in definitions of child abuse and neglect.

Cultural Perspectives

Earlier in this chapter, the manner in which perspectives of maltreatment have changed along a historical dimension was discussed. In a similar vein, individuals from different cultures might diverge considerably in what they judge to be abusive or neglectful behavior. An appreciation of these intercultural differences helps keep our current perspectives and definitions from becoming biased.

Jill Korbin (1980a, 1980b) illustrates how behaviors considered normal for one culture may appear abusive to individuals unfamiliar with those cultural practices. For example, initiation rites for preadolescent children in nonwestern cultures may include beating, induced bleeding, genital operations, or food deprivation. Punishments in nonwestern cultures may include isolation for several days, food deprivation, or cutting a child. Although these behaviors are judged as harsh and cruel by Western standards, Korbin is quick to point out that many of our own practices are seen as just as cruel by "outsiders." Our children face circumcision, painful braces for their teeth, and isolation every night in their "own rooms." One must be careful not to assume that such Western rituals or practices are acceptable simply because we are used to them, whereas the practices of other cultures are clearly abusive or neglectful because they appear foreign to us.

Korbin (1980a) discusses the importance of being able to understand behavior from both within a culture (the *emic* perspective) and as an outsider may see that behavior (the *etic* perspective). Assume, for example, that a certain cultural practice entails some pain or discomfort and perhaps some physical injury. Further, assume that this practice appears to have little inherent benefit in terms of optimal child development. The tendency in a situation such as this would be to assume that the behavior is harmful to the child and try to put a stop to it. This would exemplify the *etic*, or intercultural, perspective. From an *emic*, or intracultural perspective, the practice in question may have important implications   for acceptance by other members of that culture. Putting a stop to initiation rites in some cultures because of the pain involved may lead to the "protected" child being ostracized.   In our own culture, refusing to allow braces or cosmetic surgery because of the discomfort these procedures entail may well lead to long-term negative consequences for certain children. The practices themselves may seem cruel and unnecessary to outsiders (the *etic* perspective), but their implications within the culture are significant (the *emic* perspective).

When applying our definitions of child maltreatment, a balance between the *emic* and *etic* perspectives must be achieved.   Cultural heritage and values are important, and children must not be deprived of them because of misguided efforts at protection. Just as importantly, in western cultures as well as others, children must not be subjected to unnecessary harm or potential harm simply because a practice is traditional. The goal in both cases is optimal conditions for child development.

Definitions

Historical, theoretical, and cultural perspectives of child maltreatment should ideally converge on a set of specific, socially appropriate definitions with which individuals can recognize and respond to abuse and neglect. Definitions of abuse and neglect in our society, however, differ greatly among different groups, professions, and individuals.

When asked about definitions of maltreatment, most everyone can agree on the extremes.   The child with severe bruises or broken bones resulting from parental "discipline" or the child who is not fed, cleaned, and supervised by the parents clearly constitutes maltreatment in the eyes of most individuals. Similarly, parents keeping an unkempt house or occasionally yelling at their children for not listening clearly do not constitute maltreatment.   Situations in between these extremes are where definitional issues become cloudy.

Unfortunately, there are many more "in-between" situations than extremes. Consider the following examples:

> *Joel is an eight-year-old boy who suffers from mild learning disabilities.   His parents struggle to help him do well in school but frequently become very frustrated and occasionally hit him out of frustration.   Although Joel has never been bruised or otherwise injured during these episodes, he is clearly developing an increasingly negative attitude toward academics and acts out aggressively when frustrated in school.*

> *R.J. is a 12-year-old child whose family is very invested in their cultural heritage. As part of his "rite of passage" to manhood, R.J. must undergo a painful scarification process which will leave lasting facial scars. Although this rite is not common in R.J.'s present community, his parents are very invested in preserving their cultural heritage.*

Depending upon who is asked, these examples may or may not constitute child abuse. Yet the manner in which we label instances such as these has a direct impact on how the situations are responded to and often times whether or not they are responded to at all.

Types of definitions

Definitions of maltreatment must be addressed at two levels, general and operational. General definitions are those which describe the phenomenon of maltreatment. An example of a general definition of maltreatment is "*the presence or absence of any behavior or pattern of behaviors which interfere with optimal child development.*" This definition nicely describes child maltreatment but is of little practical use. Operational definitions, on the other hand, are the specific set of conditions which guide our day-to-day practices. An example of an operational definition of physical abuse is "*the presence of unexplained recurrent physical injuries, such injuries being of sufficient severity to leave visible evidence.*"

General definitions

The definition of child abuse and neglect which directly or indirectly provides the standard guidelines for most individuals in our society is the legislative definition. Training programs typically utilize the legislative definition as the basis for defining abuse, and research typically utilizes samples of children who have been identified as maltreated according to the statutory guidelines of that state.

Public Law 93-247, the Child Abuse Prevention and Treatment Act, provides definitions of child abuse and neglect which have served as the basis for most state legislation. Public Law 93-247, Section 3, states:

(1) the term "child abuse and neglect" means the physical or mental injury, sexual abuse or exploitation, negligent treatment, or maltreatment of a child under the age of eighteen, or the age specified by the child protection law of the State in question, by a person (including any employee of a residential facility or any staff person providing out-of-home care) who is responsible for the child's welfare under circumstances which indicate that the child's health or welfare is harmed or threatened thereby, as determined in accordance with regulations prescribed by the Secretary; and

(2)(A) the term "sexual abuse" includes:

(i) the employment, use, persuasion, inducement, enticement, or coercion of any child to engage in, or having a child assist any other person to engage in, any sexually explicit conduct (or any simulation of such conduct) for the purpose of producing any visual depiction of such conduct, or

(ii) the rape, molestation, prostitution, or other such form of sexual exploitation of children, or incest with children, under circumstances which indicate that the child's health or welfare is harmed or threatened thereby, as determined in accordance with regulations prescribed by the Secretary; and

(2)(B) for the purpose of this clause, the term 'child' or 'children' means any individual who has not or individuals who have not attained the age of eighteen.

(3) the term "withholding of medically indicated treatment" means the failure to respond to the infant's life-threatening conditions by providing treatment (including appropriate nutrition, hydration, and medication) which, in the treating physician's or physicians' reasonable medical judgment, will be most likely to be effective in ameliorating or correcting all such conditions, except that the term   does not include the failure to provide treatment (other than appropriate nutrition, hydration, or medication) to an infant when, in the treating physician's or physicians' reasonable medical judgment, (A) the infant is chronically and irreversibly comatose; (B) the provision of such treatment would (i) merely prolong dying, (ii) not be effective in ameliorating or correcting all of the infant's life-threatening conditions, or (iii) otherwise be futile in terms of the survival of the infant; or (C) the provision of such treatment would be virtually futile in terms of the survival of the infant and the treatment itself under such circumstances would be inhumane.

State statutes modeled after this federal statute generally provide more specific delineations of the conditions described in the federal statute. For example, state statutes may elaborate on *"physical or mental injury, sexual abuse or exploitation, negligent treatment...,"* may specify who is considered *"a person ...responsible for the child's welfare,"* or may elaborate on what is considered actual or threatened harm to the child. Copies of individual state's statutes are available at the county courthouse, by writing a legislative representative, or by calling the library of the state legislature.

Even with the increased specificity of state legislation, legislative definitions fall far short of the specifications needed to decide individual cases. The operational definition of terms such as negligent treatment, injury to the psychological or emotional capacity, and potential harm is left largely to the discretion of the individual making the relevant decisions. Whereas one individual may consider allowing a three-year-old to play unsupervised in the front yard neglectful, another may view this as acceptable and normal behavior. These individuals, although they may both agree that children should not be left alone in potentially dangerous situations, have quite different operational definitions of what constitutes a potentially dangerous situation.

Operational definitions

Current operational definitions have a somewhat different focus than the general definitions described above.   Whereas general definitions emphasize parental behavior, day-to-day practices are typically based on child characteristics which are indicative of maltreatment. In the previous example of the child playing unsupervised in the front yard, the lack of supervision (the parental behavior) typically does not result in allegations of neglect.   If the child is injured or abducted while playing unsupervised, however, allegations of neglect are much more likely to result. Similarly, spanking a child is typically not treated as abusive, but if the spanking leaves marks on the child allegations of abuse are very likely to result. Consequently, the child, rather than the parent, is the focus of current operational definitions.

The existing discrepancy between operational and general definitions gives rise to several problems. Most notably, some form of harm must befall the child before direct action is taken. To the frustration of child advocates, many children continue to endure abusive or neglectful parental behavior simply because the child has not yet shown clear indications of suffering.

Sources of definitional bias

When the criteria for operational definitions deviate from the accepted general definitions, definitional bias is also increased. Bias may result from individual differences in upbringing, sociocultural factors, or theoretically based differences in perceiving maltreatment. In other words, the perspectives discussed earlier in this chapter all affect the manner in which individuals operationalize maltreatment.

Individual differences in upbringing affect operational definitions of maltreatment by leading to different levels of tolerance toward adverse parent-child relations. For example, individuals brought up in authoritarian families will be more accepting of restrictive parenting styles than individuals brought up in nonauthoritarian families.

Just as individual upbringing leads to different levels of tolerance toward maltreatment, the sociocultural values to which individuals are exposed leads to biases consistent with these values. For example, violence is more pervasive in some cultural groups than in others, and individuals in these cultures are more accepting of severe physical discipline. Cultural traditions consistent with these biases may be accepted within the culture but appear abusive to individuals unfamiliar with these traditions.

Finally, bias may result from professional training or theoretical differences in how maltreatment is perceived. For example, medical personnel tend to view maltreatment from the diagnostic perspective, which focuses on pathology within the individual as the primary etiological factor. Social workers tend to view maltreatment as a result of maladaptive social conditions rather than individual pathology. Police officers may focus more on the criminal aspects of maltreatment. Biases stemming from these professional differences affect how one perceives the role of the parents, the child, the environment, and the objective or subjective indicators that maltreatment has occurred. For example, pediatricians are more likely to focus on the physical condition of the child, whereas social workers are more likely to focus on the family and environmental conditions.

In short, although general definitions of maltreatment, which focus on protecting children from physical and emotional damage, are typically consistent among different individuals, the specific applications of these general definitions differ greatly. Individuals concerned about the problem of child maltreatment must work towards integrating the various operational definitions into a set of consistent and practical definitions of child abuse and neglect.

Improving our definitions

The perspectives discussed in this chapter suggest that several factors need to be considered in developing a consistent set of operational definitions of maltreatment. With the ultimate goal of providing conditions suitable to optimal child development, parental, social, and environmental factors need to be incorporated into a workable definition.

The current emphasis on objective indicators of physical and emotional harm results in many children being exposed to parental or societal practices which have long-term negative consequences but leave no immediate scars.   Placing more emphasis on parental behavior and less on immediate evidence of harm to the child would result in the protection of many more children from the long-term effects of maltreatment, particularly emotional abuse.   Similarly, many societal conditions currently exist which do not promote optimal child development, but because the sequelae are long-term rather than immediate and sensational, these children go unprotected.   Many children are subjected to inconsistent and inadequate day care conditions, and school-age children with special needs often do not get the services they need, or worse, are treated in ways which are clearly incompatible with healthy emotional development.

Operational definitions which stress our knowledge of factors affecting child development rather than the presence or absence of objective indicators are necessary to meet our stated goals of protecting children.   Objective indicators of maltreatment are important, but they should not be the only determinants of our operational definitions.   Few adults would be comfortable if, for example, assaultive behavior toward adults was criminal only if visible physical injury resulted or if a conviction for robbery was dependent upon evidence that taking those particular items interfered with the healthy functioning of the victim.   Yet this is the case with children.   Children may be assaulted if they are not injured, left unsupervised if no negative consequences occur, and verbally abused as long as the child can temporarily maintain an acceptable level of functioning.   Focusing on the abusive or neglectful behavior rather than evidence of immediate consequences will result in much improved efficacy in our protection efforts.

Finally, definitions focusing on conditions or behaviors affecting child development will highlight social and environmental conditions conducive to maltreatment.   As suggested above, many of our social structures for caring for children clearly are not conducive to optimal child development.   Improving such conditions through primary prevention offers the most cost-effective means of combating child maltreatment.

Section summary

Child maltreatment is generally defined as behavior or conditions which are harmful to the physical, cognitive, or emotional development of the child.   This general definition is widely agreed upon, with virtually everyone supporting the proposition that children should be protected.   Operational definitions, which are the specific conditions by which general definitions are translated into day-to-day practice, are less consistent between individuals.   Individual upbringing, sociocultural factors, and professional biases all affect the manner in which maltreatment is operationalized by different individuals.   In addition, general definitions focus on parental behaviors which are detrimental to child development, but operational definitions tend to rely heavily on indicators of the detrimental effects in the child.   Operational definitions based on our knowledge of factors affecting child development would lead to better protection of at-risk children and would broaden the base of potential perpetrators beyond individual adults to social institutions as well.

Chapter summary

This chapter has explored various perspectives of maltreatment. Historical perspectives demonstrate the evolution of maltreatment as a social phenomenon and provide a framework for understanding ways in which the social, individual, and environmental factors contribute to the perpetration of maltreatment. Various theoretical perspectives differentially emphasize the social, individual, and environmental etiological factors and provide unique and complementary conceptual contributions to our understanding of child maltreatment.

By integrating historical and theoretical perspectives, one can see how the various etiological factors interrelate. Social factors contribute to maltreatment by prescribing the limits of acceptable parenting behavior. When these limits change, many individuals continue to operate under the less restrictive social values because they lack access to or do not internalize the changing value system. Because environmental stress leads to a regression to more basic attitudes or behaviors, evolving value systems are likely to be unstable and subject to the effects of environmental conditions. Finally, individual characteristics, such as dysfunctional personality characteristics, lead to behavior outside socially accepted boundaries by interfering with the ability of the individual to meet his needs with more socially accepted behavior.

Finally, this chapter briefly discussed cultural perspectives on maltreatment and presented the current general and operational definitions of maltreatment. Although most everyone agrees that children should be protected from physical and emotional harm, considerable differences exist in the ways in which individuals operationalize these general definitions. Efforts to make these operational definitions more consistent are needed, and such efforts need to focus on conditions promoting child development in addition to objective, immediate indicators of physical or emotional harm.

Society has evolved to where the protection of children is recognized as an important social goal, but different perspectives exist as to how this goal should be conceptualized and pursued. We must strive to integrate these perspectives into a consistent and practical set of definitions and practices for the protection of children from harm and the enhancement of their healthy development.

References

Aber, J.L., & Cicchetti, D. (1984). "Socioemotional Development in Maltreated Children: An Empirical and Theoretical Analysis." In H. Fitzgerald, B. Lester, & M. Yogman (eds.), Theory and Research in Behavioral Pediatrics, Vol 2. New York: Plenum.

American Humane Association (1986). Highlights of Official Child Neglect and Abuse Reporting, 1984. Denver.

Bennie, E., & Sclare, A. (1969). "The Battered Child Syndrome." American Journal of Psychiatry, 125, 975-979.

Bronfenbrenner, U. (1979). The Ecology of Human Development. Cambridge, Mass: Harvard University Press.

Bronfenbrenner, U. (1977). "Toward an Experimental Ecology of Human Development." American Psychologist, 32, 513-531.

Browne, A., & Finkelhor, D. (1986). "Impact of Child Sexual Abuse: A Review of the Research." Psychological Bulletin, 99, 66-77.

Cicchetti, D., & Rizley, R. (1981). "Developmental Perspectives on the Etiology, Intergenerational Transmission, and Sequelae of Child Maltreatment." New Directions for Child Development, 11, 31-35.

Cornford, F.M. (1975). The Republic of Plato. New York: Oxford University Press.

DeFrancis, V. (1973). Hearings before the Subcommittee on Children and Youth. 93rd Congress, on the Child Abuse Prevention Act (S. 191), 323-331.

Finkelhor, D. (1986). A Sourcebook on Child Sexual Abuse. Beverly Hills, CA: Sage Publications.

Finkelhor, D. (1980). "Risk Factors in the Sexual Victimization of Children." Child Abuse and Neglect, 4, 265-273.

Finkelhor, D. & Browne, A. (1985). "The Traumatic Impact of Child Sexual Abuse: A Conceptualization." American Journal of Orthopsychiatry, 55, 530-541.

Folks, H. (1902). The Care of Destitute, Neglected and Delinquent Children. New York: Macmillan.

Galdston, R. (1965). "Observations of Children Who Have Been Physically Abused by Their Parents." American Journal of Psychiatry, 122, 440-443.

Garbarino, J. (1977). "The Human Ecology of Child Maltreatment: A Conceptual Model for Research." Journal of Marriage and The Family, 39, 721-735.

Garbarino, J., & Gilliam, G. (1980). Understanding Abusive Families. Lexington, Mass: Lexington Books.

Gebhard, P., Gagnon, J., Pomeroy, W., & Christenson, C. (1965). Sex Offenders: An Analysis of Types. New York: Harper & Row.

Gelles, R. (1983). "An Exchange/Social Control Theory." In Finkelhor et al. (eds.). The Dark Side of Families: Current Family Violence Research. Beverly Hills, Ca: Sage Publications.

Gelles, R., & Straus, M. (1979). "Determinants of Violence in the Family: Toward a Theoretical Integration." In W.R. Burr, R. Hill, F.I. Nye, & I.L. Reiss (eds.). Contemporary Theories About the Family. New York: Free Press.

Gil, D.G. (1975). "Unraveling Child Abuse." American Journal of Orthopsychiatry, 45, 346-354.

Gil, D.G. (1970). Violence Against Children: Physical Abuse in the U.S. Cambridge, Mass: Harvard University Press.

Giovanonni, J.M., & Becerra, R.M. (1979). Defining Child Abuse. New York: Free Press.

Groth, A.N. (1982). "The Incest Offender." In S.M. Sgroi (ed.), Handbook of Clinical Intervention in Child Sexual Abuse. Lexington, MA: Lexington Books.

Groth, A.N., & Birnbaum, H.J. (1978). "Adult Sexual Orientation and Attraction to Underage Persons." Archives of Sexual Behavior, 7, 175-181.

Groth, A.N., & Burgess, A. (1979). "Sexual Trauma in the Life Histories of Rapists and Child Molesters." Victimology: An International Journal, 4, 10-16.

Hammer, R.F., & Glueck, B.C. (1957). "Psychodynamic Patterns in Sex Offenders: a Four-Factor Theory." Psychiatric Quarterly, 31, 325-345.

Kempe, C.H., Silverman, F.N., Steele, B.F., Droegemueller, W., & Silver, H.K. (1962). "The Battered Child Syndrome." Journal of the American Medical Association, 181, 17-24.

Korbin, J.E. (1980b). "The Cross-Cultural Context of Child Abuse and Neglect." In C.H. Kempe & R.E. Helfer (eds.), The Battered Child. Chicago: University of Chicago Press.

Korbin, J.E. (1980a). "The Cultural Context of Child Abuse and Neglect." Child Abuse and Neglect, 4, 3-13.

Langevin, R., Handy, L., Hook, H., Day, D., & Russon, A. (1985). "Are Incestuous Fathers Pedophilic and Aggressive?" In R. Langevin (ed.), Erotic Preference, Gender Identity and Aggression. New York: Erlbaum.

Loss, P., & Glancy, E. (1983). "Men Who Sexually Abuse Their Children." Medical Aspects of Human Sexuality, 17, 328-329.

Lynch, M.A. (1985). "Child Abuse Before Kempe: An Historical Literature Review." Child Abuse and Neglect, 9, 7-15.

Panton, J.H. (1978). "Personality Differences Appearing Between Rapists of Adults, Children, and Non-violent Sexual Molesters of Children." Research Communications in Psychology, 3, 385-393.

Polansky, N.A., Ammons, P.W., & Gaudin, J.M. (1985). "Loneliness and Isolation in Child Neglect." Social Casework: The Journal of Contemporary Social Work, 66, 38-47.

Polansky, N.A., Chalmers, M.A., Buttenweiser, E., & Williams, D.P. (1981). Damaged Parents: An Anatomy of Neglect. Chicago: University of Chicago Press.

Radbill, S.X. (1980). "Children in a World of Violence: A History of Child Abuse." In C.H. Kempe & R.E. Helfer (eds.), The Battered Child. Chicago: University of Chicago Press.

Sgroi, S.M., Blick, L.C., & Porter, F.S. (1982). "A Conceptual Framework for Child Sexual Abuse." In S.M. Sgroi (ed.), Handbook of Clinical Intervention in Child Sexual Abuse. Lexington, MA: Lexington Books.

Steele, B., & Pollock, C. (1968). "A Psychiatric Study of Parents Who Abuse Infants and Small Children." In R. Helfer & C.H. Kempe (eds.), The Battered Child. Chicago: University of Chicago Press.

Straus, M.A., Gelles, R.J., & Steinmetz, S.K. (1980). Behind Closed Doors: Violence in the American Family. Garden City, NY: Doubleday.

Straus, M.A., & Kantor, G.K. (1987). "Stress and Child Abuse." In R.E. Helfer & R.S. Kempe (eds.), The Battered Child. Chicago: The University of Chicago Press.

Wenet, F., Clark, T. & Hunner, R. (1981). "Perspectives on the Juvenile Sex Offender." In R. Hunner & Y. Walker (eds.), Exploring the Relationship Between Child Abuse and Delinquency. Montclair, N.J.: Allenheld, Osmun.

Williams, G.S. (1983). "Child Protection: A Journey into History." Journal of Clinical Child Psychology, 12, 236-243.

Zalba, S. (1971). "Battered Children." Transaction 8, (July-August), 58-61.

Chapter 2

Methodological Issues

As we become increasingly dependent upon research to guide us in this fast paced, exceedingly complex society, decisions based on the misinterpretation or misapplication of research become increasingly detrimental.

In simpler times, long ago, our actions were guided primarily by our experiences. The world of an individual was relatively small, and what one needed to function could be, for the most part, learned from friends, neighbors, and elders. Today, the pace and complexity of society preclude one individual from directly experiencing even a small fraction of what it takes to survive. Most of what we know has been discovered, developed, or created by individuals with whom we are unfamiliar, and transmitted by literature, television, or by word of mouth from someone many times removed from the actual experience.

Because of this dependence upon so many unknown sources of information, the processes by which information is derived and transmitted are of utmost importance. Methodological issues should be as much a part what we learn as the facts themselves, for it is these methods which determine the parameters of the facts. For example, we may read that abused children fit a certain behavioral profile, but unless we are also provided with information about the children, the nature of the abuse, and the circumstances under which these conclusions were drawn we are in no position to apply this information in other situations. In fact, information presented without the applicable methodological limitations can easily do more harm than good.

Like all other disciplines, the knowledge which has accumulated over the past decades in reference to child abuse and neglect is integrally tied to the manner in which these phenomena have been studied. Most of the early information which accumulated on maltreatment was derived from clinical observations. More recently, empirical research and theory based propositions have added much to our knowledge base.

These different methods of study and the nature of the information they provide are the subject of the current chapter. The information which has accumulated in reference to child abuse and neglect is impressive, but, at the same time, we know relatively little about these phenomena. As discussed in Chapter 1, many potential etiological factors have been identified, but to date we can only hypothesize about how these factors interact to elicit abusive or neglectful behavior. Similarly, many sequelae of maltreatment have been identified, but in most cases the methodology employed to identify the sequelae cannot tell us if the history of maltreatment was the cause, the result, or simply a correlate of the sequelae. These issues must be addressed if we are to effectively apply our knowledge to the treatment and prevention of child maltreatment. Methodological issues discussed in this chapter include the strengths and limitations of clinically derived information and issues relevant to definitions, sample selection, causation, and generalization in the available empirical research.

Clinically Derived Information

Most of the early literature on child abuse and neglect was based on impressions derived from clinical experience. For example, social workers may have noticed that the neglected youngsters which they saw tended to be less playful than other children, or pediatricians may have noticed that physically abusive parents seemed immature. These impressions then served as the basis for generalizations about other victims or perpetrators.

Impressions through observation are our most common way of learning about others. We notice that certain types of people have certain characteristics and then generalize these beliefs to the broader population. Similarly, we may notice that certain actions precede certain outcomes and therefore attribute the outcomes to the actions. For example, one may notice that many physically abused children have speech problems and conclude that physical abuse causes speech problems.

Observations of this nature are very useful for generating hypotheses about the relationships between different variables. They are, however, insufficient to warrant firm conclusions about the relationships. Conclusions derived from experience may prematurely overlook other plausible explanations. For example, the observed lack of playfulness in the above example of neglected children may be due to other factors common to the sample of neglected children, such as living in an area which does not provide access to a park or playground. Careful research is needed to rule out alternative explanations for the relationships we observe in our day-to-day experiences. If our initial impressions are not empirically verified, our actions may be misguided. In fact, one of the traditional stumbling blocks for the advancement of science has been the tendency to cling to impressions which seem sensible or appealing but which are not entirely valid.

Validation with Research

The goal of systematic research is to determine if our impressions are indeed valid. If we wanted to confirm our suspicion that neglected children are indeed less playful than other children, we would design a research study that controlled for extraneous variables. A sample of neglected children would be selected, and their playfulness would be compared to a sample of nonneglected children who were similar to the neglected children on all other dimensions, such as residence, race, socioeconomic status, age, etc. Systematically comparing the children in this way would rule out the possibility that other factors were responsible for the observed lack of playfulness. If this relationship were then confirmed, one would still not know whether neglect *causes* a lack of playfulness (perhaps less playful children are more likely to be neglected), but one could be relatively sure that there is a relationship between the two. A longitudinal study would be needed to determine if neglected children come to be less playful or if less playful children come to be neglected.

Ideally, such research could be systematically designed and implemented, and our impressions would be confirmed or disconfirmed. Real-life research, however, has its own set of limitations. In fact, research on child abuse and neglect is fraught with methodological shortcomings. Several authors have documented a number of methodological limitations common to the maltreatment literature, including inadequate definitions, inadequate sample size and selection, lack of appropriate comparison groups, and, in many cases, inadequate research designs (e.g., Lamphear, 1986; Leventhol, 1982; Toro, 1982). These limitations must be understood before the available literature can be adequately interpreted. The following sections discuss several of the current methodological problems with the research on child abuse and neglect and explores how each of these issues affects the interpretation of the available research literature.

Definitions

Definitions, explicit or implied, are fundamental to the understanding of any phenomenon. Unless the parameters of what is being discussed are understood, miscommunications will abound. For example, if Bill is telling Mary about a wonderful new cure for the "most annoying ailment" (referring to the common cold), but Mary assumes he is talking about headaches, she is unlikely to derive much useful information from the conversation. Similarly, if Bill is talking about the characteristics of parents who "abuse" their children, his operational definition of abuse must be clear before the information can be understood and applied by his listeners.

The literature on child maltreatment uses a variety of definitions of varying generality. Some authors discuss "maltreatment", which typically encompasses physical abuse, neglect, emotional abuse, and sometimes also sexual abuse. Other authors specify the nature of the maltreatment (e.g., physical abuse, neglect, etc.), while still others may detail the specific inclusion criteria, such as the presence of long-bone fractures. Further, many published studies simply utilize research samples comprised of cases which have come to the attention of local authorities. These cases are defined by the legislative definition of maltreatment, but, as discussed in Chapter 1, the manner in which the legislative definition is operationalized is subject to considerable bias. Consequently, cases of maltreatment defined by the legislative definition may be quite variable in regard to the nature and severity of the abuse or neglect.

Definitional ambiguity and inconsistency diminish both the validity of individual studies and the confidence with which various studies can be compared. With many statistics, high variability within one or more groups obscures true group differences, leading to the conclusion that such differences do not exist. For example, consider three types of physically abusive parents. The first type involves individuals who become abusive when disciplining their children, the second includes individuals who have abused their children as a reaction to external stressors, and the third type involves individuals with dysfunctional personality characteristics which place them at risk to abuse. If perpetrators with these various profiles were all grouped together in one sample under the descriptor "physically abusive parents" and compared to a group of nonabusive parents, the statistical analyses might indicate, because of the high variability between parents, that there are no group differences between the abusive and nonabusive parents.

Similar problems occur if attempts are made to compare separate studies when the sample definitions are not concise and consistent. If each of the three profiles of abusive parents referred to in the above paragraph emerged in a separate study as characteristic of abusive parents, attempts to integrate the three studies would be very difficult because of what would appear to be inconsistent findings. Although each hypothetical study investigated "physically abusive parents," the profiles which emerged from the studies would be very different. Further, for each of the profiles, one study would produce positive findings and two would produce negative findings, leading to the conclusion that none of the characteristics are strongly associated with abuse.

Because of definitional problems and sample differences such as those described above, the literature on child maltreatment appears more like many distinct studies than an integrated field of research. For the above reasons, however, studies with negative results may often be entirely compatible with studies with positive results. The differences in research findings may simply reflect unique aspects of a complex phenomenon, but not until definitions are precise and used in a consistent manner will we be able to adequately account for these differences. When sample definitions are inconsistent or inadequately specified, the various pieces of the puzzle simply cannot be put together.

Research Samples

Consistent and specific sample definitions are the starting point for interpretable research. Adequate definitions, however, are not in themselves sufficient to render findings which are reliable and valid. Research interpretation also depends upon the research design and characteristics of the groups being studied. The sample size, the specificity of the sample, and the characteristics of the control group to which the maltreatment sample is compared all affect the inferences which can be drawn from the research.

Samples and research design

Sample characteristics must be considered in conjunction with the research design. For example, research on the characteristics of victims and perpetrators of child maltreatment is typically cross-sectional in nature, that is, individuals assessed at one particular point in time are compared on the basis of known differences, such as whether or not they have experienced maltreatment. The scores on the personality tests of parents known to have abused their children, for example, may be compared to the scores of nonabusing parents to see if any personality characteristics might be associated with abuse. The comparison group may be individuals who are assessed at the time of the study (e.g., when the MMPI profiles of abusive and nonabusive parents are compared) or a previously compiled standardization sample (e.g., when

MMPI profiles of abusive parents are examined to see if they deviate from the norm).

In cross-sectional research, the sample of interest and the comparison sample are essentially selected from two different groups (i.e., maltreatment vs. nonmaltreatment). The samples are known to differ in respect to maltreatment, but there may be other variables on which the groups differ as well. For example, the families comprising a maltreatment sample may frequently change residence, whereas the families of the nonmaltreated children may be more stable. Whether or not this incidental difference is identified, it is confounded with the difference in maltreatment status. In other words, if the maltreated children are observed to have poorer social skills than the comparison group, one cannot be sure if these deficits are due to the maltreatment or to the lack of stable residence. Any group differences which are identified may in fact be associated with either the maltreatment or with the confounding variable. Because maltreatment is a complex phenomenon, the potential for confounds in the research is enormous.

The role of confounds in a research study is affected by both the statistics used and the composition of the sample. Statistics will not be discussed in this chapter, except to state that when reading the literature one should be aware of those statistics which explicitly correct for or exclude confounds (e.g., analyses of covariance, partial correlation) and those statistics which make no provisions for the confounds (e.g., t-test, analyses of variance). These statistics and their applications are explained in a number of research texts, such as Winer (1971). The following sections briefly discuss how sample size, sample selection, and characteristics of the comparison sample affect research findings.

Sample size and specificity

Sample size and specificity both affect the validity of research interpretation. As sample size increases, so does the confidence with which one can infer that the research findings are due to the manipulated variable rather than one or more uncontrolled variables.

With larger samples the uncontrolled variables are more dispersed among the subjects and are less likely to have a systematic effect. For example, assume that a sample of five physically abused children were assessed on a measure of empathy and compared to a sample of five nonabused children. If four of the physically abused children also had a history of being emotionally abused, any positive findings could be attributed to the emotional as well as physical abuse, and any negative findings would not disconfirm a relationship between physical abuse and empathy. If, however, a sample of 50 physically abused children were assessed in the same manner with the same results, the chances of having a disproportionate number of children who were emotionally abused would decrease and the results would be more likely to represent the true relationship between physical abuse and empathy.

Just as larger samples improve validity, samples which have been selected in a very specific manner aid research interpretation. As mentioned above, the more differences there are between the samples being compared, the less reasonable it is to assume that one of those differences, such as maltreatment, is solely responsible for group differences on the research measures. In the above example, all confounding effects of emotional abuse could be removed from any size sample simply by excluding from the sample children who have experienced emotional abuse. Research samples which include only specific types of individuals greatly facilitate research interpretation, but are rare in the maltreatment literature.

Although increasing sample size and specificity is, theoretically, a very effective way to increase the probability that the presumed associations are valid, such selection procedures are often extremely difficult to institute. Different variables are often related in ways that prevent them from being practically separated. In the above example, the physical and emotional abuse may be highly correlated. In other words, a high percentage of children who have experienced physical abuse have also been victims of emotional abuse, and finding a sample of children who have experienced *only* physical abuse may be virtually impossible. When such conditions exist, it is very difficult to disentangle the effects of the variables by trying to increase sample size or use more selective sampling procedures. A more practical way to disentangle the variables is by using a comparison group which differs on the variable of interest.

Comparison groups

The appropriate use of comparison or control groups provides one of the single best techniques for isolating the effects of particular variables or interventions. Comparing the research sample to a sample similar in all ways except for variable of interest (e.g., maltreatment status) will lead to a high degree of confidence that the variable of interest is related to the observed effects or associations.

For example, the effects of physical and emotional abuse in the above example, even if highly correlated, can be disentangled by comparing physically and emotionally abused children to children who are emotionally, but not physically, abused. In this way the effects of physical abuse will be isolated, since the effects of emotional abuse should be similar for both groups. Similarly, matching the comparison group for race, SES, sex, age, intelligence, etc., helps to assure that these variables are not contributing to the observed differences between the groups.

Research on the perpetrators and victims of maltreatment frequently falls short of the standards described in the above paragraphs. The research samples are often small, and control or comparison groups are often poorly matched or not used at all. Consequently, the confidence with which we can conclude that certain characteristics in the parents or sequelae in the children are related or unrelated to maltreatment is greatly reduced. This limitation is particularly important for intervention efforts in cases of maltreatment.   If characteristics associated with maltreatment are also associated with other factors such as poverty, then overlooking these alternative relationships will lead to misguided or inadequate intervention designs.

Cause and Effect

The ultimate goal in the study of maltreatment is to discover what causes maltreatment and what the sequelae of maltreatment involve.   Cross-sectional research, the most common design in the maltreatment literature, does not directly address the question of causation. If cross-sectional research indicates that a certain characteristic is associated with maltreating parents or their children, we do not know if that characteristic is the result of the maltreatment, if it contributes to the occurrence of maltreatment, or if it is a function of some other variable related to the maltreatment.

For example, language delays have been found to be more prevalent in samples of neglected children. These results are typically interpreted as indicating that parental neglect leads to language delays in children. The research, however, could also mean that children with language delays are more likely to be neglected. Further, the possibility that no causative link exists cannot be ruled out. The language delays may be the result of earlier conditions, such as premature birth, and these earlier conditions may also give rise to or result from conditions which place the child at risk for neglect.

The two primary methods to address causation involve longitudinal research and inference. Longitudinal research involves studying the same families over time and noting factors which precede the development of conditions such as maltreatment, the actual development of such conditions, and the impact of such conditions on subsequent development. Because the whole developmental process is studied, causation is more easily identified. Unfortunately, longitudinal research is time-consuming and expensive, involves its own set of confounds such as sample and experimenter mortality, and can easily become overwhelming because of the complexity of the variables.

Inference, although much less reliable than longitudinal research, is more frequently used to address causation. Inference involves the development of a logical causative chain which is consistent with other relationships in which cause-effect links have been supported. For example, one can infer that language delays result from neglect in part because related research has suggested that language development is facilitated by contingent verbal stimulation. By definition, neglect is often associated with less appropriate verbal interaction between the parent and child.

Extreme caution must be exercised when inferring causation. Even though inferences typically "make a lot of sense," they can easily cause more subtle or complex causative processes to be overlooked. As mentioned above, most of our beliefs about the causes and effects of maltreatment are based on inference. Consequently, the confidence with which various inferences are made should be kept in mind in our day-to-day practices.

In short, our knowledge of the causes and effects of maltreatment is limited. Most of our beliefs about causation are based on inference rather than on carefully designed empirical studies. Consequently, individuals involved with perpetrators or victims of maltreatment must be sensitive to the confidence with which various inferences are made and not overlook alternative factors which are contributing to the problem. In many instances we fail to challenge cause and effect inferences when an alternative explanation would fit the data we have collected. An invalid inference in an area such as child abuse, where lives of children are at stake, can be exceedingly dangerous.

Generalization

The final section addresses two additional methodological dangers: 1) the danger of overgeneralization based on a small and nonrepresentative data base, and 2) improper use of research results.

Research samples should ideally be selected so they are representative of the entire population of interest. In this way the research findings can be assumed to apply to all individuals in that population, not just the individuals in the research sample. For example, if one wanted to determine the average height of men in the United States, the sample should include individuals representing a variety of regions, races, occupations, etc. If the sample was limited to basketball players, perhaps because their heights are readily available, the research results would most likely not be a valid representation of the height of men in general.

Research samples in the study of child maltreatment are often poorly representative of the larger population. The samples are typically comprised of low SES individuals and cases in which the maltreatment is relatively severe. Consequently, most of our empirically based knowledge applies to this select group. Very little is known about maltreatment in middle and upper class families and less severe forms of maltreatment. Similarly, our knowledge of maltreatment is based entirely on reported cases. Whether or not these research findings apply to cases of maltreatment which go undetected or unreported is not known.

Because our knowledge is based on a relatively nonrepresentational segment of the population of maltreating families, this knowledge should not be automatically generalized to describe all maltreating families. Less severe forms of maltreatment may be associated with different parent and child characteristics, and higher SES may or may not affect the nature of maltreatment in these families. Our samples are, however, typically representative of the cases of maltreatment which are most commonly reported. Consequently, generalization to this population for the purposes of prevention and intervention is appropriate.

Finally, one additional caution involving the practical application of maltreatment research findings is necessary. The majority of maltreatment research is designed to determine if certain characteristics are overrepresented in maltreatment samples. Even if the methodological difficulties described above are overcome, the findings of this type of research are of little help in *identifying* perpetrators or victims of maltreatment.

For example, physical abuse may indeed lead to aggression in young children, but aggression may also result from a multitude of other factors, such as social skill deficits, communication problems, or frustration. If methodologically sound research shows that most physically abused children exhibit signs of aggression, we still have no information relevant to the number of aggressive children who are maltreated.

In other words, most of what we know about the characteristics of perpetrators and victims of maltreatment does not translate into a profile which can be used to identify these individuals from the general population. This question would be answered by obtaining, for example, a sample of aggressive children and determining how many of these children have been physically abused.

Unfortunately, there is little objective evidence to guide us in determining which characteristics are strong versus weak indicators of maltreatment. Except for certain physical characteristics in children which are the immediate consequences of inflicted injury, physical neglect, or sexual activity, most of the parent or child characteristics associated with maltreatment can also be found in nonmaltreated samples. Consequently, most of the identified characteristics can only be used to guide assessment and intervention, not to identify families in which maltreatment is present. A lucrative area for future research would be to more carefully investigate the percentage of maltreated children in samples of children identified as aggressive, depressed, etc., to determine the reliability of these characteristics as indicators of maltreatment.

Chapter Summary

This chapter discussed several methodological issues relevant to the interpretation and application of the available literature on maltreatment. The research studies on maltreatment that have been reported in the literature have many limitations. Small and nonhomogeneous samples, poorly matched control groups, and definitional problems have limited the usefulness of much of the maltreatment research. Definitions of research samples are often very general and are many times inconsistent between studies. Inadequate comparison groups are often used, and little research exists which directly addresses current beliefs about causation. Further, samples are typically comprised of low SES individuals and contain only relatively severe cases of maltreatment.

These limitations greatly limit the extent of our knowledge about maltreatment. Although many studies have been conducted, the various findings cannot be integrated into a unified body of knowledge. The relationships between maltreatment and the many characteristics thought to be associated with maltreatment are not known, and our beliefs about the causes and effects of maltreatment are primarily based on inference. In other words, many bits of information are known, but how these pieces fit together has yet to be determined. Research with larger, more representative, and better defined samples and more adequate research designs are needed to expand and enhance what we know about maltreatment and improve our efforts at prevention, identification, and treatment.

Although the methodological limitations discussed in this chapter may at first seem to present insurmountable obstacles for the application of the available literature, the overall picture is not that discouraging. Although most of our hypotheses about child abuse and neglect are in need of further validation, if we remember we are dealing with hypotheses, and not proven facts, we can proceed to discuss many the many facets of maltreatment about which we are continually learning. We must be cautious in our conclusions, however, and continually strive to reinforce them with high quality research.

References

Lamphear, V. (1986). "The Psychosocial Adjustment of Maltreated Children: Methodological Limitations and Guidelines for Future Research." Child Abuse and Neglect, 10, 63-69.

Leventhol, J.M. (1982). "Research Strategies and Methodologic Standards in Studies of Risk Factors for Child Abuse." Child Abuse and Neglect, 6, 113-123.

Toro, P.A. (1982). "Developmental Effects of Child Abuse: A Review." Child Abuse and Neglect, 6, 423-431.

Winer, B.J. (1971). Statistical Principles in Experimental Design. New York: McGraw-Hill.

Chapter 3

Parent and Family Characteristics

"To most abusive parents, they are not abusive -- they are parents."

A father recently described the impact of his visit to the child protection services agency:

"As I sat in the waiting room, I saw a huge cop bring this little tiny girl in. She looked so helpless I figured right away he had taken her away from her parents. I thought to myself, 'My God, what kind of people could abuse a little girl like that?' I couldn't help but think of the newspaper article I had read about kids who are beaten, sexually molested, not fed. I could never understand that.

Then, something terrible happened. It suddenly occurred to me that I was in the waiting room for the same reason. It hit me that my reasons for hitting, shaking and yelling at David were good, but they did not excuse me from being an abusive parent. It tears me up to think about how I've hurt that kid, but that is over now."

(Two weeks later.)

"I'm doing a lot better with David. I've only hit him twice and those times he really deserved it. I still don't know why he... ."

David is a lot of children. Their parents love them, want the best for them, and yet mistreat them. What causes parents to abuse or neglect their children? Is it something about the parents, or the children, or are there situations which will cause anyone to mistreat a child?

Maltreatment is a complex, multifaceted phenomenon and there are no simple answers as to why parents abuse or neglect their children. Many risk factors, both environmental and intrapersonal, have been proposed and subjected to some degree of research. These risk factors are the subject of the current chapter.

Risk factors which contribute to the potential for maltreatment fall into three general categories.   These categories, which were first encountered in the earlier discussion of etiological theories (see Chapter 1), involve 1) differences in experience which give rise to maladaptive parenting beliefs and behaviors, 2) environmental conditions leading to stress, and 3) intrapersonal characteristics associated with increased risk in the perpetrators.   Each of these areas is discussed further in the following pages and examples of the research relevant to each area are presented.

The final section of this chapter is devoted to the special topic of teenage parents. Teenage parents represent a group at particular risk for maltreating their children, and the needs and problems of this population of parents warrant special consideration. At the end of the chapter, the characteristics of maltreating parents are summarized in an assessment format, making the information easily accessible for day-to-day applications.

DIFFERENCES IN EXPERIENCE

"I just never thought of what I was doing as abusive" is a statement familiar to anyone having worked with abusive or neglectful parents. Although such a statement sometimes reflects denial or an attempt to avoid criticism, it often is an honest appraisal of the situation.   Many parents who mistreat their children simply are unaware of the harmful effects of their behavior, especially when the damage is emotional rather than physical.

Sources of experience-based differences

The behavior and beliefs of any parent are largely determined by the cumulative sum of prior experiences with children and childrearing. Some individuals develop their knowledge and attitudes about childrearing primarily from their own upbringing, others incorporate experiences from literature to which they have been exposed or television they have viewed, while still others look to friends and neighbors for parenting information.

There are three primary ways an individual may internalize standards for childrearing which are compatible with maltreatment (see Figure 3-1).   Such standards may be a function of culturally-based biases in childrearing, such as when a potentially harmful disciplinary practice (i.e., corporal punishment) goes unchallenged.   Second, inappropriate standards for childrearing may arise from abusive treatment by one's own parents, coupled with isolation from other models of appropriate parenting behavior. Finally, individuals may simply have had inadequate exposure to parenting models, in which case their standards for childrearing may arise from alternative models, such as how adults treat each other.   With each of these three processes, parents may be unaware that their standards of childrearing may be consistent with child abuse and neglect.

Manifestations of experience-based differences

Experience-based differences in parenting beliefs or knowledge may contribute to abusive or neglectful behavior in three general ways (see Figure 3-1). Parents may hold beliefs about discipline or childcare which are compatible with maltreatment, their repertoire of parenting skills may be inadequate to respond to the complex demands of caring for children, or they may have insufficient knowledge about child development and the capabilities of young children.   These manifestations of experience-based differences in parenting, which are elaborated below, may contribute to maltreatment in isolation or in combination with other risk factors.

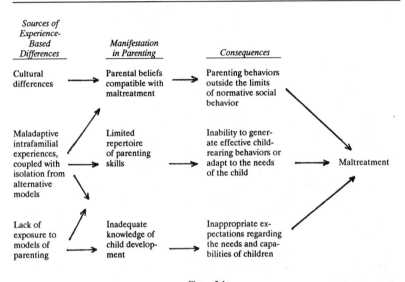

Figure 3-1

Experience-based differences in childrearing

Parental belief systems

Parental beliefs represent the parents' conceptions of desirable or appropriate actions for themselves and their children. Harm may befall children when parents are misinformed about the parameters of socially acceptable childrearing. For example, parents who have learned that severe physical punishment teaches children to behave will be more likely to use such punishment on a routine basis. Such beliefs can be culturally based or arise from a parent's idiosyncratic experiences within his or her own family. For example, Showers and Bandman (1986) found the majority of perpetrators in 78 cases referred for physical abuse with electric cords viewed discipline of this nature as appropriate and the authors attributed this acceptance in part to sociocultural differences in perceptions of appropriate discipline.

Maladaptive beliefs of this nature may account for much emotional abuse in today's society. Although no research addresses this issue, clinical experience suggests that many parents use yelling, explicit and implicit put-downs, and criticism as primary ways of disciplining and teaching children. These behaviors negatively affect children but are not typically viewed as inappropriate by parents. Rather, parents express concern after their children begin to show developmental sequelae such as lack of motivation or low self-esteem. Even then, many parents do not associate their behavior with the sequelae but rather view the problem as arising from within the child. Just as the physical discipline accepted by other cultures may be seen as physically abusive, common disciplinary practices in the typical American home may be seen as verbally abusive. Because such disciplinary practices are common, however, most individuals would view harsh verbal reprimands as entirely acceptable with children.

Limited repertoire of parenting skills

"I know what I'm doing is not working, but she gets me so frustrated I just lock her in her room until her father gets home." Parents who exhibit abusive or neglectful behavior sometimes realize the behavior is dysfunctional but are unable to generate more effective alternatives. As etiological factors, an inadequate repertoire of parenting skills differs from maladaptive beliefs in that parents subscribing to a certain set of beliefs truly believe their behavior is not dysfunctional, whereas parents who lack the repertoire of alternatives may see their behavior as dysfunctional but lack the necessary information to change their behavior in an adaptive way. Parents may persevere in or escalate maladaptive behavior patterns simply because they possess no better options, even though they may not be comfortable with these behavior patterns.

Just as beliefs about child development and behavior arise from prior experience, parenting skills and strategies must be learned at some time in an individual's life. The majority of such "training" currently occurs in informal ways, such as by observing one's parents and friends or by some other form of exposure, such as television, newspapers, or books. Parents whose exposure to such childrearing information is limited or biased in some fashion may have a more difficult time of parenting because of inadequate preparation.

For example, parents who know only how to discipline their children by yelling or hitting may become abusive when these forms of discipline are escalated because they do not initially lead to any changes in behavior. Parents who rely heavily on corporal punishment, for instance, are at risk for abuse when their children become adolescents because they feel they must often punish much more severely to have a visible impact on their children. Similarly, if parents cannot generate effective techniques to control their children, they may simply give up and neglect may result.

Although there is no research which directly compares the behavioral repertoire, in terms of discipline, of abusive and nonabusive parents, several studies have found maltreating parents to be more rigid or inflexible in their parenting behaviors (e.g., Milner & Wimberly, 1980). In some cases, this inflexibility may well reflect a basic lack of awareness of alternative behaviors. Determining the extent to which parents possess the awareness of a broad range of childrearing behaviors is an important first step in preventing child abuse, for until a parent has this base of skills, they will be likely to experience difficulty in their relationship with their child and the child may be viewed as a source of stress and frustration. On the other hand, if the parents possess a foundation of parenting skills but continue to mistreat their child, the problem involves factors which are preventing the parents from using their knowledge in their day-to-day functioning, and the sources of these problems must be explored.

Knowledge of child development

Insufficient knowledge of normal child development may lead to unrealistic or inappropriate expectations[1] for children and consequent abuse or neglect. For example, individuals who do not realize that young children cannot anticipate danger or reason out solutions to problems may leave children unsupervised, not realizing the situation is potentially harmful. On the other hand, children who are expected to be capable of unrealistic abilities may be harshly punished because they are "not trying" or subjected to emotional abuse because their relative shortcomings cause them to be viewed negatively by their parents.

The early literature, although primarily clinical in nature, tended to support the hypothesis that abusive parents held unrealistic expectations for their children (Spinetta & Rigler, 1972). More recently, Spinetta (1978) found differences in abusive parent's expectations of their children as compared to the expectations of nonmaltreating parents. In addition, the greatest differences were found between the low-income abusers and the middle-income controls, suggesting that sociocultural differences as well as maltreatment contributed to the differences in knowledge-based expectations.

Experience-based differences in childrearing and the intergenerational cycle

Attitudes and behavior patterns which have developed from past experience are often taken for granted. Especially in areas such as childrearing, there has been very little effort to intervene or question the family's traditional way of raising their children. Consequently, parenting practices tend to be passed along from one

----

[1]The term "expectation" is used in two ways in the child maltreatment literature. The distinction is typically not delineated in the literature but is important for distinguishing two different types of problems. As used in this section, expectations refer to knowledge or information-based beliefs regarding children's capabilities and normal behavior. Individuals with inappropriate expectations would hold these expectations for all children because they are based on misinformation. With the advent of cognitive psychology, expectations have also come to be used to refer to perceptions or attitudes based on an individual's cognitive style or mood. For example, negative expectations have been shown to be associated with depression. Expectations in this sense are not based upon misinformation, but rather a misperception. The expectations are applied in a more selective manner than knowledge-based expectations, such as when a parent expects negative behavior from his/her child, but this negative expectation does not apply to other children. Recent research on parental expectations (e.g., Larrance and Twentyman, 1983) primarily address expectations based on attitude or affect rather than knowledge. This line of research is discussed below in the section on individual characteristics.

generation to the next, leading to a tendency for parenting practices to repeat themselves. In abusive families, this cycle has been termed the intergenerational cycle of maltreatment. The intergenerational cycle of maltreatment implies that individuals who are mistreated as children are at greater risk to subsequently mistreat their children.

Although a history of childhood maltreatment in samples of maltreating parents is by no means a unanimous finding in the research literature (see Friedrich & Wheeler, 1982, and Jayaratne, 1977, for reviews), the majority of studies confirm this assumption. For example, Hunter et al. (1978) found histories of maltreatment in 90% of a sample of 10 families reported for maltreatment versus only 17% of the 245 not reported. Korbin (1986) found that 8 of 10 women jailed for fatally abusing their children had been abused as children, and another had been the victim of "culturally sanctioned" abuse. Newberger et al. (1986) found that, in a sample of 409 families, at-risk parents reported having been more severely disciplined as children than matched comparison parents. The intergenerational cycle is one of the few aspects of maltreatment that is virtually unanimously agreed upon.

The role of isolation in the intergenerational cycle

Unless exposed to alternative childrearing methods, children who are maltreated are bound to adopt similar attitudes and behaviors when they become parents. Because there is no formal mechanism to train or educate parents in our society, exposure to more adaptive parenting must come from experience with other families or from the mass media. Many maltreating families, however, tend to remain isolated from these information sources, preventing such exposure from occurring. Consequently, isolation may increase the risk for maltreatment not only by reducing social support networks as commonly discussed but also by maintaining maladaptive parenting practices.

Isolation may take several forms. Individuals may simply lack social connections, as is conceptualized by connectedness at the mesosystem level of functioning (Garbarino, 1977). On the other hand, individuals may have social connections but may not have access to materials which provide parent-related education such as television, magazines, etc. Individuals may actually have strong social connections, but the social group they are a part of may be isolated from the larger society, as is the case with certain religious sects. Finally, individuals may not be socially isolated per se, but because of their lifestyles, priorities, etc., they may simply not be exposed to information regarding child development and appropriate parenting. Isolation in any of these forms will decrease the exposure to a variety of parenting styles and behaviors, subsequently preventing the benefits that such exposure would bring.

Several comparative research studies support the contention that maltreating families are often more isolated than nonmaltreating families. Newberger, Hampton, Marx, and White (1986) studied 48 abuse cases, 41 FTT cases, 97 accident cases, and 23 ingestion cases along with a sample of 209 matched comparison children and found that isolation was most pervasive in the abuse families. Hunter, Kilstrom, Kraybill, and Loda (1978) assessed the families of 255 premature infants, 10 of which were reported for maltreatment during the first year of life, and again found family isolation to be overrepresented in the maltreatment sample. Similarly, Polansky, Ammons, and Gaudin (1985) studied 76 neglectful families and 80 matched low-income control families and confirmed relatively greater isolation and loneliness in the neglectful families.

Both isolation and exposure to maltreatment as children appear to be common in the histories of maltreating parents. This combination of factors is sufficient to develop and maintain a repertoire of maladaptive parenting beliefs and behaviors and increase the risk of abusive or neglectful behavior toward children of the next generation.

Section summary

Differences in experience related to parenting and child development can lead to maltreatment by perpetuating maladaptive belief systems regarding childrearing, by limiting knowledge of more adaptive parenting techniques, and by reducing access to information about child development. Parents who mistreat their children because prior experience has led to maladaptive parenting styles typically do not view their own behavior as inappropriate. These parents need to be educated in terms of more adaptive parenting techniques.

Early exposure to maltreatment, along with isolation from exposure to more adaptive parenting alternatives, increases the risk for maltreatment because exposure to appropriate parenting models is unavailable. Our society currently has no formal means of training parents, so parenting skills are largely passed on from one generation to another. Isolated families, because they are not exposed to changing attitudes, new information, etc., are particularly likely to persevere with maladaptive parenting styles.

The available research confirms that abusive and neglectful families are often more isolated than nonmaltreating families. The causative link between isolation and maltreatment, however, has not been identified. Although limiting access to parenting information is one mechanism by which isolation contributes to maltreatment, isolation may also lead to maltreatment by increasing stress levels in at-risk families. The following section explores the relationship between stress and maltreatment.

STRESS

Adverse environmental conditions leading to stress are frequently discussed as contributing to child abuse and neglect. Cicchetti and Rizley (1981) discuss adverse environmental conditions both as long-term causative factors and as direct precipitants of maltreatment. Justice and Justice (1976) view stress associated with constantly changing environmental conditions as being the hallmark of life in abusive families. These authors also see the stress created by the child as the most direct precipitant of maltreatment. Ecological theorists discuss stress on many social levels as directly and indirectly contributing to abusive behavior (e.g., Garbarino, 1977).

Several studies confirm that maltreating families experience greater levels of stress than nonmaltreating families. Justice, Calvert, and Justice (1985) compared 23 abusing couples and 23 nonabusing couples on stress levels and factors that mediate responses to stress. Parents who abused their children were found to experience higher levels of stress. When these parents were compared to nonabusing parents who also experience high levels of stress, they were found to be more likely to condone violence as a means of solving problems and coping with stress. Gaines et al. (1978) and Mash et al. (1983) both found abusive parents to report more stress than nonabusive parents on self-report questionnaires. Using interviews and case analyses, Hunter et al. (1978) and Oliver (1985) found comparatively more stress in abusive than nonabusive samples.

The effects of stress

The effects of stress on humans are complex. Hans Seyle (1950, 1956) coined the term "general adaptation syndrome" to describe a sequence of three stages of reaction to stress. The first stage involves an immediate, intense reaction to the stressor. The second stage involves attempts to adapt to the stressor by using various coping mechanisms, and if the attempts to cope are unsuccessful, a final stage of exhaustion occurs. Reactions to stress typically involve developmentally regressive behaviors, that is, behaviors which represent basic, primitive instinctual or learned responses.

Child maltreatment can occur at any of the three stages of adaptation to stress (see Figure 3-2). When children constitute an immediate stressor, such as by crying, noncompliance, or other behavior which creates anxiety or anger in parents, the parents may react with physical or verbal aggression. The likelihood of such a reaction is increased if aggressive tendencies have been previously internalized through modeling and reinforcement and represent a frequently used means of dealing with conflicts.

Initial reactions to stress may also involve *displaced* aggression. Children are at risk for being the target of displaced aggression because the family is often seen as a "safer" outlet for frustrations encountered elsewhere (e.g., Straus & Gelles, 1980). For example, frustrations occurring in environments such as the workplace often cannot be vented because of the potential consequences for the parent. Unfortunately, the consequences of aggression within the family are often much less apparent than in social situations outside the family, and, consequently, there are fewer immediate sanctions to inhibit intrafamilial violence.

The second level of the general adaptation syndrome involves efforts to cope with the stressor beyond the initial reaction. For example, an individual who loses his job may initially react with anger and aggression, then subsequently resort to alcohol abuse to cope with the long-term effects of unemployment. Attempts to cope with stress at this level can involve a variety of actions, each for the purpose of reducing the anxiety associated with the stressor. Similar to the initial reaction, attempts to cope at this level will be comprised of actions which have been previously internalized by the individual. These behavior patterns may be adaptive or maladaptive, and many may be consistent with child abuse or neglect.

Examples of how efforts to cope with environmental stressors can lead to maltreatment are numerous. The use of alcohol or drugs is a common way of coping with stress in American society. The use of such substances leads to reduced inhibitions and impulse control, both factors which have been associated with physical and sexual abuse (e.g., Finkelhor, 1986). Drug and alcohol use can also become an obsession, very often resulting in a preoccupation which can easily lead to neglecting other aspects of one's life, including children. Examples of such "obsessions" are common with the recent rise in "crack" cocaine use. This drug quickly becomes the most important thing in life and consumes people in such a way that they are completely unable to care for themselves or those around them.

Another way of coping with stress is to simply remove oneself from the stressful environment. Such escape can be physical or mental, and when it occurs neglect may result because children are left to fend for themselves.

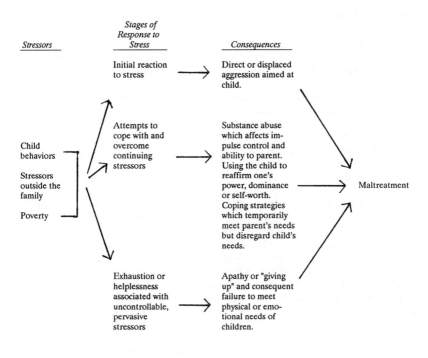

Figure 3-2

Processes by which environmental stress may contribute to maltreatment

When stress results from feelings of social, emotional, or occupational inadequacy, individuals may cope by asserting their authority over children. Such dominance, in the extreme, may take the form of sexual exploitation or attempts at physical or emotional control over children. These coping strategies, while socially maladaptive, are functional for the parent because they temporarily provide the sense of adequacy or efficacy the parent lacks.

When stress persists despite various efforts to cope, exhaustion or learned helplessness associated with pervasive, uncontrollable stressors may set in. In this final stage of coping, individuals may come to believe their efforts are futile, and consequently may give up their attempts at adaptive functioning. These circumstances may result in depression, apathy, and failure to expend energy on demanding tasks such as childrearing.   Day-to-day functioning becomes a chore, the family environment may deteriorate, and children may often be left physically and emotionally uncared for. Some of the neglectful mothers characterized by Polansky and his colleagues as suffering from the "apathy-futility syndrome" (e.g., Polansky et al., 1981) may be functioning at this level of adaptation to stress.

Dealing with stress

Improving stress management with parents represents an important intervention point in child abuse and neglect. The disorganization associated with stress and anxiety increases an individual's motivation to restore order and may open them up to try new coping strategies. If adaptive coping strategies can be learned, the likelihood that future stress will lead to maltreatment is decreased. Simply reducing adverse or stressful conditions, however, as many public assistance programs do, is only a temporary solution.   Future difficulties and frustrations are inevitable, and unless adaptive coping techniques are well learned and reinforced, future stress is bound to cause regression to prior maladaptive behaviors.

Section summary

Many of the families in which child abuse and neglect occur are subject to increased levels of environmental stress. Stress may be associated with maltreatment in a variety of ways. Parents may "lash out" at children as a reaction to the anxiety or frustration produced by the child. Children may be the focus of displaced aggression from stress occurring elsewhere, such as in the parent's workplace. Sustained efforts to cope with stress may embody actions which are directly or indirectly associated with child maltreatment, such as substance abuse or assertion of one's dominance, either physically or sexually, over the child. Finally, pervasive and uncontrollable stress may lead to a giving up or learned helplessness. This state of exhaustion may lead to an inability to care for the physical and emotional needs of children. Families under stress are in need of support and the support must focus both on addressing the immediate source of the stress and helping the family learn more effective ways of coping with future stress.

Both experience-based differences in parenting and difficulties due to environmental stress are typically seen as a function of external or environmental factors. For example, stress is often seen as a function of financial difficulties, housing problems, etc., and experience-based differences in parenting are primarily the result of sociocultural and environmental conditions which allow for the perpetuation of inadequate childrearing practices.

Both stress and maladaptive parenting practices, however, can also result from cognitive and character deficits.   Certainly, some parents abuse or neglect their children despite awareness of more appropriate behavior and a relatively stress-free environment. In fact, the assumption that the perpetrators are in some way disturbed is widely held and has guided the majority of the research and writing on abusive or neglectful parents. The following section explores the intrapersonal characteristics which are thought to increase the potential risk of individuals to perpetrate maltreatment.

CHARACTERISTICS OF PERPETRATORS

The earliest literature on maltreatment viewed the perpetrators of child abuse and neglect as qualitatively different or deviant from nonperpetrators. Efforts to identify the characteristics which distinguished perpetrators from nonperpetrators were common, and only recently has the emphasis moved in the direction of sociocultural and environmental factors. Although individual characteristics are no longer considered to be the primary cause of maltreatment, efforts to develop a character profile of the abusive or neglectful parent continue. These intrapersonal risk characteristics are now thought to interact with environmental and sociocultural factors to create situations conducive to maltreatment.

Several traits may be directly or indirectly associated with maltreatment. Contrary to earlier beliefs, there appears to be no single personality profile which is directly and invariably related to maltreatment. Most of the characteristics which have been identified in perpetrators can also be found in samples of nonperpetrators and no personality characteristics have been identified which, when present, guarantee that maltreatment will occur. Rather, a variety of characteristics exist which place individuals at risk for perpetrating maltreatment.

Characteristics associated with perpetrators are summarized in Figure 3-3. A variety of cognitive, personality, and behavioral traits has appeared in literature but, as discussed in chapter two, methodological problems limit our knowledge about the specific nature and roles of these factors in causing maltreatment. Although much has yet to be learned about perpetrator characteristics contributing to the risk for maltreatment, each of the characteristics discussed below appears to represent factors which may contribute in some manner to child abuse and/or neglect.

Physical/Medical Characteristics

Physical or medical problems have received little attention in the literature on adult perpetrators of maltreatment, even though physical injuries are the primary indicators of maltreatment in children, and maltreated children are thought to often become maltreating adults. A few studies addressing the incidence of physical problems with perpetrators are available and suggest that physically abusive and sexually abusive parents may have a greater incidence of certain physical abnormalities.

Physical abuse and neglect

Smith, Honigsberger, and Smith (1973) reported abnormal EEG in 8 of 35 parents who had abused their children. Oliver (1985) found that 6.8% of a sample of 278 maltreating parents to have a history of chronic or recurrent epilepsy.

There is also evidence that physically abusive parents may be more easily aroused by social stimuli and that abusive and neglectful parents may be slower to habituate to arousing stimuli. Friedrich et al. (1985) measured a series of variables in samples of abusive, neglectful, and control mothers. As measured by changes in skin conductance, abusive and neglectful mothers were less able to habituate to audiotapes of either an infant's cry, white noise, or a pure tone. Frodi and Lamb (1980) also found that, while nonabusive parents relaxed to a videotape of an infant smiling, abusers responded with physiological arousal. Such response styles may cause certain adults to become overly aroused or irritated by children's actions and this anxiety may lead to incidents of abuse.

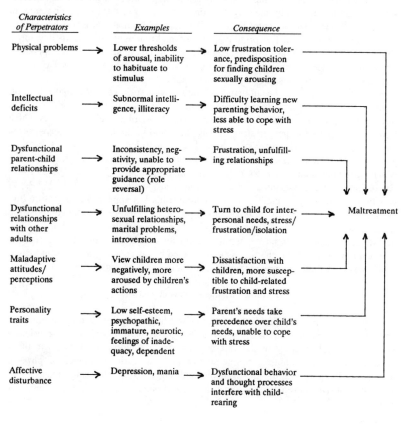

Figure 3-3

Individual characteristics associated with maltreating parents

Sexual abuse

Several studies suggest that perpetrators of sexual abuse may also show unusual patterns of physiological responding, particularly to sexual stimuli. Studies using physiological measures have demonstrated that molesters show more arousal to slides of female and male children than nonmolesters (Freund, 1967; Quinsey et al., 1975). Although the child molesters in these studies typically claimed adult females as their preferred sex object, they demonstrated the largest penile responses to slides of female children. The penile tests also confirmed that female-object child molesters had peak arousal to female children, and male-object pedophiles to male children (Quinsey et al., 1975).

Atwood & Howell (1971) found that the pupils of child molesters dilated to slides of children and constricted to slides of adult females, an opposite pattern from that demonstrated by a comparison group. These studies suggest that pedophiles may have an arousal preference for children, but whether or not all child molesters, including incest offenders, have such a preference is not clear.

A few studies focus on the relationship between biological factors such as hormone levels or chromosomal makeup and sexual arousal to children. There are reports of physiological abnormalities among some child molesters (e.g., McAuliff, 1983), and reports of success in treating them with medication. Elevated testosterone levels have also been noted in pedophiles (Berlin & Coyle, 1981).

In short, physical and medical characteristics have received relatively little attention as factors associated with maltreatment.   Although such factors may contribute to the occurrence of abuse or neglect in certain cases, relatively little is known about specific ways in which physical or physiological abnormalities may affect maltreatment and whether they represent causative factors or simply correlates.

Intellectual Deficits

Intellectual deficits may serve as risk factors by decreasing an individual's ability to acquire parenting skills, learn about child development, empathize with the needs of children, or adapt to the variety of challenging situations which childrearing presents. More generally, intellectual deficits may interfere with an individual's ability to adaptively cope with stress in any domain.

Physical abuse and neglect

A number of studies have suggested that certain samples of abusive and neglectful parents demonstrate intellectual deficits.   For example, Brunnquell, Crichton, and Egeland (1981) studied a series of variables in 267 at risk mothers, and found IQ as measured by the Shipley-Hartford to differentiate between mothers who later provided adequate care, mothers who provided inadequate care, and a random sample of mothers from the original pool.   Adequate-care mothers achieved the highest IQ scores, and inadequate-care mothers achieved the lowest IQ scores.

Similarly, Oliver (1985) found that 13% of a sample of 278 parents from families in which intergenerational maltreatment was evident had been characterized by subnormal intelligence (IQ's "usually between 50 and 70"). In addition, 27% of this sample was characterized as illiterate or semiliterate.

Again, whereas these numbers indicate some manner of association between intellectual deficits and risk for maltreatment, it cannot be determined from the research if this relationship is causative or simply correlational in nature.   It is possible that parents with subnormal intellectual levels have greater difficulty parenting, or it is also possible that other factors, such as poor sociocultural conditions, place individuals at risk for both poor intellectual development and maladaptive parenting styles.

Parent-Child Interactions

The characteristics which differentiate maltreating from nonmaltreating parents in terms of parent-child relationships have been widely discussed. Physically and emotionally abusive parents are often characterized as rejecting, harsh, and unpredictable, while neglectful mothers are variously characterized as treating their children in angry, distant, and inconsistent ways. Sexually abusive parents are often characterized as either overly dominating or inappropriately dependent upon their children.

TABLE 3-1

**Published studies investigating parent-child interactions
in maltreating families**

Study	Sample					Summary of Results
	PA	*N*	*EA*	*C*	*Behavior Problem*	
Aragona & Eyberg (1981)		9		9	9	N - Negative and controlling (during child-directed play)
Burgess & Conger (1978)	17	17		17		PA - Lower rates of verbal and physical interaction N - More negativity toward children
Mash, Johnston & Kovitz (1983)	18			18		PA - More directive and controlling
Nastasi & Hill (1982)	6	I*		6	6	PA - Did not adapt behavior to demands of parent-child task
Smith & Hanson (1975)	214		53 families			PA - Inconsistency, lacked demonstrativeness on overinvolved/severe or lack of discipline

*Included in the physically abusive sample.

Physical abuse and neglect

Several studies have been designed to validate our impressions about the ways in which the parent-child interactions of maltreating parents may be different than those of nonmaltreating parents. Table 3-1 summarizes several of these studies. Smith and Hanson (1975) studied the characteristics of 214 parents of battered children and compared them to a sample of nonbattering parents empirically equated for (but not matched for) social class. The battering parents were characterized by inconsistency in their relationships with their children. For example, these parents were reported to variously lack demonstrativeness toward their children or be overly involved with them and to be overly physically punishing or extremely lax in their supervision.

Other studies have found abusive and neglectful parents to be generally less warm and positive with their children. Burgess and Conger (1978) observed the interactions of abusive, neglectful, and control families and found that the abusive families exhibited lower rates of verbal and physical interaction. The neglectful parents showed more negativity in their interactions. Herrenkohl et al. (1984) also observed parent-child interactions and found maltreatment associated with more parental rejection and less child warmth. Income level, as well as maltreatment, was associated with parent behavior, with lower incomes also being associated with more parental rejection and less child warmth.

Several studies have also shown that maltreating parents do not adapt their interactions to changing environmental demands in the manner that nonmaltreating parents do. Aragona and Eyberg (1981) studied low income Caucasian families in which the children had been identified as neglected, as having a behavior problem, or having no identified problems. They observed parent-child interactions during play and reported that the nature of the play settings made a difference in the interactions. The neglectful mothers were more negative and controlling during child-directed play, and the mothers of behavior-problem children were more negative and controlling during parent-directed play.

Nastasi and Hill (1982) also observed mother-child interactions of abused and/or neglected, behavior disordered, and nonproblem children. Their observations, conducted during free play and structured task-oriented play, showed that the mothers of the maltreated children were the only group that did not increase their guidance from the unstructured to the structured situation. Children in all three groups reacted to the different tasks in a similar manner.

Mash, Johnston, and Kovitz (1983) found abusive mothers did increase their guidance from play to task situations but in a somewhat maladaptive manner. As compared to nonabusive mothers, abusive mothers became more directive and controlling when the demands placed upon them and their children were increased.

In short, it appears that parents, particularly mothers, of physically abused and neglected children exhibit behaviors which are maladaptive in a way that may be unique to this population. They appear to interact less and be more negative in their interactions. In addition, they appear to be less adept at providing useful and appropriate guidance to their children. Such deficits are likely to lead to frustration in dealing with children and are also likely to interfere with optimal child development, particularly in the areas of problem solving and interpersonal skills.

Sexual abuse

One additional frequently discussed characteristic of parent-child relationships, particularly in regard to sexual abuse, is role reversal. Role reversal refers to the apparent tendency of these children to become caretakers of their parents' needs rather than vice versa.

Although role reversal is commonly accepted as a characteristic of incestuous families, this characteristic has not subjected to adequate empirical study to warrant firm conclusions. The extent to which children in nonmaltreating families "care" for their parents -- and whether or not there are qualitative differences in the ways nonmaltreated children treat their parents -- is not known. It is possible that the behaviors consistent with role reversal are not unique to maltreating families but occur more frequently because maltreating parents act in ways which reinforce these behaviors. Because of the frequency with which role reversal is associated with maltreatment, it is important that it be more carefully studied to better delineate the nature of this relationship.

Relationships with Adults

The above section explored differences in perpetrators' and nonperpetrators' relationships with children. It has also been suggested that perpetrators also have difficulty relating to adults, and, in the case of sexual abuse, that these difficulties represent a direct causative factor for the abuse.

Physical abuse and neglect

Interpersonal deficits have been noted in samples of physically abusive and neglectful parents, and the deficits are typically viewed as correlates rather than as causative factors. Friedrich et al. (1985) found that abusive and neglectful parents scored lower on the socialization scale of the California Personality Inventory, with neglectful mothers scoring the lowest. Hymen (1977) found physically abusive fathers to be more introverted than comparison fathers, and Smith and Hanson (1975) discussed the interpersonal relationships of physically abusive parents as more often being characterized by unhappiness and hostility.

Sexual abuse

Several studies suggest that male sexual abusers may have problems with adult females. In a study of 200 sex offenders, Hammer & Glueck (1957) report "fear of heterosexual contact" as a common finding. Panton (1978) found that child molesters tended to be socially anxious and inadequate. They felt insecure in their relationships with others and expected rejection and failure in adult heterosexual advances. Child molesters have also been shown to harbor unusual amounts of sexual anxiety which may contribute to the problems relating to females (Goldstein et al., 1973). General social skills deficits may also contribute to problems relating to adult women (Wilson & Cox, 1983). Interpersonal problems such as these are thought to directly contribute to the potential for sexual abuse with adults turning to children because of their lack of fulfillment in adult relationships.

In general, however, the research which demonstrates interpersonal deficits in maltreating parents does not address whether these interpersonal problems directly contribute to the occurrence of maltreatment or whether they are another manifestation of more basic underlying problems. It is possible that frustration in adult heterosexual relations could directly contribute to sexual relations with children, or that other types of maltreatment could result from the resentment, indifference, or stress which arises when parents cannot get along with other adults. On the other hand, it is possible that other characteristics such as intellectual deficits, maladaptive, social or interpersonal attitudes, or affective disturbance could interfere with both adult and child relationships. In this case, the interpersonal deficits noted would represent another manifestation of a more fundamental deficit affecting relationships in general.

TABLE 3-2

**Examples of studies assessing the attitude or perceptions
of maltreating parents**

Study	Sample			Summary of Findings
	PA	*N*	*C*	
Friedrich, Tyler & Clark (1985)	14	13	15	PA & N - Rated infant's cry as more aversive
				N - Rated cry as more irritating and demanding
Frodi & Lamb (1980)	14		14	PA - Greater physiological arousal to tapes of infants and rated the crying infant as more aversive
Larrance & Twentyman (1983)	10	10	10	PA & N - Negative expectations for their children. Viewed their children as more responsible for failure and less responsible for success.
Mash, Johnston, & Kovitz, (1983)	18		18	PA - Mothers rated children more negatively, no differences in children's behavior noted
Wood-Shuman & Cone (1986)	5 (18 at risk)		20	PA & At-Risk - Rated videotaped scenes of children more negatively

Attitudes and Perceptions

Behavior is closely related to perceptions and attitudes.   If one perceives another's behavior as threatening, he/she is likely to react in a defensive manner.   If one perceives that his or her child's misbehavior or failure to live up to parental expectations is malicious, anger or frustration toward that child may result.   Such misperceptions or attitudes may lead to maltreatment by causing parents to overreact or react inappropriately to the situation.

Studies which assess attitudes and perceptions of parents typically utilize one of two methods.   The first method involves comparing parents' viewpoints to an objective standard.   If parental viewpoints do not match the objective standard, it can be assumed their viewpoint is inaccurate or biased in some manner.   The second method involves comparing responses of maltreating and nonmaltreating parents to the same stimulus.   If the two groups differ in how they assess or respond to the stimulus, it can be assumed that the maltreating parents differ from the norm in these respects.   Comparing groups, however, does not necessarily provide information about which group may be more or less accurate in their perceptions.   Table 3-2 gives examples of several studies which assess the perceptions of physically abusive and neglectful parents.

Appraisal of children's behavior

Many studies are available which demonstrate that abusive parents rate their children as behaviorally disordered.   In most cases such ratings probably reflect a higher degree of behavioral disturbance in these children (e.g., Aragona & Eyberg, 1981).   In some cases, however, there is evidence that such ratings reflect parental misperceptions rather than an accurate appraisal of their children's behavior.   For example, Mash, Johnston, and Kovitz (1983) collected both behavioral observations and parental ratings of children's behavior from physically abusive and nonmaltreating mothers.   Although no between-group differences were noted in the children's behavior, the abusive mothers rated their children as significantly more behavior disordered than the nonabusive mothers.   In other words, the perceptions of the maltreating mothers were not consistent with the behavior of their children but were negatively biased.

Research comparing the perceptions of maltreating and nonmaltreating parents can involve comparing physiological responses to as well as parental ratings of children's behavior.   Physiological responses reflect arousal to a stimulus, which in turn provides clues to the manner in which a stimulus is perceived or the effect it has upon the individual.   For example, Frodi and Lamb (1980) compared the physiological responses of physically abusive and nonabusive mothers to videotapes of children. The abusers responded to a videotaped cry with greater cardiac and skin conductance arousal.   Further, the abusers showed physiological arousal to a smile segment, whereas the nonabusers relaxed to this segment.   These findings suggest that abusers may be overly reactive to children, but they may also reflect that abusers become more easily aroused in general.   Finally, Frodi and Lamb also found that abusive parents rated the crying infant as more aversive than did the nonabusive parents, supporting the contention that they do in fact find certain aspects of children's behavior more annoying than do other parents.

Similar findings were reported by Friedrich et al. (1985). Maltreating mothers differed in their subjective ratings of audiotapes of children, with control mothers rating children's crying as less "angry" than abusive or neglectful mothers. Further, neglectful mothers rated the cry as most irritating. Wood-Shuman and Cone (1986) also found that abusive and at-risk mothers rated videotaped scenes of children more negatively. Abusive mothers rated the scenes most negatively, comparison mothers least negatively, and the ratings of at risk mothers fell between the other two groups.

The above research suggests that abusive and neglectful parents become more easily aroused by children. Related research also suggests that these parents view their children more negatively in other ways as well. Larrance and Twentyman (1983) studied attributions and expectations by comparing stimulus-picture ratings of abusive, neglectful, and control mothers. Both abusive and neglectful mothers demonstrated more negative expectations for their children than did the control parents. In addition, abusive mothers attributed their own children's transgressions and failure to stable and internal causes, whereas external and unstable attributions were made for both their child's success and another child's transgressions. Nonmaltreating parents' attributions were the opposite of this pattern. These findings indicated that abusive and neglectful parents viewed their children in a negative light, making attributions which are likely to promote parental anger and dissatisfaction rather than pleasure.

In short, the research on attitudes and perceptions of maltreating parents generally confirms the assumption that these parents often hold maladaptive views of their children. They view their children more negatively and become more angry and aroused by children's actions. Although these attitudes and perceptions may be either the cause or the result of behavior patterns associated with maltreatment, they indicate that these parents are more likely to react to their children in maladaptive ways. If the stress resulting from children's behavior is viewed as a common precipitant of abuse, as suggested by Justice and Justice (1976), the increased sensitivity of certain parents to this stress may increase the probability of abuse by these parents.

Personality Traits

When child abuse emerged as a national issue in the early 1960's, a common misconception was that most perpetrators suffered from severe mental illness. Although psychotic individuals are typically incapable of adequately caring for children, it is now generally accepted that mental illness of this severity accounts for only a small percentage (less than 5%) of all cases of maltreatment. The most frequently discussed and studied characteristics thought to distinguish perpetrators from nonperpetrators are now personality traits.

The personality traits most frequently discussed depend upon the type of maltreatment. Physically abusive parents are most frequently discussed as impulsive, angry, and sociopathic. Emotionally abusive parents are characterized as angry and resentful. Neglectful parents (usually the mothers are identified) are generally described as apathetic, immature, or dependent. Sexually abusive adults are thought to be immature or childish, have low self-esteem, and be distrustful of others. The available research suggests that some perpetrators, although certainly not all, have comparatively higher levels of many of these personality traits.

TABLE 3-3

Studies of the personality traits of maltreating parents

Study	Sample PA	N	EA	SA	C	Measures	Summary of Findings
Brunnquell, Crichton, & Egeland (1981)	32	I*			32	Composites derived from measures of personality, intellectual, social and environmental variables	Groups best differentiated by a composite of IQ, anxiety, locus of control, dependence, reciprocity and succorance
Friedrich, Tyler, & Clark (1985)	14	13			15	MMPI (shortened) MAACL CPI	PA & N - F & Pd (psychopathic deviate) N - Sc (schizophrenia) PA & N - greater anxiety and hostility
Gabinet (1979)	22				90 90 (psychiatric patients)	MMPI	Mania scale elevations
Hammer & Glueck (1957)				200 (sex offenders)		Rorschach TAT H-T-P Blacky	Low self-esteem Sexually immature
Hunter, Kilstrom, Kraybill, & Loda (1978)	10	I*			245	Interview Case analysis	Impulsive Apathetic Childish-dependent

Hymen (1977)	37	37	16 PF	PA mothers - immature fathers - introverted
Land (1986)	89		MMPI	Pd & Ma scale elevations
Mash, Johnston, & Kovitz (1983)	18	18	Sense of competence scale	Low parenting self-esteem
Melnick & Hurley (1969)	10	10	Psychological tests	Low self-esteem, low family satisfaction
Milner & Wimberly (1980)	65	65	Child Abuse Potential Inventory	Rigidity, unhappiness, distress
Panton (1978)		28 (30 rapists) (30 child rapists)	MMPI	SA - low self-esteem, self-doubt feelings of inadequacy, insecurity
Smith & Hanson (1975)	214	53	Interview Psychological tests	Neurotic Hostile
Smith, Hanson, & Noble (1973)			Eyesenck PI	Neuroticism

*Included in PA sample.

imon way to study the personality characteristics of maltreating
re their profiles on psychological tests to the available norms or to
maltreating comparison samples. Table 3-3 provides examples of
dies.   Studies are available with samples of physically abusive,
sexually abusive individuals, but,   again,   emotional abuse is
und...   d in the literature.

Physical abuse

The personality traits of perpetrators are most commonly studied with samples
of physically abusive parents. The MMPI profiles of these parents are frequently
characterized by elevations on the Pd (Psychopathic deviate) and Ma (Mania) scales
(e.g., Friedrich et al., 1985; Gabinet, 1979; Land, 1986). The Pd scale of the MMPI is
sensitive to family problems and reflects characteristics such as a lack of feelings or
emotions, disregard for social norms, and behavioral irresponsibility. The Ma scale
reflects, among other things, emotional instability, impulsivity, and restlessness.

Layden and Bascuas (1987) studied the MMPI profiles of physically abusive
parents using a technique called cluster analyses. Cluster analyses was used to find
groupings of similar MMPI profiles, and four types of profiles which characterized the
abusive parents were found. The clusters included sociopathic (Pd, Ma elevations),
guilty/depressed (Pd, D elevations), normal profile abusers, and a small group of
psychotic abusers (F, Pa, Sc elevations). Their identification of a group of abusers
with normal personality profiles provides further evidence of the variability in
maltreating parents and highlights the need to incorporate multiple etiological factors
in our explanations of maltreatment.

Other personality tests have found physically abusive parents to be overly rigid,
immature, hostile, dependent, impulsive, and to suffer from low self-esteem (see
Table 3-3). Each of these characteristics can interfere with an individual's ability to
cope with stress and can also lead to the deficits in interpersonal behavior discussed
earlier. Further, because the behavior of individuals with such traits is often more
dependent on their own dysfunctional needs than on the demands of the particular
situation, the probability of environmentally inappropriate behavior is increased when
such traits are present.

Neglect

Neglectful parents have also been found to differ from nonabusive parents on
certain personality measures. Friedrich et al. (1985) found that neglectful parents,
like physically abusive parents, had elevated MMPI scores on the F and Pd scales. In
addition, the neglectful parents had elevated Sc scale scores, suggesting a greater level
of general thought disorder. Samples which include neglectful parents along with
physically abusive parents have noted greater levels of immaturity and apathy than are
typically found in physically abusive samples alone (e.g., Hunter et al., 1978; Hymen,
1977). Immaturity and apathy are also discussed as contributing to the loneliness and
isolation which so often characterizes neglectful families (e.g., Polansky et al., 1981).
Personality traits associated with neglect appear to more consistent with depression
and inadequacy, as compared to physically abusive parents whose traits appear more
related to interpersonal disturbance.

Sexual abuse

Finally, sexually abusive individuals are typically thought to have personality characteristics consistent with immaturity and inadequacy. For example, Panton (1978) found that the MMPI profiles of nonviolent child molesters reflected low self-esteem, self-doubt, feelings of inadequacy, and insecurity. In a sample of 224 probational male sex offenders given the Bender-Gestalt test, Peters (1976) found greater levels of immaturity, regression, dependency needs, and feelings of phallic inadequacy. These characteristics are consistent with the belief that sexually abusive individuals are frequently childlike in their personalities and may consequently find that their needs are better met in relationships with children (e.g., Panton, 1978). The above is only a sampling of the available literature on the personality traits of perpetrators. This research is varied, and most of the characteristics which "fit" the abusive or neglectful profile have been verified in at least one study. Studies exist in which physical abusers have been found to be impulsive and hostile, and neglectful parents have been shown to be apathetic and dependent. Perpetrators of sexual abuse have been found to be immature or emotionally regressed. Perpetrators of maltreatment in general appear to have low self-esteem, unfulfilled emotional needs, and are often classified as more "neurotic" than the general population.

Variability of traits

Despite the availability of research which points to various personality traits in perpetrators of maltreatment, the development of a unified personality profile is made impossible by the variability of traits identified across different studies. This variability is in part due to differences in the methodologies and measures used but is probably more due to actual differences among the characteristics of the perpetrators. A variety of personality deficits may lead to maladaptive behavior and coping styles, any of which may result in maltreatment given the relevant set of environmental circumstances. Again, the personality traits identified are risk factors, and any of a variety of personality characteristics may interfere with adaptive functioning and consequently increase a parent's potential for abusing or neglecting their children.

Affect

Affect is a general term referring to mood. Disturbances of affect generally involve pervasive or extreme unhappiness or, conversely, unusually high spirits or mania. Both depressive and manic states have many related features. Depression is associated with negativity, low energy, pessimism, disturbances of eating and sleeping and low self-esteem. Mania is associated with overactivity, impulsiveness, and often a disregard for the consequences of one's behavior.

Many of the features of affective disturbance have been previously discussed as characterizing perpetrators. Personality tests have shown elevated levels of depression and mania in abusive and neglectful samples and interviews and questionnaires often indicate low self-esteem in abusive parents. Relatively few studies, however, have looked at the prevalence of affective disorders as clinical syndromes in abusive and neglectful parents.

Famularo, Barnum, and Stone (1986) studied affective disorders in perpetrators of physical abuse or neglect and suggest that depression often characterizes those parents. Using the *Research Diagnostic Criteria*, they evaluated 50 parents whose children had been removed because of child abuse and/or neglect and 38 matched comparison parents. Thirty-six percent of the maltreatment sample had histories which met the diagnostic criteria for major or minor depression, as compared to only 13% of the comparison sample. In addition, 2 (4%) of the maltreating parents had histories consistent with bipolar disorder. Despite histories of frequent contact with social service agencies, most of these parents had not been previously diagnosed, and only one of the maltreating parents had received pharmacological treatment for an affective disorder.

Oliver (1985) also assessed depression in a sample of 278 parents whose families exhibited an intergenerational cycle of maltreatment. A high incidence of depression was found for the mothers, with 34% showing past or present evidence of depressive states. Only 5.3% of the fathers, however, showed evidence of depression.

Finally, Polansky et al. (1981, 1985) provide evidence of high levels of isolation and loneliness in neglectful mothers, even though these mothers do not appear to lack access to social support networks. The authors identify character disorders, such as the "apathy-futility syndrome" and "infantilism," which seem to characterize neglectful mothers and interfere with their ability to access and derive support from the available social support networks. His characterization of the neglectful mothers suggests that depression may be contributing to the isolation and loneliness these mothers experience.

The prevalence and treatment of affective disorders in abusive and neglectful parents, particularly mothers, merit further attention in the maltreatment literature. The pharmacological treatment of affective disorders is well researched in the medical literature but is largely overlooked in the treatment of abuse and neglect. Further research should explore the efficacy of such treatment in cases of abuse or neglect where there is evidence of possible disturbances of affect.

Section summary

Many characteristics have been identified which differentiate samples of maltreating and nonmaltreating parents. Although various studies have found maltreating parents to have more physical problems, cognitive limitations, interpersonal problems, and disturbances of personality and affect, none of these characteristics are exclusively associated with individuals who abuse or neglect their children. Consequently, a unified personality profile of abusive or neglectful parents does not exist.

The characteristics discussed in this chapter should be viewed as risk factors which make an individual more prone to abusive and neglectful behavior. In a given individual, the presence of a greater number of such risk factors increases the likelihood that abusive or neglectful behavior can occur. On the other hand, some parents who mistreat their children exhibit no signs of deviance in regards to cognitive, physical or personality characteristics, and maltreatment should consequently not be viewed as exclusively a function of deviant individuals. Only by considering sociocultural factors and environmental conditioning, along with the individual characteristics, can maltreatment be adequately understood.

TEENAGE PARENTS

The final section in this chapter considers a topic of increasing relevance to maltreatment -- teenage parents. Although the birth rate among older women appears to be declining, the birth rate among teenagers continues to rise (Phipps-Yonas, 1980). In addition, there is some evidence, albeit mixed, that teenage parents may be more prone to be reported for abusing or neglecting their children (e.g., Bolton, Lanar, and Kane, 1980). Although a close examination of the available data suggest that age alone may not be the primary contributing variable to maltreatment by teenage parents, many of the developmental correlates of adolescence are likely to make parenting at this age more difficult (Kinard & Klerman, 1980).

If one reviews the parental characteristics discussed throughout this chapter, it becomes evident that an impressive number of these characteristics are a normal part of adolescent development. For example, teenage parents may often lack or not take advantage of information relevant to pre- and postnatal care, may be more subject to, and less able to cope with, the effects of environmental stress, and may exhibit many of the individual characteristics or traits which have been associated with maltreatment in adults. This section explores the characteristics and needs of teenage parents as they relate to child abuse and neglect. The general areas discussed parallel the earlier discussion of parental characteristics, including differences in childrearing experience, the effects of stress, and intrapersonal characteristics.

Difference in childrearing experience

Teenage parents learn how to parent the same way adults do, through their experiences as children and exposure to other parents or families. Teenage parents, however, are often less likely than their adult counterparts to have access to various sources of parenting information and may be more likely to not take advantage of, or actually reject, the information that is available. Because they are striving to develop a sense of independence, adolescents frequently are not receptive to what others, particularly adults, tell them. Further, teenage mothers may receive less input from their partners, with many teenage boys being unable or unwilling to accept the responsibilities of parenting. The responsibilities of parenting may also lead to greater isolation from their peers, and because of age differences and developmental considerations (e.g., years), fulfilling social relations with adults are less likely to develop. Consequently, many of the usual sources of parenting information are limited or unavailable with teenagers.

Stress

Adolescents are also likely to encounter greater levels of environmental stress than adults. Developing adolescents experience rapid cognitive, emotional, and physical growth and must struggle with rapidly shifting emotions and moods. The additional demands of caring for a child can only exacerbate this stress.

Adolescents also face coping with financial and social concerns in an adult-oriented world. Job opportunities are much more restricted for teenagers than they are for adults. In addition, adolescents who have children often drop out of school, further limiting their chances for a financially and emotionally fulfilling career. Similarly, difficulty in generating a fulfilling social life may lead to stress. The lifestyles of teenage parents are often very different from the lifestyles of their peers. Even though their needs for peer support and acceptance are as strong as the needs of other adolescents, teenage parents are much more restricted in their social activities. Yet if a teen parent chooses to participate in the social activities of her peer group, her parental responsibilities may be neglected. The choices faced by teenage parents are difficult and often mean choosing between the developmental needs of the parent and child.

In addition to increased environmental stress, adolescents are often less able to cope with this stress. Teenagers are in many ways still children, and they have not yet developed confidence in their ability to solve adult-size problems. Insecurities abound, and coping strategies are more likely to involve denial, substance abuse, regression, or other ineffective techniques. In the absence of parental support and caretaking for the adolescent parent, these teenagers may resort to abuse as an outlet for their frustrations, or neglect may occur because these parents are unable to meet their own needs, let alone the needs of their children.

Individual characteristics

Many of the individual characteristics which increase the risk of maltreatment in adults are normal in teenagers. Adolescents are struggling to develop a sense of identity and independence and do not want to be told what to do. Consequently, interpersonal conflict, particularly with authority, is common. The struggles of normal adolescent development can also lead to behavior which appears immature, defensive, antisocial, and irresponsible. Although such characteristics often occur as a part of normal adolescent development, they may create significant problems if there are children who must be cared for.

Characteristics which increase risk for maltreatment in adolescent parents must be handled differently than similar characteristics with adults. Teenagers need time to resolve their salient developmental issues, and therapy to "change" these characteristics is often not an appropriate solution. Rather, teenage parents need support and opportunity to develop. If the demands and stress of parenting can be temporarily relieved through family or other support services, many of the conflicts of adolescence can be resolved and both the parent and child can develop into healthy, fully functioning individuals.

Section summary

The numbers of teenage parents in our society are continuing to increase. Because of the developmental needs of these parents, they present a high risk population for abusing or neglecting their children. Teenage parents are less likely to seek out and be provided with information about pre- and postnatal child care, are more subject to and less able to cope with environmental stress, and have many developmentally normal personality characteristics which might interfere with parent-child relationships. Consequently, the needs of maltreating teenagers must be addressed differently than the needs of maltreating adults. Most notably, efforts must be made to facilitate the normal developmental processes and provide the necessary support so that teenage parents can become healthy, fully functioning adults while still providing for the needs of their children.

Domain - Identify Strengths and Weaknesses	*Treatment Recommendations*
I. Childrearing experiences	I. Educational needs:

A.   Beliefs about discipline/ childrearing
   B.   Repertoire of parenting skills
   C. Knowledge of child development	

II. Stress	II. Social supports & counseling

A.   Immediate stressors
   B.   Long-term stressors
   C.   Manner of coping with stress
	A. Social supports
	   B. Social supports
	   C. Stress management counseling

III. Intrapersonal characteristics	III. Treatments and supports needed

A.   Physical/medical
   B.   Intellectual
   C.   Parent-child interactions (consistency, supportiveness, flexibility)
   D.   Relationships with adults
   E.   Attitudes and perceptions
   F.   Personality traits (impulsive, angry, socio-, pathic, immature, dependent, distrustful, etc.)
   G. Affect (depressive, manic)	

Figure 3-4

Assessment summary of the characteristics of maltreating parents*

*A comprehensive assessment covering these areas will require a multimethod approach, including interviews, observations, family history, medical examination, and psychological assessment.

CHAPTER SUMMARY

This chapter has discussed the characteristics associated with abusive and neglectful parents. Differences in experience related to parenting may lead to inappropriate childrearing behaviors because parents do not perceive their behaviors are maladaptive or because they are unaware of alternative behaviors. Environmental stress may precipitate abuse or neglect when initial reactions of anger or frustration are directed at the children or when efforts to cope with or readjust to stress create conditions conducive to maltreatment. Finally, individual characteristics, such as intellectual deficits, interpersonal problems, or personality traits, may place individuals at risk for maltreatment by interfering with the ability to effectively parent or cope with stress. Teenage parents, because of their age and developmental status, are particularly susceptible to the conditions associated with maltreatment and may be at greater risk for maltreating their children than adults of similar background.

The reasons adults abuse or neglect children are varied and complex. In any individual case, a multiplicity of factors may contribute to the potential for maltreatment. These various factors must each be addressed if efforts to prevent future maltreatment are to be effective. Figure 3-4 summarizes the perpetrator characteristics discussed in this chapter with a format which can be easily adapted for assessment purposes. By assessing each area which may contribute to maltreatment, individual treatment and prevention efforts can be made maximally effective.

The majority of perpetrator characteristics contributing to maltreatment are related to an individual's upbringing. Exposure to adaptive parenting, ways of coping with stress, and personality traits are all integrally tied to conditions and experiences of childhood and early family life. The following chapter further explores the effects of maltreatment on children and may provide additional insight to the developmental factors which contribute to the intergenerational cycle of child abuse and neglect.

REFERENCES

Aragona, J.A., & Eyberg, S.M. (1981). "Neglected Children: Mother's Report of Child Behavior Problems and Observed Verbal Behavior." Child Development, 52, 596-602.

Atwood, R., & Howell, R. (1971). "Pupilometric and Personality Test Scores of Female Aggressors, Pedophiliacs, and Normals." Psychonomic Science, 22, 115-116.

Berlin, F., & Coyle, G. (1981). "Sexual Deviation Syndromes." Johns Hopkins Medical Journal, 149, 119-125.

Bolton, F.G., Lanar, R.H., & Kane, S.K. (1980). "Child Maltreatment Risk Among Adolescent Mothers: A Study of Reported Cases." American Journal of Orthopsychiatry, 50, 489-504.

Brunnquell, D., Crichton, L., & Egeland, B. (1981). "Maternal Personality and Attitude in Disturbances of Childrearing." American Journal of Orthopsychiatry, 51, 680-691.

Burgess, R.L., & Conger, R.D. (1978). "Family Interaction in Abusive, Neglectful, and Normal Families." Child Development, 49, 1163-1173.

Cicchetti, D., & Rizley, R. (1981). "Developmental Perspectives on the Etiology, Intergenerational Transmission, and Sequelae of Child Maltreatment." New Directions for Child Development, 11, 31-55.

Famularo, R., Barnum, R., & Stone, K. (1986). "Court-ordered Removal in Severe Child Maltreatment: An Association to Parental Major Affective Disorder." Child Abuse and Neglect, 10, 487-492.

Finkelhor, D. (1986). A Sourcebook on Child Sexual Abuse. Beverly Hills, CA: Sage Publications.

Freund, K. (1967). "Diagnosing Homo- or Heterosexuality and Erotic Age Preference by Means of a Psychophysiological Test." Behavior Research and Therapy, 5, 209-228.

Friedrich, W.N., Tyler, J.D., & Clark, J.A. (1985). "Personality and Psychophysiological Variables in Abusive, Neglectful, and Low-Income Control Mothers." The Journal of Nervous and Mental Disease, 173, 449-460.

Friedrich, W.N., & Wheeler, K.K. (1982). "The Abusing Parent Revisited: A Decade of Psychological Research." The Journal of Nervous and Mental Disease, 170, 577-587.

Frodi, A.M., & Lamb, M.E. (1980). "Child Abusers' Responses to Infant Smiles and Cries." Child Development, 51, 238-241.

Gabinet, L. (1979). "MMPI Profiles of High-Risk and Outpatient Mothers." Child Abuse and Neglect, 3, 373-379.

Gaines, R., Sandgrund, A., & Power, E. (1978). "Etiological Factors in Child Maltreatment: A Multivariate Study of Abusing, Neglecting, and Normal Mothers." Journal of Abnormal Psychology, 87, 531-540.

Garbarino, J. (1977). "The Human Ecology of Child Maltreatment: A Conceptual Model for Research." Journal of Marriage and The Family, 39, 721-735.

Goldstein, M., Kant, H., & Hartman, J., (1973). Pornography and Sexual Deviance, Los Angeles: University of California Press.

Hammer, R.F., & Glueck, B.C. (1957). "Psychodynamic Patterns in Sex Offenders: A Four-Factor Theory." Psychiatric Quarterly, 31, 325-345.

Herrenkohl, E.C., Herrenkohl, R.C., Toedter, L., & Yanushefski, M. (1984). "Parent-Child Interactions in Abusive and Nonabusive Families." Journal of the American Academy of Child Psychiatry, 23, 641-648.

Hunter, R.S., Kilstrom, N., Kraybill, E.N., & Loda, F. (1978). "Antecedents of Child Abuse and Neglect in Premature Infants: A Prospective Study in a Newborn Intensive Care Unit." Pediatrics, 61, 629-635.

Hyman, C.E. (1977). "A Report on the Psychological Test Results of Battering Parents." British Journal of Social and Clinical Psychology, 16, 221-224.

Jayaratne, S. (1977). "Child Abusers as Parents and Children: A Review." Social Work, 22, 5-9.

Justice, B., Calvert, A., & Justice, R. (1985). "Factors Mediating Child Abuse as a Response to Stress." Child Abuse and Neglect, 9, 359-363.

Justice, B., & Justice, R. (1976). The Abusing Family. New York: Human Sciences Press.

Kinard, E.M. & Klerman, L.V. (1980). "Teenage Parenting and Child Abuse: Are They Related?" American Journal of Orthopsychiatry, 50, 481-488.

Korbin, J.E. (1986). "Childhood Histories of Women Imprisoned for Fatal Child Maltreatment." Child Abuse and Neglect, 10, 331-338.

Land, H.M. (1986). "Child Abuse: Differential Diagnosis, Differential Treatment." Child Welfare, 65, 33-44.

Larrance, D.T., & Twentyman, C.T. (1983). "Maternal Attributions and Child Abuse." Journal of Abnormal Psychology, 92, 449-457.

Layden, P., & Bascuas, J. (1987). "An Empirical Typology of Physically Abusive Parents." Paper presented at the 58th Annual Convention of the Eastern Psychological Association, Arlington.

Mash, E.J., Johnston, C., & Kovitz, K. (1983). "A Comparison of the Mother-Child Interactions of Physically Abused and Nonabused Children during Play and Task Situations." Journal of Clinical Child Psychology, 12, 337-346.

McAuliff, S. (1983). "Is Sexual Deviance a Biological Problem?" Psychology Today, March, 84.

Melnick, B. & Hurley, J.R. (1969). "Distinctive Personality Attributes of Child-Abusing Mothers." Journal of Consulting and Clinical Psychology, 33, 746-749.

Milner, J.S., & Wimberly, R.C. (1980). "Prediction and Explanation of Child Abuse." Journal of Clinical Psychology, 3, 875-884.

Nastasi, B.K., & Hill, S.D. (1982). "Interactions Between Abusing Mothers and Their Children in Two Situations." Bulletin of the Psychonomic Society, 20, 79-81.

Newberger, E.H., Hampton, R.L., Marx, T.J., & White, K.M. (1986). "Child Abuse and Pediatric Social Illness: An Epidemiological Analysis and Ecological Reformulation." American Journal of Orthopsychiatry, 56, 589-601.

Oliver, J.E. (1985).   "Successive Generations of Child Maltreatment: Social and Medical Disorders in the Parents." British Journal of Psychiatry, 147, 484-490.

Panton, J.H. (1978).   "Personality Differences Appearing Between Rapists of Adults, Children,   and   Nonviolent   Sexual   Molesters   of   Children."   Research Communications in Psychology, 3, 385-393.

Phipps-Yonas, S. (1980).   "Teenage Pregnancy and Motherhood: A Review of the Literature." American Journal of Orthopsychiatry, 50, 403-431.

Polansky, N.A., Ammons, P.W., & Gaudin, J.M. (1985).   "Loneliness and Isolation in Child Neglect.   Social Casework: The Journal of Contemporary Social Work, 38-47.

Polansky, N.A., Chalmers, M.A., Buttenweiser, E., & Williams, D.P. (1981). Damaged Parents: An Anatomy of Neglect.   Chicago: University of Chicago Press.

Quinsey, V., Steinman, C., Bergensen, S., & Holmes, T. (1975).   "Penile Circumference, Skin Conduction, and Ranking Responses of Child Molesters and "Normals" to Sexual and Nonsexual Visual Stimuli." Behavior Therapy, 6, 213-219.

Seyle, H. (1950).   The Physiology and Pathology of Exposure to Stress.   Montreal: Acta.

Seyle, H. (1956).   The Stress of Life.   New York: McGraw-Hill.

Showers, J.S., & Bandman, R.L. (1986).   "Scarring for Life: Abuse with Electric Cords." Child Abuse and Neglect, 10, 25-31.

Smith, S.M., & Hanson, R. (1975).   "Interpersonal Relationships and Childrearing Practices in 214 Parents of Battered Children." British Journal of Psychiatry, 127, 513-525.

Smith, S.M., Hanson, R., & Noble, S. (1973).   "Parents of Battered Babies: A Controlled Study." British Medical Journal, 4, 388-391.

Smith, S.M., Honigsberger, L., & Smith, C.A. (1973).   "E.E.G. and Personality Factors in Baby Batterers." British Medical Journal, 2, 20-22.

Spinetta, J.J. (1978).   "Parental Personality Factors in Child Abuse." Journal of Consulting and Clinical Psychology, 46, 1409-1414.

Spinetta, J.J., & Rigler, D. (1972). "The Child Abusing Parent: A Psychological Review." Psychological Bulletin, 77, 296-304.

Wilson, G., & Cox, D. (1983). "Personality of Pedophile Club Members." Personality and Individual Differences, 4(3), 323-329.

Wood-Shuman, S., & Cone, J.D. (1986). "Differences in Abusive, at Risk for Abuse, and Control Mothers' Descriptions of Normal Child Behavior." Child Abuse and Neglect, 10, 397-405.

Chapter 4

Characteristics
of the Children

Adam's bruises have long since healed. He now attends preschool regularly. Yet, when one observes Adam it is obvious he is not like other children. When he tries to join others in play he is often not accepted. He is easily frustrated and quickly resorts to aggression. He is often unresponsive when given directives by adults. Although Adam desperately wants to be liked and included, his behavior usually elicits anger and rejection.

Jenny does not participate in her kindergarten class. Her teachers say she is overly shy. Jenny's speech is very immature, and when she talks she often makes inappropriate comments. Jenny wants to learn like the other children, but is frightened.

Becky is a 12-year-old girl who rarely attends school. Her time is spent partying with friends, many of whom are much older than her. People who know her say she's a great person, that she's always surrounded by fun and good times. Before going to bed at night, Becky often cries. She says she is worthless and often wonders if life is worth living.

Physical abuse, sexual abuse, emotional abuse, and neglect of children have been found to affect children in almost all areas of functioning. Different children are affected in different ways, with some children showing dramatic, pervasive, and sensational symptoms and others being affected in more silent, subtle ways. Some of the consequences of maltreatment are obvious, such as bruises or brain damage in a child who has been hit. Because characteristics such as these are a direct and immediate result of maltreatment, they are considered indicators of maltreatment. Other consequences, such as dysfunctional interpersonal behavior in neglected or sexually abused children, are less obvious and are referred to as sequelae rather than indicators of maltreatment.

Although the most visible results of abuse, such as burns or scars, are the most sensational, the more subtle consequences are often the most detrimental on a long-term basis. Sequelae such as disturbed interpersonal relations, pervasive distrust, and low self-esteem may affect an individual long into adult life.

Although our knowledge of human development is not advanced enough to specifically delineate the nature of the relationships between negative experiences early in life and later adult functioning, the cumulative effects of experience on development cannot be denied. Consequently, early identification and intervention with at-risk children are critical to insure healthy development. If the conditions leading to maladaptive behavior can be remediated early in life, both the individual and the larger society are going to benefit.

TABLE 4-1

Physical Characteristics of Maltreated Children

Physical Abuse		Neglect
Bruises, lacerations, welts, abrasions, fractures, or burns as follows:		Underweight, malnourished
		Poor hygiene
Unusual location	- cheeks, lips, mouth, ear lobes	
	- back, buttocks, back of legs	Fatigue, constant falling asleep
	- external genitalia	
	- burns on soles of feet, palms of hands, back or buttocks	Bald spot on infant's head
Unusual appearance	- clustered or patterned	Unattended physical problems or medical needs:
	- resembling the shape of an instrument	
	- on several different surface areas	- chronic anemia
	- cigar or cigarette burns	
	- immersion (glove or sock-like) burns	- severe diaper rash
	- rope burns (esp. on neck)	
Suspicious circumstances		- skin rashes
	- no explanation	
	- explanation does not fit injury	- tooth decay/gum disease
	- patterns to the occurrence of injuries (e.g., after absences from school)	- head/body lice
	- repeated injuries or injuries in various stages of healing	- ringworm
Whiplash syndrome in infants		Nonorganic Failure to Thrive
Nonorganic Failure to Thrive		

Sexual Abuse		Emotional Abuse
Swelling, bruising or irritation around	- genital areas	Physical symptoms of anxiety:
	- anal areas	- psychogenic skin disorders
	- mouth	- pain with no physical basis
Torn, stained, or bloody underclothing	Vaginal discharge	- ulcers
Pain/discomfort in walking or sitting	Anal ulcers	- unexplained vomitting
Genital pain or itching	Venereal diseases	
Difficulty in urination	Pregnancy	

The goal of this chapter is to familiarize the reader with the indicators and sequelae associated with child abuse and neglect. The physical effects of maltreatment are discussed first.   Physical symptoms are the most objective indicators of maltreatment and are the primary basis for our current operational definitions of child abuse and neglect (see chapter 1). The developmental sequelae of maltreatment are then presented. Areas of functioning which have been shown to be affected by maltreatment include cognitive abilities, socioemotional development, affect, and behavior.   The specific sequelae within each of these areas of functioning are numerous and most have the potential for negatively affecting long-term development.

PHYSICAL CHARACTERISTICS OF MALTREATED CHILDREN

Physical characteristics associated with maltreatment include physical injuries, burns, and failure to thrive. Table 4-1 shows the physical characteristics which have been identified as being associated with maltreatment.

Physical injuries and burns have received attention in the literature as *indicators* of physical abuse. In other words, enough is known about the cause of these physical injuries and burns to show that their presence is almost always indicative of abuse.

Failure to thrive, on the other hand, may or may not be the result of maltreatment. Causes of failure to thrive other than physical abuse and neglect have been noted and discussed, and consequently failure to thrive is generally considered associated with, but not necessarily indicative of, maltreatment. Familiarity with the research findings on failure to thrive is important for educated decision making regarding maltreatment and related intervention.

Physical Injuries

The physical injuries resulting from physical abuse range from mild cuts and bruises to more pervasive, often permanently debilitating, injuries. Because physical injuries are often clearly visible on the body and usually cause the child significant immediate distress, they are the most immediate indicators of child maltreatment and often the precipitant of identification and intervention.

Although every child suffers accidental physical injury, there are several circumstances under which physical injuries should be considered suspicious and appropriate action taken.   These circumstances may involve the location or appearance of the injury or the explanations for the injury provided by the parents.

Location

Children who are accidentally injured are usually bruised or cut over bony prominences such as elbows, knees, or forehead. Once a child learns to walk, the shin becomes a common site for mild bruises. The nature of these injuries is usually consistent with falls, walking into objects, or rough-and-tumble play.

Consider the two-year-old who enjoys chasing around with other children but who has not yet developed the coordination and common sense to exercise appropriate judgment. This child will frequently suffer scrapes on his knees from

Accidental

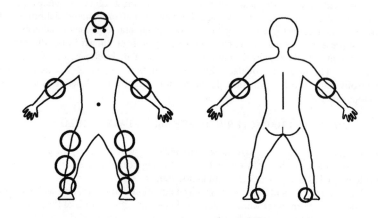

Nonaccidental

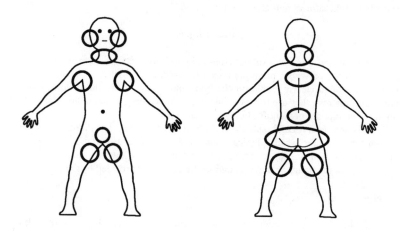

Figure 4-1
Locations of accidental and nonaccidental injuries.

falling down, bruises on the front of his legs from running into things, and scrapes or bumps on his elbows, chin, or forehead from tripping and falling. When observed in a naturalistic setting, this child will usually appear energetic, playful, and curious. Similarly, older children may suffer injuries from dangerous play such as sports, bike riding, tree climbing, etc. Again, the appearance of these injuries fits the cause, involving scrapes, cuts, or bruises on the arms, hands, lower legs, etc.

Children suffering from nonaccidental or inflicted injury, on the other hand, typically suffer bruises or welts on the cheek (from being slapped), on the buttocks, lower back, or upper leg (from being severely spanked), or on the neck (from being choked). Figure 4-1 depicts areas commonly associated with accidental and nonaccidental injury. The areas associated with nonaccidental injury involve locations unlikely to be contacted during typical falls or bumps. Further, nonaccidental injury may involve areas of soft tissue, such as the buttocks. Figure 4-2 shows bruising to the buttocks which is indicative of maltreatment.

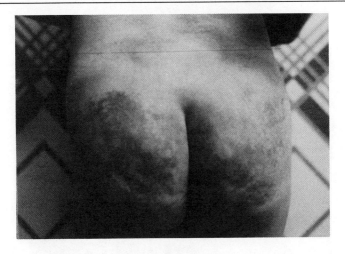

Figure 4-2
Injuries to the buttocks resulting from severe spanking.

(Photograph courtesy of the Broward County Child Protection Team.)

Appearance

Just as the location of an injury may be indicative of maltreatment, the appearance of certain injuries may suggest that they were inflicted rather than accidental. Patterned physical injuries or injuries which bear resemblance to an instrument which can be used for striking are usually indicative of child abuse. Hand marks, teeth marks, loop-shaped or parallel cuts or scars, and rectangular bruises are usually indicative of inflicted injury.

Figure 4-3 shows parallel scars such as those resulting from being repeatedly struck with a stick, rod, or cord. Figure 4-4 shows a loop-shaped scar resulting from being hit with a doubled over cord. The most common locations for injuries resulting from abuse with an electric cord are the arms, thighs, and back (Showers & Bandman, 1986).

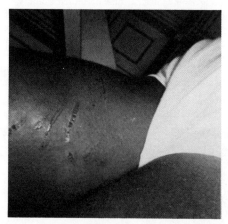

Figure 4-3
Parallel scars from a long, thin object such as a stick, rod, or cord.

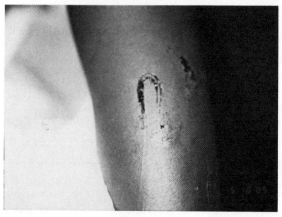

Figure 4-4
Loop-shaped scar from being hit with a doubled-over cord.

(Photographs courtesy of the Broward County Child Protection Team.)

Figure 4-5 shows several rectangular injuries resulting from being hit with a belt. Rectangular scars or bruises can also result from being hit a ruler, shoe, or other flat object. The bruise pictured in Figure 4-6 is noteworthy because it clearly represents a shape, perhaps that of a belt buckle. Bruises which bear a resemblance to a particular object were probably caused by that object.

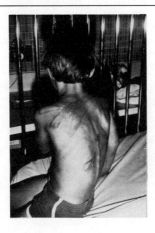

Figure 4-5
Rectangular injuries from being beaten with a belt.

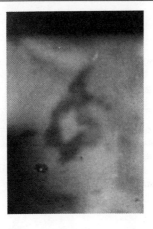

Figure 4-6
A bruise which resembles the shape of an object suggesting inflicted injury.

(Photographs courtesy of the Broward County Child Protection Team.)

Other physically abusive actions which leave recognizable injuries include slapping, grabbing, and biting. A severe slap will leave a bruise which shows where a finger or fingers hit. Grabbing, squeezing, and choking may also leave bruises, often patterned according to pressure points of the fingers or fingertips. For example, grabbing a child's face may leave a thumb mark on one cheek and a wider bruise or series of finger bruises on the other side. Biting will almost always leave telltale teeth marks. If the teeth marks are adult size, immediate concern is warranted. Schmitt (1987) suggests that if distance between the canines (third tooth on each side) is greater than three centimeters, the bite should be considered as having come from someone with their permanent teeth (see Figure 4-7).

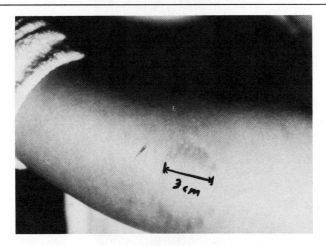

Figure 4-7
A bite mark with the distance between the canines highlighted.

(Photograph courtesy of the Broward County Child Protection Team.)

Injuries such as those described in the above paragraphs should almost always raise suspicion because of their appearance or location. Several types of injuries, however, can appear less remarkable but still be indicative of child abuse. This is the case when the cause of an injury can or is not adequately explained or other suspicious circumstances are associated with the injury.

Suspicious circumstances

A common reason for physical abuse to go unreported or untreated is that parents provide accounts that the injuries are accidental in nature, and these accounts are accepted at face value. If closer examination reveals that an injury does not fit the parent's explanation or if the explanation is inappropriate to the child's developmental stage, maltreatment should be considered.

Very young children (under two years of age) rarely sustain bone fractures and, because of their lack of mobility, infants under ten months of age rarely sustain severe injuries of any nature. Consequently, explanations for these injuries which involve the child being responsible for the injury are not plausible. Explanations for serious injuries in very young children such as an infant falling down or a one-year-old running into something are questionable at best. Similarly, children in the early stages of walking are unlikely to gain enough speed to do any significant damage to themselves by running into a fixed object.

Explanations for injuries which purport that a child inflicted injury upon himself or herself are also inadequate to explain most injuries, be they severe bruises, bone fractures or dislocations, or muscle injuries. Children do not "love pain," and it is unlikely that an otherwise normal child will inflict any type of severe injury upon himself or herself. Similarly, describing a child as "accident prone" is insufficient to explain a history of physical injury. When caregivers can only offer such vague or inadequate accounts of significant physical injuries, further investigation is warranted.

Suspicious circumstances can involve the nature of the injury as well as explanations for its cause. Injuries which occur in patterns or which are similar to injuries previously acquired may be inflicted. For example, a child who is frequently absent from school and often shows evidence of injury upon return may be being abused. Similarly, multiple bone fractures in various stages of healing or a history of fractures may reflect inflicted injury. Schmitt (1980) suggests that children suspected of being physically abused receive trauma x-rays, because bone fractures in various stages of healing or fractures which have not received immediate medical attention are highly diagnostic of child maltreatment.

Abuse and brain trauma

Several injuries of a more serious and lasting nature have also been described as indicative of child abuse. Subdural hemotoma (bleeding beneath the dura mater, a layer of protective tissue between the brain and skull) was one of the earliest symptoms noted to be associated with physical child abuse (Kempe et al., 1962). Symptoms of subdural hemotoma in infants include fever, irritability, bulging fontanelle (separations between the skull bones which have not yet hardened) or enlargement of the head, and clouded consciousness (Merritt, 1979). Convulsive seizures are also associated with subdural hemotoma and are one of the more common presenting symptoms (Merritt, 1979).

In addition to intracranial bleeding, direct blows to the head without intracranial bleeding can lead to brain damage. A variety of symptoms can result, and the nature of the symptom is largely dependent on where the brain damage occurs. Martin et al. (1974) review some of the symptoms of brain damage, including hypotonia (difficulty or pain in motor functioning) and soft signs commonly associated with neurological impairment. Such soft signs often involve language impairment, fine motor or coordination problems, a lack of behavioral or cognitive flexibility, or difficulty with perception or sensation. Neurological damage has also been found to result from serious whiplash associated with infants being shaken (Caffey, 1972; 1974). The "Whiplash Shaken Infant Syndrome," as this phenomenon has been termed, involves intracranial and intraocular bleeding in the absence of external signs of head trauma. Dykes (1986) reviews the literature on the Whiplash Shaken Infant Syndrome and discusses the incidence of the symptoms, alternative causative mechanisms, and outcome.

Difficulties or disabilities resulting from brain trauma are usually lasting. Treatment does not cure the deficit but rather teaches ways to cope. Prevention of such injuries is the best reason for efforts to identify potentially abusive families and intervene before the damage is done.

Injuries such as those described in the above sections, because of their location, appearance or related circumstances,   are the most objective indicators of maltreatment. It should be noted, however, that even with highly suspicious injuries, care must be taken in concluding that the child has been abused. Certain medical conditions may give the appearance of inflicted injury or make the child prone to repeated injuries such as broken bones.

Schmitt (1980, p. 137) describes naturally occurring physical conditions which may cause signs similar to some of the indicators of abuse described above. These conditions include birthmarks, bluish spots on the skin which occur concomitantly with pubic lice, and symptoms associated with allergic or viral reactions. Figure 4-8 shows parallel bruises on the neck which are the result of "coining," a technique used by the Vietnamese to treat a variety of symptoms such as fever or headache. Coining involves rubbing hot oil on the skin and massaging in a downward motion with the edge of a coin (Yeatman, Shaw, Barlow, & Bartlett, 1976). While the marks appear highly suspicious, the cause is not typically considered abusive.

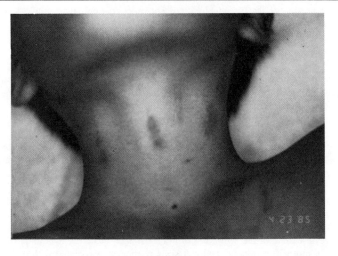

Figure 4-8

Parallel "scars" resulting from "coining," a Vietnamese treatment
for symptoms such as fever or headache.

(Photograph courtesy of the Broward County Child Protection Team.)

Although ruling out alternative causes for suspicious physical injuries is vitally important in cases of suspected child maltreatment, the availability of alternative explanations for the injuries should not be used as an excuse to avoid reporting the case to protective services. Only qualified medical personnel can make the decision as to the cause of the apparent injuries; child care workers, psychologists, teachers, and others have only the responsibility to the child of assuring that the necessary medical attention is received.

Burns

Like other physical injuries, burns may be indicative of maltreatment because of their appearance or because the explanation provided does not fit the injury. Burns which are indicative of maltreatment include cigarette burns, burns which reflect the shape of an instrument, acid burns, or immersion burns.

Cigarette burns are distinctive in appearance, leaving round or semicircle scars the size of a cigarette or cigar. They may occur in clusters and often are found on the palms of the hand or soles of the feet. Burns by other instruments also tend to leave distinctive marks. Irons, stove elements, heat radiators, etc. will all leave burns with which resemble the instrument which caused the burn.

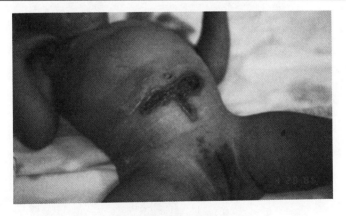

Figure 4-9

Burn reflecting a caustic substance flowing
down into a space in the child's diaper.

(Photograph courtesy of the Broward County Child Protection Team.)

Abusive burns may also occur when hot liquids or caustic substances are thrown at or placed on children. Burns of this nature often show patterns based on the flow of the liquid. Figure 4-9 shows an inflicted burn which involved some of the liquid flowing down where there was a space in the child's diaper.

The flow of the liquid, as indicated by the burn, may often be used to determine if the burn was intentional or accidental. Feldman (1987, p. 204) suggests that one way of differentiating accidental spilling, such as a child pulling a pan off the stove, from intentional throwing of a liquid is that accidental burns often involve the underside of the chin (from looking up) and the armpit on the side which the child used to reach up and pull the container. If there is no indication that these areas were burned, it is less likely that the child caused an accidental spill.

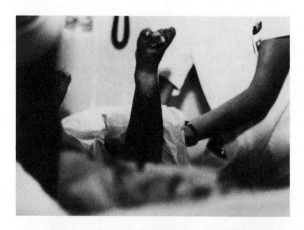

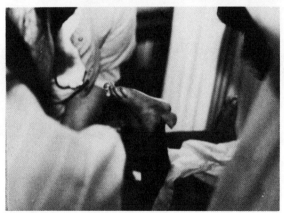

Figure 4-10

Sock-like immersion burn resulting from the
child's leg being held in scalding water.

(Photographs courtesy of the Broward County Child Protection Team.)

Immersion burns involve sock-like or glove-like burns from placing the child's feet or hands in hot water. Figure 4-10 shows an immersion burn resulting from placing a child's feet in scalding water. The identifying characteristic of these burns is the clean, well-delineated burn line. Alternatively, immersion may result in doughnut-shaped burns on the buttocks and surrounding areas. These doughnut-shaped burns result from a child being held in a sink or tub of water which is too hot for the child; the area in contact with the bottom of the tub will typically remain unburned or less severely burned, thus resulting in the "doughnut" impression (Feldman, 1987, p. 201).

Finally, explanations which do not fit the appearance of the burn may be indicative of abuse. Explanations for burns such as "the child fell into the tub" are inadequate to explain most immersion burns. Children who fall into hot water will thrash about, and the consequent splashing will be reflected in poorly delineated burn lines. If the parents claim that a child burned himself or herself, but the burn is clearly delineated on a broad surface of skin (such as the palm of the hand), the explanation should be considered questionable. If a child accidentally contacts something hot, their reflexes will cause a quick withdrawal, and the burn will be unlikely to indicate direct extended contact.

Section summary

A variety of physical injuries may be indicative of child physical abuse. Unusual or developmentally inappropriate cuts, bruises, welts, or other injuries may be inflicted. Injuries which resemble an instrument, which are patterned or clustered in an organized way, or which cannot be adequately explained all may be indicative of physical abuse. Similarly, burns which are well delineated, reflect the shape of an instrument, or show suspicious flow patterns may be indicative of physical abuse. Severe physical trauma in very young children warrants investigation, especially if the caretaker is unable to give an adequate account of the injury. Although some highly suspicious injuries may be the result of circumstances other than abuse, only qualified medical personnel can make the final determination.

Injuries Indicative of Sexual Abuse

Certain physical injuries are noteworthy because they may be indicative of sexual abuse. Bruises, cuts, swelling, or pain around the genital area, particularly in young females, is highly suspicious. Trauma to the genital area may also be reflected indirectly by blood on the undergarments.

Bruises around the mouth or inside the mouth (e.g., on the soft palate) may be a result of forced or coerced oral sex. Bruises of this nature may also result from forced feeding, which would also be considered abusive and warrant intervention. Difficulty or pain in urination may also be the result of sex related injuries, and venereal diseases and pregnancy are always the result of sexual contact.

Indicators of Neglect and Emotional Abuse

Several physical conditions are indicative of neglect or emotional abuse. These conditions are often less "horrifying" than the injuries associated with physical and sexual abuse, but the long-term effects on the child may be just as detrimental.

Children who are physically neglected may be underweight, malnourished, and appear dirty and unkempt. Neglected children may also experience constant fatigue and fall asleep at unusual times.

A variety of physical problems or medical needs may be indicative of physical neglect, especially if they are unattended. Deficiency diseases such as beriberi and scurvy are the result of inadequate nutrition, while severe diaper rash, persistent skin rashes, tooth decay, and gum disease may result from failure to insure or provide adequate hygiene. Infants who are left unattended may also develop a bald spot on the back of the head or a slight flattening of head because of uneven pressure due to laying in one position for long periods of time.

Emotional abuse is not usually discussed as leading to physical problems, but verbal abuse or emotional neglect may lead to anxiety and concomitant physical symptoms. Psychogenic skin disorders, persistent pain or illness with no organic basis, and ulcers may be symptoms of an emotionally unhealthy environment. When children suffer such anxiety-based disorders or symptoms, further assessment of the family conditions and parent-child relationships is warranted.

Failure to Thrive

The physical characteristics described above have received attention in the literature primarily as indicators of physical abuse. Failure to thrive (FTT), on the other hand, is typically discussed as a consequence of abusive family life rather than being directly associated with a specific instance of abusive behavior. Consequently, FTT is not direct evidence of maltreatment but should be treated as evidence that the child is experiencing difficulty in some area of functioning. In children who present with failure to thrive, further assessment is needed to clarify the specific area of difficulty.

The research on failure to thrive has typically involved studying FTT in maltreated samples rather than identifying the frequency of maltreatment in FTT samples. The findings consequently pertain to FTT as sequelae of abuse. Little can be said about the reliability of FTT as an indicator of maltreatment.

Failure to thrive is medically defined as "a child who has some time during the first three years of life suffered a marked retardation or cessation of growth" (Kempe, Cutler, and Dean, 1980). This definition implies knowledge of the child's prior physical developmental status so that the current status can be compared. In practice, FTT is also associated with developmental lags in height, weight, and head circumference in the absence of prior knowledge about the physical status of the child. In this context, comparisons are made to standard growth charts rather than the child's prior physical status.

Failure to thrive may have a known organic cause or occur in the absence of any discrete causative factor (Kristiansson & Fallstrom, 1987). When no organic cause is evident (i.e., nonorganic failure to thrive) environmental factors such as an abusive parent-child relationship are often thought to be responsible for the developmental delays. Nonorganic failure to thrive has been variously called abuse dwarfism, deprivation dwarfism, psychosocial dwarfism, and reversible hyposomatotropinism (Money, Annecillo, and Kelly, 1983).

Early studies on the developmental characteristics of maltreated children suggested that FTT was overrepresented in maltreated samples. Elmer and Gregg

(1967) found that 32% of a sample of severely physically abused infants were below the third percentile in height and weight. More recently, Elmer (1978) reported that a sample of 17 recently abused children weighed less than a sample of 17 matched comparison children.

Confounds in the research of FTT

Both the long-term implications and causes of FTT in maltreated samples have been debated. In the study by Elmer (1978), the weight differences between maltreated and comparison children were negligible at one- and eight-year follow-ups. She suggested that the effects of poverty are detrimental to both maltreated and nonmaltreated children, and, when these effects are controlled for, the physical development of maltreated children is not significantly different that the physical development of nonmaltreated children reared in similar conditions of poverty.

Martin, Beezley, Conway, and Kempe (1974) also concluded that the failure to thrive syndrome observed in abused children may very probably be a function of low socioeconomic status, specifically poor nutrition associated with poverty. In other words, FTT may a more a function of physical neglect than of physical abuse. Kempe, et al. (1980, pp. 170-175) discuss several factors which may lead to FTT, which can be associated with either an abusive or neglectful family environment, or be a result of poverty. These factors include feeding problems, medical problems, and inadequate parent-child interaction.

The difficulty in studying the causes and implications of FTT is exacerbated by the changes in developmental status which occur after identification of the affected children. There is evidence that recovery from FTT often begins after identification and intervention. The rate of recovery appears to be in part dependent upon the duration of the prior abuse, the child's age at the time of the intervention, and the duration of the intervention (Kristiansson & Fallstrom, 1987; Money, Annecillo & Kelly, 1983). Consequently, the actual relationship between FTT and maltreatment is difficult to assess, with any study of the long-term consequences being confounded by the effects of the intervention. Samples in which both the nature of the maltreatment and the intervention are carefully defined are needed to delineate the variables which contribute to FTT. As discussed in chapter 2, however, adequately defined research samples are infrequent in the maltreatment literature, and until this problem is overcome, the relationship between FTT and maltreatment will remain obscure.

Section summary

The available data indicate that physical growth deficits appear to be associated with maltreatment, although the exact cause of the deficits (physical abuse, neglect, or poverty in general) is still unclear. An environment which is generally insufficient for adequate child growth and development, rather than specific instances of child abuse, may be the primary cause of the growth deficits.

Whether the cause of FTT is physical abuse, neglect, or a generally impoverished environment, it appears that identification of FTT children and provision of services to provide for the minimal basic needs of those children are sufficient to promote physical development to levels commensurate with other children from families of similar means. Consequently, early identification and provision of services are essential for promoting recovery in FTT children. The specific interventions which are most effective for remediating growth deficits need to be delineated, and this will require improved research, especially in reference to the definitions of the children being studied.

COGNITIVE SEQUELAE OF MALTREATMENT

Child abuse and neglect have been found to affect cognitive functioning in a variety of ways. Research on the cognitive functioning of maltreated children typically involves comparing the developmental or intellectual status, as measured by standardized tests, of maltreated and nonmaltreated children. The characteristic most often discussed is language development. Other characteristics which have been studied include general intellectual level and other factors affecting learning, such as task relevant attributions and persistence.

Problems affecting assessment

When discussing the cognitive abilities of maltreated children, it is important to remember that most measures of intellectual ability are integrally related to, but different from, motivation and behavior. Maltreated children often exhibit behavior problems, and consequently accurate assessment of their intellectual levels may be difficult.

Intellectual ability and behavior or motivation may become most confused in measures of school performance or achievement. For example, because school learning is cumulative, the degree to which behavior and motivation affect school performance measures increases with the age of the child. In other words, a first-grade child who has not done his work will be relatively less delayed on measures of achievement than will a fourth-grade child who has had several years of motivational problems. Yet the abilities of the two children may be very similar. Caution must be exercised not to confuse true intellectual deficits with related problems which interfere with performance and school achievement.

The effects of maltreatment on cognitive functions

Child abuse and neglect can lead to cognitive deficits in a number of ways (see Figure 4-11). For example, physical abuse can lead to brain damage and consequent impairment of functions associated with the damaged area. A lack of environmental stimulation associated with neglect may be the cause of general intellectual and learning delays. Similarly, failure to provide for a child's basic needs, such as adequate food and rest, may result in that child having concentration difficulties or being generally listless and unmotivated.

Maltreatment can lead to cognitive and learning deficits in less direct ways as well. Parents who are generally unresponsive to their child's overtures or whose interactions with their children are based solely on the parent's needs may raise children who are distractible or have difficulty functioning in a structured learning environment. In other words, children cannot learn attention and structure from an inconsistent and unpredictable environment. Similarly, children from a chaotic or isolated home environment may simply be unable to interact effectively with others, a skill which is essential for adequate performance in school and on most current measures of cognitive functioning.

Little research directly addresses the affects of sexual or emotional abuse on cognitive functioning, but these types of abuse may lead to increased distractibility and decreased school-related motivation, both which adversely affect learning and performance. Sexual and emotional abuse can also interfere with school performance by leading to poor attendance and decreased classroom participation. In other words, an environment in which the needs or problems of parents are given priority over the needs of the children will not be conducive to successful academic experiences.

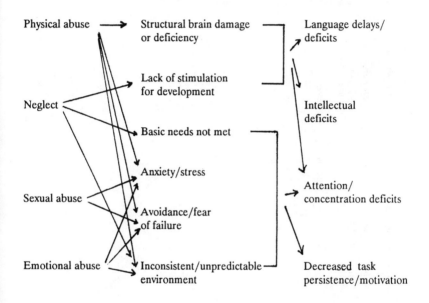

Figure 4-11

Relationships between maltreatment and cognitive deficits.

Specific cognitive sequelae of maltreatment are discussed below. Although research on the cognitive sequelae of sexual and emotional abuse is scarce, studies investigating the cognitive sequelae of child physical abuse and neglect are common in the literature. Because language development is closely related to most standardized measures of cognitive functioning, the literature relevant to language development is discussed first. Subsequently, the literature on general intellectual ability and other cognitive factors which affect learning will be discussed.

TABLE 4-2

Studies addressing language development in maltreated children

Study	PA	N	SA	Other	Control	Age	Measures	Findings
Allen & Oliver (1982)	13	7		31	28	2-5 yr	Pre-school Language Scale	Language delays associated with neglect but not physical abuse.
Appelbaum (1977)	30				30	2-29 m	Denver	Physically abused children were relatively delayed.
Blager (1979)	13 (abuse not recent) 18 (abuse recent)	7				3-8 yr 4-7 yr	Language tests	Delays exhibited by recently abused children but not by sexually abused children or children in which the physical abuse was not recent.
Blager & Martin (1976)	10 10					30-48 m 45-98 m	PPVT Various tests of language development. Spontaneous speech sample.	Younger children showed delays on tests, whereas older children showed delays on unstructured assessments (e.g., spontaneous speech sample).
Elmer (1977) (follow-up)	17			17	25	9 yr	Language evaluation	No group differences.
Friedrich, Einbender, & Leucke (1983)	11				10	4-5 yr	McCarthy	PA - Lower verbal scores.
Giblin, Starr, & Agronow (1984)	14				14	2-29 m	Bayley, McCarthy	No group differences.
Johnson & Morse (1968)	101						Speech assessment	19% exhibited speech problems.
Martin (1972)	42						WISC Revised Yale Developmental schedules	38% showed language delays relative to overall intellectual functioning.

Language Development

The research on language development has suggested that both physical abuse and neglect may be associated with language delays. There is some evidence that neglect may be the primary cause of language delays, although physical abuse of sufficient severity to cause structural damage to language areas of the brain will certainly lead to related language deficits. Clinical experience also suggests that both sexual and emotional abuse may lead to regressive tendencies and consequent immature or inappropriate speech, but these impressions have not yet been empirically verified. Table 4-2 summarizes the results of several studies which address language development in maltreated children.

Early studies reported significant language deficits in physically abused children (e.g., Blager & Martin, 1976; Johnson & Morse, 1968; Martin, 1972). The majority of these studies, however, did not use comparison groups, so the abuse cannot be isolated as the cause of the language deficits.

Studies using suitable comparison groups have found language delays in some samples but not in others. Appelbaum (1977) found relative language delays in physically abused infants, and Friedrich et al. (1983) found lower verbal scores on the McCarthy Scales with preschool-age children. Giblin, Starr, and Agronow (1984), however, did not find language delays in preschool-age children, and no differences were found in Elmer's follow-up sample of school-age children (Elmer, 1977). Several factors may be responsible for these apparently discrepant findings. The age of the children, the recency of the maltreatment, and the nature of the maltreatment all appear to contribute to the inconsistent research findings. Although sample differences make comparisons across studies difficult (see chapter 2), it appears that language deficits may be most pronounced in younger samples and in samples where the maltreatment is relatively recent. In addition, there is some interesting research which suggests that neglect may have a greater impact on language than other types of abuse.

Neglect and language deficits

Allen and Oliver (1982) studied abused, neglected, abused and neglected, and nonmaltreated children, with a special effort to assure that abuse and neglect were not confounded. They found that neglect was associated with receptive and expressive language delays, and furthermore, when the effects of neglect were controlled for, physical abuse did not appear to be associated with language delays. In fact, neglect only was found to be more detrimental than the combination of physical abuse and neglect. These findings are consistent with the current authors' research. Neglected children achieved lower scores than either physically abused or nonmaltreated children on the verbal scale and general cognitive index of the McCarthy Scales (Segal, Iverson, & Layden, 1985).

The findings that neglect may be the primary contributing factor to language delays are also consistent with other research investigating social factors in language acquisition, which suggests that appropriate parental responsiveness is important for language development (e.g., Snow & Gilbreath, 1983). Children must be exposed to appropriate and contingent language in order for their own emerging verbalizations to be refined. If such exposure is not available or if the language to which they are exposed is inconsistent or inappropriate, language deficits will result. In other words, language delays most likely result from inadequate or inappropriate language stimulation. Regardless of whether a child is considered abused or neglected, lack of exposure to language will lead to slower language development, and exposure to inappropriate or noncontingent verbal stimulation will result in qualitative speech abnormalities.

Further, because children are exposed to more sources of language as they grow older, the nature of their language problems is likely to change. Specifically, young children who are verbally neglected are likely to exhibit delays in language acquisition. Older children, as their overall exposure to language increases, may catch up in terms of acquisition but may continue to show deficits in the more refined aspects of language such as structure or syntax. Consequently, language deficits are likely to be qualitative rather than quantitative in older children, particularly if they have exposure to other children and adults who help foster language acquisition.

Intellectual Functioning

Maltreated children frequently appear intellectually impaired. Although there is research support for the hypothesis that maltreated children, as a group, score lower on IQ tests than nonmaltreated children, there is sufficient variability in most studies to warrant caution in generalizing the findings to all maltreated children. Specifically, intellectual impairment must not be confused with problems which may on the surface appear similar, such as withdrawal or lack of acquired information.

Early studies on the intellectual status of maltreated children involved comparing the maltreated children's IQ scores with the available normative standards. Elmer and Gregg (1967) found that over one half of a sample of 22 severely abused children had WISC IQs below 80. Similarly, Martin, Beezley, Conway, and Kempe (1974) found that 35% of physically abused children had IQs below 85. Martin (1972) and Morse, Sahler, and Friedman (1970) found 33% and 42% of their samples of abused children, respectively, scored in the mentally retarded range of intellectual functioning.

These studies suggest that children from abusive families are delayed in intellectual functioning, but, as in all studies without matched comparison samples, they do not specify abuse as the cause of the deficits. Other variables common to the research samples, such as poverty, may also have contributed to the observed intellectual deficits.

Several studies have attempted to verify the above conclusions by using suitable comparison groups to more convincingly implicate physical abuse and/or neglect as the causes of the observed intellectual deficits. Table 4-3 summarizes the results of several of these studies. Intellectual or developmental delays have been noted in samples of infants, preschool, and school-age children. In addition, both physically abused and neglected children have been found to exhibit intellectual deficits.

The studies presented in Table 4-3 used suitable comparison groups, thus strengthening the association between maltreatment and the observed deficits. The findings, however, are largely based on cross-sectional designs and have typically used samples in which the abuse was relatively recent. Similar to other developmental variables, such as FTT and language development, the interpretation of the research becomes more complex when longitudinal data are considered.

TABLE 4-3

Studies assessing the intellectual/developmental functioning of maltreated children

Study	Sample				Age	Measure	Findings
	PA	N	Other	Control			
Appelbaum (1977)	30			30	2-29 m	Bayley	Abused children delayed on both mental and motor scales.
Barahal, Waterman, & Martin (1981)	17		I*	16	6-8 y	Slossen	Maltreated children scored slightly lower.
Elmer (1977) (follow-up)	17	17		25	9 y	School Records	No group differences at follow-up.
Friedrich, Einbender, & & Leucke (1983)	11			10	4-5 y	McCarthy	Physically abused children scored lower on General Cognitive Index.
Hoffman-Plotkin & Twentyman (1984)	14	14		14	3-6 y	Stanford-Binet PPVT Merrill-Palmer	PA & N children did not differ, but both delayed relative to controls.
Relich, Giblin, Starr, & Agronow (1980)	13			13	24-53 m	McCarthy or Bayley	No group differences were noted.
Sandgrund, Gaines, & Green (1974)	60	30		30	5-12 y	WISC	Both abused and neglected children achieved lower IQ's than controls.

*Included in PA sample.

Elmer and Gregg (1967) found an elevated proportion of mental retardation in their abused samples, and Elmer (1977) reports general mental and language delays in young abused children; however, these differences were greatly diminished at follow-up. As with findings on physical development, the authors suggest that over time the effects of poverty tend to equalize group differences. A recent study by Bradley and Caldwell (1984) tends to support the impact of poverty in causing the observed developmental delays. They found that the quality of the home environment of nonmaltreated children, as infants, was significantly related to both IQ and achievement in first grade. It is difficult to determine, however, if the developmental differences disappear because the effects of poverty "equalize" the children, as the above research might suggest, or because changes in the family or child's environment resulting from the identification of the maltreatment and subsequent intervention facilitate development in the maltreated children. Future research needs to more carefully address the factors associated with recovery of cognitive functioning upon identification of maltreatment.

Other Factors Affecting Learning

Deficits of language and intellect have direct implications for an individual's academic, social, and behavioral functioning. Children with such deficits will learn more slowly, and the learning will require more effort. Communication and social deficits may result, and children may develop negative attitudes toward learning situations. Several cognitive variables other than intellectual development may affect children in similar ways. These variables include attention, motivation, and task-relevant attributions or attitudes.

Clinical experience with maltreated children suggests that any type of maltreatment can interfere with motivation and concentration. Maltreated children appear slower to initiate tasks and often seem to lack persistence. They also seem to have difficulty concentrating and often seem detached from tasks with which they are involved. Research which directly addresses these impressions is limited, however, and that which is available has produced mixed findings.

Several studies have included task-related measures in their investigations of the functioning of maltreated children. Egeland, Sroufe, and Erickson (1983) found that physically abused preschool-age children were distractible and lacked persistence in task-related behaviors. Neglected children were characterized as having a general inability to deal with their environment in a constructive, goal-oriented manner. Hoffman-Plotkin and Twentyman (1984) found both abused and neglected children aged two to four years to be less ready to learn as indicated by parent and teacher report. In addition, Barahal et al. (1981) found six- to eight-year-old abused children were impaired on several variables functionally related to academic performance. They were more egocentric and viewed outcomes as being more externally determined, characteristics which are likely to lead to impaired interest and motivation.

On the other hand, Friedrich et al. (1983) found no differences in task persistence between the abused and nonabused children in their sample. Slade, Steward, Morrison, and Abramowitz (1984) also found no difference on task persistence between physically abused and control children. Slade et al. did find, however, that abused children accepted less responsibility for failure on a task than did nonabused children, which led the authors to conclude that abused children differ in their cognitive appraisal of task outcomes which are aversive in nature.

The mixed research findings regarding characteristics such as attention and persistence, coupled with frequency with which maltreated children are described as distractible and unmotivated, indicates a need to further explore these characteristics in maltreated samples. Research utilizing samples in the classroom would be particularly useful, and the inclusion of specific family characteristics in sample classification may account for more variability than the general classifications of abused, neglected, or nonmaltreated. At present, however, deficits in attention, persistence, and motivation should be decided on a case by case basis and not be considered characteristics of maltreatment in general.

Section summary

Deficits in language development, intellectual ability, and other factors associated with learning have long been thought to characterize maltreated children.

Language deficits have been verified in a number of samples of physically abused and/or neglected children. Children under five are more likely to exhibit deficits on standard tests of language acquisition or development, whereas older children are more likely to show deficits in the structure or fluency of their speech. In the absence of structural damage to language areas in the brain, the conditions associated with language deficits appear to involve amount and nature of the children's exposure to language. Consequently, neglected children, because they presumably are provided with inadequate parent-child stimulation, are more likely to show language deficits than children subjected to other forms of maltreatment. Many abused children, however, may also be deprived of adequate parent-child verbal interactions, and language deficits may result.

Intellectual deficits have also been found to be associated with physical abuse and neglect. Both language and intellectual deficits tend to be most pronounced in samples of younger and/or recently maltreated children. The long-term implications of these deficits in maltreated children are less clear. The deficits appear to attenuate somewhat as time passes, but it is not clear if identification and intervention lead to recovery or if other factors, such as poverty, equalize the maltreatment and comparison groups.

Finally, the extent and manner in which maltreatment affects cognitive factors such as attention, concentration and motivation are unclear. Research is available which suggests that maltreated children suffer in these respects, but several studies are also available which have found no group differences on these measures. The variability between studies suggests that certain factors associated with maltreatment can affect attention and motivation, but the relationship is not well enough delineated to isolate the relevant variables.

SOCIOEMOTIONAL SEQUELAE

Socioemotional development refers to the child's emerging relationships with others and self. Healthy socioemotional development implies psychological health as reflected in a positive self-concept, functionally adaptive perceptions and behavior patterns, and healthy, fulfilling relationships with others in the world.

Child abuse and neglect is thought to affect all facets of socioemotional development. Maltreated children have been described as aggressive, withdrawn, fearful of others, anxious and compulsive, generally unable to get along with peers, and suffering from low self-esteem (e.g., Galdston, 1965; Martin & Beezley, 1977; Terr, 1970). Physically abused children are most often characterized as aggressive and fearful. Neglected children are frequently said to be withdrawn, lethargic, and unresponsive to the overtures of others. Sexually and emotionally abused children are most often described as developing clinical symptoms such as regressive behaviors, role reversal, and inappropriate social behavior.

Research on the socioemotional development of maltreated children has involved a variety of methods to investigate a wide array of interpersonal behaviors, social perceptions, and psychological attributes. The literature on socioemotional development in maltreated children is complex, and at first glance may appear to hold many contradictions. A closer examination of the literature, however, reveals that many of the apparent contradictions may be accounted for by differences in methodology and sample, such as the research setting and age of the child being studied.   The four aspects of socioemotional development to be discussed in this section involve attachment, interpersonal behavior, social perceptions, and self-esteem.

Attachment

Attachment, as discussed in the child development literature, refers to the quality of the relationship between an infant and his or her caregiver.   Quality of attachment is typically assessed using the "strange situation" paradigm, which involves subjecting an infant to a new room and a female stranger, both with and without the mother present, and noting the child's reaction (Ainsworth et al., 1978).   The manner in which the infant reacts to the caregiver leaving and returning during the various situations is the primary indicator of the quality of attachment.   Based upon these observations, infants are classified as anxious-avoidant, anxious-resistant, or securely attached.

Maltreated children have been shown to have less secure and less stable attachments with their caregivers.   Generally, about one fourth of maltreated infants in most research samples are classified as securely attached by the above scheme.   In contrast, about three fourths of nonmaltreated infants are typically classified as securely attached.   For example, Schneider-Rosen and Cicchetti (1984) found that 67% of 18 maltreated infants were classified as insecure as compared to only 26% of the nonmaltreated infants.

Evidence that the attachments of maltreated children are also less stable than those of nonmaltreated children is provided by Egeland and Sroufe (1981).   They found that, at twelve months of age, maltreated children were disproportionately underrepresented in the secure attachment group (38% secure attachments as compared to 75% in the nonmaltreated sample).   Because of changes in the attachment classifications of the maltreated children, no group differences were evident when the children were reassessed at eighteen months of age.   The authors suggest that increased family support and out-of-home care for some of the abusive families may have led to an improvement in the quality of some of these children's attachments between the twelve- and eighteen-month assessments.   They also note, however, that the largest classification change for neglected children was from the resistant to the avoidant group, suggesting that the attachments of these children were simply less stable than the attachments of nonmaltreated children.

Most developmental researchers agree that the insecure attachments of maltreated children are the result of maladaptive parent-child interaction patterns (e.g., Ainsworth et al., 1978; Egeland and Sroufe, 1981).   The research methodology employed to study attachment, however, does not directly address the question of causation.   The children in these studies had already been maltreated, and the possibility that the insecure attachments contributed to, rather than resulted from, the maltreatment cannot be ruled out.

Call (1984) discusses how, in some cases, attachment disorders may precede, rather than result from, maltreatment.   He notes that poor-quality attachments are almost universal in infants seen for nonorganic failure to thrive.   Although cause and effect have not been definitively demonstrated, he believes that in some cases attachment disorders in infants place the infant at risk for developmental problems which, in turn, create additional difficulty and stress for the parent.   In this way, Call suggests that attachment disorders of infancy may directly or indirectly increase the child's risk for maltreatment.

Section summary

Whether attachment disorders place a child at risk for maltreatment or represent a consequence of an abusive or neglectful environment, the research shows that insecure attachments are overrepresented in samples of physically abused and neglected children. In addition, the attachments of maltreated children appear to be less stable than those of nonmaltreated children. Because the adaptive resolution of early developmental tasks lays the foundation for later developmental processes, early intervention with maltreated infants, beginning with their earliest attachment experiences, is critical to their later development.

Interpersonal Behavior

Disturbed interpersonal behavior is one of the most commonly discussed characteristics of maltreated children. A sampling of the various characterizations of maltreated children which appear in the literature includes aggressive, withdrawn, socially inappropriate, immature, angry, hostile, and unresponsive (e.g., Galdston, 1975; Kempe & Kempe, 1978; Sebold, 1987; Terr, 1970). Table 4-4 lists the various interpersonal characteristics most frequently discussed as being associated with maltreatment.

TABLE 4-4
Common descriptions of the interpersonal behavior of maltreated children

Physical Abuse	*Neglect*
Aggression	Aggression
Withdrawal	Withdrawal
Avoidance	Suspicious/distrustful of others
Fearful of others	Unresponsive
Angry	Hostility
"Frozen watchfulness"	
Hostility	

Sexual Abuse	*Emotional Abuse*
Sexually aggressive or pre-occupied	Aggressive
Overly compliant	Suspicious
Seductive	Avoids eye contact
Distrustful	Unable to make friends
Fearful of opposite sex	Overly compliant
"Role reversal"	Overly noncompliant
Withdrawn	Bizarre or inappropriate
Isolated	interpersonal behavior

TABLE 4-5

Studies investigating the interpersonal behavior of maltreated children

Study	PA	N	SA	EA	Other	Control	Age	Measures	Findings
Appelbaum (1977)	30					30	2-29 m	Denver Infant Beh. Record (Bayley)	Lower scores on personal-social development. Few differences were noted on infant behavior record.
Camras, Grow, & Ribordy (1983)	17					17	3-6 y	Teacher ratings	PA children rated less socially competent.
Egeland, Sroufe, & Erickson (1983) (follow-up)	24	24		19	19	85	42 m (4-5 y)	Observations Observations Teacher ratings	42 m - Maltreatment groups more negativistic, noncompliant, and less enthusiastic than controls. (PA - most noncompliant, EA - most avoidant, N - most dependent). 4-5 y - PA & O (psychologically unavailable mothers) were less compliant than controls.
Friedrich, Urquiza, & Beilke (1986)			85				3-12 y	CBCL	Greater prevalence of both internalizing and externalizing behavior problems than CBCL normative sample.
George & Main (1979)	10					10	1-3 y	Observations	PA children more aggressive toward both peers and caregivers. Also less responsive to caregivers.
Hoffman-Plotkin & Twentyman (1984)	14	14				14	3-6 y	Parent rating Teacher rating Observations	PA & N children rated by parents and teachers are more aggressive and less socially mature. Observations showed PA children were more aggressive.

Study					Age	Measures	Findings
Howes & Espinosa (1985)	26	4	21	26	3-5 y	Observations	Peer relations of PA children deficient in newly formed peer group, but not in well established peer groups.
Iverson, Tanner, & Segal (1987)	7	9		18	3-5 y	Behavior Observation Record	PA children interacted as much as controls, but were less effective in their interactions. Neglected children interacted less than others.
Jacobson & Straker (1982)	19			38	5-10 y	Observations	PA children were less socially interactive, but no differences in overt aggression were found.
Kinard (1980)	30			30	5-12 y	Psychological tests	PA children exhibited more responses consistent with aggression.
Lewis (1980)	12	I*		14	8-32 m	Observations	PA children less positive and more avoidant of caregivers. No differences in peer interactions were noted.
Reidy (1977)	20	16		22	80 m	TAT Observations Teacher ratings	PA more aggressive than N & C on TAT and in free play. Both PA & N rated more aggressive than C in school setting.
Watkins & Bradbard (1984)	12	I*	I*	12	3-5 y	Observations	No group differences in reference to "caregiving" behaviors.

*Included in PA sample.

Unfortunately, the enthusiasm for describing the interpersonal behavior of maltreated children, in the absence of accumulated systematic research, has led to such a variety of characteristics being identified that it is near impossible to integrate the information into a reasonable descriptive framework.   The available research suggests that the nature of the maltreatment may interact with developmental status to influence the manner in which interpersonal difficulties become manifest, but samples in most maltreatment research are too poorly defined to clarify these relationships.   Very generally, however, the accumulated evidence does suggest that maltreated children as a group tend to be overtly or covertly aggressive and less socially effective in their interactions.

The majority of the research on the interpersonal behavior of maltreated children has involved physically abused and neglected samples.   More recently, comparisons of sexually abused and nonmaltreated children have begun to appear in the literature.   Little comparative research on emotionally abused children is available.   Table 4-5 summarizes several studies on the interpersonal behavior of maltreated children.

Infants

The literature on infant attachment discussed in the preceding section is relevant to interpersonal behavior as well.   Infants classified as avoidant may exhibit behaviors such as ignoring their mothers, moving away from their mothers, engaging in little affective interchange, or verbally requesting to be left alone.   Resistant infants may show little effort to interact and may resist their mother's efforts to initiate contact (Ainsworth et al., 1978; Gersten et al., 1986).   These behaviors, although only indirectly addressed as part of the more general attachment classification scheme, suggest that physical abuse and neglect may lead to interpersonal difficulties as early as the first year of life.

Several studies indicate that young maltreated children have interpersonal deficits in a variety of settings.   George and Main (1979) found that physically abused children, one to three years of age, were more aggressive toward their peers and more frequently "harassed" their caregivers, both verbally and nonverbally, than nonmaltreated children.   In addition, the abused children were less responsive to friendly overtures from their caregivers.   Finally, unlike any of the children in the comparison group, some of the abused children in this study threatened to assault, or actually assaulted, their caregivers.

Preschool-age children

Physically abused children between the ages of three and five have also been found to be more aggressive than either neglected or nonmaltreated children (Reidy, 1977; Hoffman-Plotkin & Twentyman, 1984).   Children of this age are typically observed in daycare or preschool settings.   The aggression may take the form of physical or verbal assault on peers or teachers, destructive behavior, or angry outbursts.   Neglected children, as well as abused children, have been rated by parents and teachers to be more aggressive and less socially mature than nonmaltreated children (e.g., Hoffman-Plotkin & Twentyman, 1984; Reidy, 1977).   Behavioral observations, however, tend to confirm increased levels of aggression only in physically abused children. Neglected children, on the other hand, tend to exhibit less interpersonal interaction than the other children (Hoffman-Plotkin & Twentyman, 1984; Iverson, Tanner, & Segal, 1987).

In a recent study by the current authors (Iverson et al., 1987), the interpersonal behavior of physically abused, neglected, and nonmaltreated children was observed during free play on the playground. The children's behavior was recorded on the Behavior Observation Record (Iverson & Segal, 1986), a form designed to capture both the presence or absence of interpersonal behavior and the quality of the interpersonal behavior which the children exhibited. The observations verified that neglected children interacted with others less than the other children. The majority of their time was spent playing alone or watching others from a distance. Abused children, on the other hand, showed levels of interaction similar to the nonmaltreated children but showed very definite deficits in the effectiveness with which they interacted with other children. Specifically, their attempts to join or approach others often elicited rejection or no response, while the approach behaviors of the nonmaltreated children more often led to acceptance by the children being approached.

School-age children

School-age children have also been found to show signs of interpersonal anger and aggression, but the manner in which these signs are manifested appears to be more complex and subtle than with preschool age children.   Kinard (1980), for example, found that psychological test responses consistent with aggression distinguished a group of abused from nonabused children, with the abused children producing more responses of an aggressive nature. Direct measures of aggression, however, do not always show differences in aggression in school-age children. Jacobson and Straker (1982) found that abused children were less socially interactive but failed to find any group differences in overt aggression.

The apparent decrease in the overtness of the aggression demonstrated by older physically abused children is not surprising when other developmental factors are considered. Young children have less impulse control, are unable to view their own behavior through others' eyes, and have not yet developed sense of social boundaries. Consequently, aggressive or antisocial tendencies are likely to be directly manifested in a variety of settings, including in the presence of adult observers. Older children are more sensitive to the situational context and usually have sufficient impulse control to avoid acting out in obviously maladaptive ways.   Consequently, older children may be less overtly aggressive, but aggressive tendencies may be exhibited in unsupervised peer group activities, in situations where the demands exceed the impulse control (such as the classroom), or on unstructured activities such as projective tests. Consequently, the absence of overt or public acting out should not lead one to assume that anger or aggressive feelings are absent but should lead to more careful assessment of these areas in different settings and with a variety of assessment instruments.

Sexual and emotional abuse -- interpersonal sequelae

Sexually and emotionally abused children are underrepresented in research on interpersonal behavior, but, as was presented in Table 4-4, these children are thought to exhibit a variety of inappropriate interpersonal behaviors.   Clinical impressions abound with sexually abused children being described as withdrawn, aggressive, seductive, fearful, isolated, immature with their peers, and distrustful (e.g., Lindberg & Distad, 1985; Sebold, 1987). Emotionally maltreated children have been described as aggressive, passive or withdrawn, demanding, compliant, suspicious of others, and antisocial.

Very little research is available to verify these impressions and explore whether or not they are directly associated with the maltreatment. Recent research on sexual abuse, however, offers tentative confirmation of some of these impressions.   For example, Friedrich, Urquiza, and Beilke (1986) studied 24 male and 61 female victims of sexual abuse between the ages of three and twelve years. Although no comparison group was used, they did find an increased prevalence of behavior problems in reference to the norms on the Achenbach Child Behavior Checklist. Children under five were characterized by their mothers or caregivers as more often demonstrating internalizing behaviors (e.g., depression, somatic concerns) and children over five were more frequently said to demonstrate externalizing behaviors (e.g., aggression, cruelty).   Unfortunately, research utilizing direct observation is not available to confirm these parental impressions.   Even though the ratings may reflect actual differences in interpersonal behavior, direct observations of the children are needed to verify the parent perceptions and determine the situational specificity of these behaviors.

One final study deserves particular comment because of the inclusion of a group of children whose mothers were "psychologically unavailable" in addition to the usual maltreatment groups. Egeland, Sroufe, and Erickson (1983) assessed preschool age children from families classified as physical abusive, verbal abusive, neglectful, and families whose mothers were psychologically unavailable. In addition, a sample of children with a history of adequate care served as a comparison group. In reference to social behavior, they found that the children whose parents were psychologically unavailable were characterized as more angry and noncompliant than the other groups, including the other maltreatment groups.

Psychological unavailability may be an inherent characteristic of other types of maltreatment. Physically abused, neglected, sexually abused, and emotionally abused children may all lack access to a parent who appropriately responds to their needs. When parents do not respond to the needs of the child, the child is likely to become frustrated and angry, and at best it is unlikely that the child will be sensitive or appropriately responsive to the needs of others.   Consequently, the interpersonal behavior of these children is more likely to reflect the child's needs than the environmental demands, and dysfunctional behavior is likely to result. The extent to which this process contributes to the interpersonal deficits in children exposed to different types of maltreatment needs to be further explored.

Section summary

The research addressing the interpersonal sequelae of maltreatment indicates that children who are abused or neglected are more likely than nonmaltreated children to exhibit dysfunctional interpersonal behavior. The early attachments of physically abused children are characterized by a general inability to derive security and comfort from their caregivers. As these children grow older, their behavior often appears more aggressive in nature and is more likely than the behavior of nonmaltreated children to elicit negative or rejecting responses.

Neglected children, on the other hand, tend to exhibit a general avoidance of interpersonal interaction. They are often characterized as avoidant as infants, and as they grow older they seem to engage in less peer interaction than either physically abused or nonmaltreated children.

Although little research with sexually abused samples is available, it appears that these children may also exhibit increased levels of dysfunctional interpersonal behavior. However, many of the most commonly discussed characteristics of sexually and emotionally abused children, such as role reversal, need to be more adequately studied to verify their relationship to maltreatment. Until comparative research is available, caution needs to be exercised when applying these characterizations to maltreated children as a group.

Despite the evidence that the interpersonal behavior of maltreated children differs from that of nonmaltreated children, there is still a question about the specific causes of these differences. The study by Egeland et al. (1983) suggests that psychological unavailability of the mother may contribute to interpersonal deficits, but the role of modeling and psychological factors, such as fear and frustration, may also be important causative factors. Whatever the cause, children subjected to any form of maltreatment by a parent are at risk for interpersonal problems with both peers and adults, and these difficulties can interfere with social functioning on both an inter- and intrapersonal level.

Social Perceptions

Social perceptions have to do with the manner in which individuals perceive and interpret social situations or cues. Because responses depend upon how stimuli are perceived, children who misinterpret social situations or the cues of others are likely to behave in situationally inappropriate or maladaptive ways. Further, perceptions are often biased by prior experience and the manner in which an individual "constructs" and responds to his or her world provides clues about the world from which that individual comes.

For example, a child who interprets helpful advice (e.g., "try doing it this way") as a critical attack may become unnecessarily angry or defensive. Excessive negativity of this nature may reflect a history of being verbally attacked and criticized and may cause individuals to interpret much of what happens to them as adverse. Because maltreated children often appear distrustful, negativistic, pessimistic, depressed, or angry, it has been hypothesized that these children may be perceiving and responding to their world in a negatively biased way. Figure 4-12 shows the process by which perceptions of this nature can mediate behavior.

A limited number of studies directly address the social perceptions of physically abused and neglected children. As with adults, perceptions in children are assessed by studying their appraisal of an objective, standard stimulus or by comparing their views or responses with those of nonmaltreated children. For example, Camras, Grow, and Ribordy (1983) found that physically abused children, relative to nonabused children, were deficient in their ability to decode facial expressions. Presumably these children will be less sensitive to facial cues, a critical component of effective communication. Similarly, Barahal, Waterman, and Martin (1981) found six-to eight-year-old physically abused children were more rigid and egocentric in their interpretations of others' perspectives and in their verbalizations regarding social roles. In other words, the physically abused children were less able to assess the attitudes and intentions of others, instead basing these social interpretations on their own needs and biases.

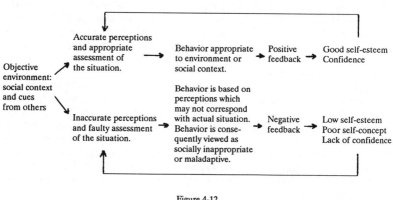

Figure 4-12
Social perceptions as mediators of behavior.

There is also empirical support for the contention that the perceptions of maltreated children are consistent with their prior experiences of abuse or neglect. Dean, Malik, Richards, and Stringer (1986) analyzed the stories of maltreated and nonmaltreated children between the ages of six and fourteen years. Although themes of inequality between children and adults were evident in the stories of all children, maltreated children evidenced more personal responsibility for the unkind acts of adults. Maltreated children between the ages of six and eight additionally viewed adults as being less likely to reciprocate the kind acts of children. Finally, Smetana, Kelly, and Twentyman (1984) assessed views on moral transgressions and psychological distress with abused, neglected, and control children from the same day-care center. Abused children were more likely to view psychological distress as universally wrong, whereas neglected children were more likely to judge unfair distribution of resources as universally wrong. Abused and control children, but not neglected children, considered moral transgressions to merit less punishment when committed by themselves. All groups accurately distinguished moral and social convention.

In short, the research on the social perceptions of maltreated children indicates that these children are less able to accurately assess external social cues and the actions of others. Instead, they develop ways of perceiving the world, which, although maladaptive, are consistent with their prior experiences. Physically abused children hold views which are likely to lead to inaccurate interpretations of others actions, and both abused and neglected children have been shown to appraise various situations in a self-defeating manner.

As mentioned above, behavior based on maladaptive perceptions is likely to be dysfunctional or socially inappropriate.   Unfortunately, once particular ways of viewing the world have been internalized, these biases affect how all social situations are perceived.   In other words, children who misinterpret situations in a self-defeating manner are less likely to derive objective information from new situations.   In this way, biased or inaccurate ways of perceiving the world are self-perpetuating.   The best way to facilitate adaptive, positive views is to assure that children are exposed to positive, esteem-enhancing experiences throughout their early development.

Self-Esteem

Self-esteem refers to perceptions an individual has of himself or herself.   Positive self-esteem implies perceiving one's self as a worthwhile individual who is deserving of good things.   Negative self-esteem involves considering one's self to be of little value and consequently deserving of blame and negative treatment.   Like social perceptions, the way one assesses himself or herself is based on experience and, in turn, determines how new information is internalized.   For example, a child with a negative self-image is less likely to take responsibility and feel good about succeeding on a task, instead tending to attribute the success to external factors such as the simplicity of the task or luck, which in turn, reinforces the negative self-image.

Because perceptions of one's self develop largely from experiences, any type of maltreatment is thought to negatively affect a child's self-esteem.   For experiences to affect self-esteem, however, the child must take personal responsibility for these experiences.   For example, if a child can attribute parental mistreatment to problems with the parents, self-esteem is less likely to be negatively affected.   Unfortunately, most young children are developmentally unable to make such external attributions and are more likely to conclude that they are the direct or indirect cause of the maltreatment.

Physical abuse and neglect

Research on the self-esteem of physically abused children suggests these children do have lower self-esteem than nonmaltreated children.   Using the Piers-Harris Self Concept Scale, Kinard (1980) found physically abused children to more often endorse items reflecting low self-esteem.   Kazdin, Moser, Colbus, and Bell (1985) also found physically abused children to demonstrate lower self-esteem as measured by a self-report inventory.   Based on observations and teacher ratings, Egeland et al. (1983) found both physically abused and neglected children to exhibit low self-esteem.

Sexual and emotional abuse

A recent study by Ney, Moore, McPhee, and Trought (1986) did not directly assess self-esteem but did investigate the effects of various types of maltreatment on children's perceptions of themselves and their world.   The nature and severity of the maltreatment affected the children's perceptions, with sexually and verbally abused children showing the most dysfunctional perceptions.   For example, these children believed they were responsible or at fault for instances of either mild or severe maltreatment. As discussed above, such perceptions are likely to contribute to the development of a negative self-image and begin a a self-defeating cycle of feeling bad about oneself.

Section summary

Maltreatment appears to have dramatic negative consequences for the socioemotional functioning of children, both in their early attachments with caregivers and in their later relationships with both peers and adults. Physically abused children often appear overtly or covertly aggressive and are less able to generate effective social interactions with others. Neglected children appear to be generally socially withdrawn, although they may also become socially inappropriate or aggressive in certain situations. Sexually abused children have been characterized by a variety of interpersonal problems, including aggression, withdrawal and sexual inappropriateness. In addition, maltreated children in general have been found to have self-defeating ways of perceiving themselves and the world around them. Such perceptions are likely to lead to dysfunctional social behavior, which further reinforces their negative self-concept, and creates a cycle causing these children great difficulty in their overall development.

Despite the quantity of research on the socioemotional development of maltreated children, many more characteristics have been identified than have been studied. Characteristics such as suspiciousness, role reversal and fear of others are frequently attributed to maltreated children, but the nature and extent of these characteristics have not been delineated. Caution must be exercised when utilizing these characteristics in decision making because little is known about how they develop and their prevalence in nonmaltreated children. In short, the research on the socioemotional functioning of maltreated children needs to be expanded to include the variety of sequelae which have been discussed but not yet verified with careful research.

AFFECT

Affect is a term which refers to mood or emotional display. Clinicians have long purported that maltreated children in general display more negative affect than nonmaltreated children. Maltreated children are often described as angry, fearful, sad, depressed, and effectively inappropriate.

Several studies address affect in maltreated children. For example, Egeland et al. (1983) found that physically abused children assessed at forty-two months of age were less enthusiastic and exhibited more negative affect than did verbally abused, neglected, or nonmaltreated children. Children of verbally abusive or psychologically unavailable parents, on the other hand, were described more angry than the other children.

Physically abused children have been found to show extremes of affect, positive as well as negative. Giblin, Starr, and Agronow (1984) assessed affect in abused and nonabused children from five to forty-nine months of age. When affect was assessed relative to home environment, abused children favored on home environment showed more positive affect than the control children favored on home environment.

Similarly, abused children not favored on home environment showed more negative affect than control children not favored on home environment. These results suggest that abused children may have an affective hypersensitivity to environmental stimuli, and the prevalence of negative affect typically observed may be a function of the pervasive negative environments to which these children are generally exposed.

Depression, an affective disorder, has been considered as a diagnostic entity for children exhibiting certain constellations of sequelae typically associated with maltreatment (e.g., Blumberg, 1981; Kinard, 1982). Such characteristics as low self-esteem, maladaptive social perceptions, and dysfunctional interpersonal behavior are all characteristic of depression, as well as being sequelae of maltreatment. In addition, the sequelae of abuse described by Kinard (1980), which include abused children being more sad, unpopular, and poorly behaved, and the higher incidence of self-destructive behaviors observed in abused children (Green, 1978) are typically discussed as consistent with childhood depression.

Kinard (1982) discusses the experiences of uncontrollability and deprivation in the upbringing of maltreated children and points out that experiences of this nature have been shown to be etiologically related to depression in adults. As discussed in Chapter 3, the stress associated with pervasive and uncontrollable aversive experiences may lead to feelings of helplessness and exhaustion, and maltreatment may be etiologically related to depression in the same manner. Blumberg (1981) also discusses failure to thrive as being a possible manifestation of childhood depression.

Although the relationship between maltreatment and depression has received some preliminary attention in the literature, this relationship has not been empirically studied. The reasons for this notable absence in the research literature are twofold. First, there is currently no well-defined syndrome of childhood depression. Second, research samples of maltreated children are typically too small to allow the study of any broad, multidimensional construct such as depression. Because so many of the sequelae of maltreatment are consistent with symptoms of depression, however, the relationship between maltreatment and childhood depression appears to a fruitful avenue for future research.

Section summary

Disturbances of affect appear common among maltreated children. Verbally abused and neglected children appear more angry than nonmaltreated children, and physically abused children seem to show more negative affect in general. In some cases, physically abused children may also show inappropriately positive affect, suggesting that they may have a general hypersensitivity to affective stimuli. Although sexually abused children are also thought to frequently display inappropriate affect and signs of depression, little research is available which directly addresses these impressions. Many of the experiences and characteristics of maltreated children, however, appear to be consistent with the syndrome of depression and this relationship needs to be more fully studied in the future.

BEHAVIORAL SEQUELAE

The final section in this chapter addresses the behavioral sequelae of maltreatment. Many of the behavioral characteristics of maltreated children have been touched upon in prior sections, because the socioemotional sequelae of maltreatment are often inferred from behavior. For example, anger may be inferred from aggressive or avoidant behavior, and low self-esteem is often inferred from self-depreciatory behavior or a lack of motivation. This final section presents a number of behavioral characteristics which have not yet been addressed in previous sections of this chapter.

Table 4-6 lists several characteristics associated with the behavior of maltreated children. All types of abuse are thought to be related to delinquency, truancy, running away, and self-destructive behaviors. Behaviors indicative of anxiety are also common in all types of maltreatment. In addition, sexually and emotionally abused children are often said to be regressed or infantile in their behavior.

TABLE 4-6

Behavior sequelae of maltreatment

Physical Abuse

- Self-abusive behavior
- Lying
- Stealing
- Truancy
- Tics
- Stuttering
- Unpredictable

Neglect

- Irregular school attendance
- Begging, stealing or hoarding food
- Lying
- Theft
- Vandalism
- Running away
- Daydreaming
- Bizarre eating habits
- Nailbiting
- Tics
- Stuttering
- Unpredictable

Sexual Abuse

Excessive daydreaming/fantasizing
Excessive sexual play/masturbation
Self-abusive behavior
Truancy
Running away
Regressive/infantile behavior
Suicidal gestures
Insomnia

Emotional Abuse

Self-abusive behavior
Hoarding food
Referral to self in the third person
Thumbsucking
Nailbiting
Habit disorders - sucking, biting, rocking
Obsessive or compulsive behaviors
Insomnia
Enuresis
Truancy
Running away
Destructive behavior

Because behaviors such as those listed in Table 4-6 are often infrequent and situationally specific, most efforts to empirically confirm their relationship to maltreatment have involved after-the-fact case analyses or second-hand reports with checklists or rating scales. For example, Green (1978) documented increased levels of self-destructive behavior in physically abused children on parent and psychiatrist interviews. Using teacher reports, Morgan (1979) found physically abused children to be characterized as unpredictable and prone to outbursts in the classroom. Using the Child Behavior Checklist and comparing to the available norms, Friedrich et al. (1986) found sexually abused children have a greater number of behavior problems, including aggression, withdrawal, and a preoccupation with sexual matters. None of these studies, however, were based on direct observations of the children.

Even the behavioral characteristics known to be associated with maltreatment have not had their specific relationship to various types of maltreatment delineated. For example, the sexual preoccupation associated with sexual abuse (e.g., Friedrich et al., 1986) has not been investigated to determine its prevalence in children who have experienced other types of maltreatment. Common sense suggests that sexualization would be specific to sexually abused children, but preoccupations such as excessive masturbating may be used as an "escape" for physically or emotionally abused children as well. Similarly, many of the behavioral sequelae in Table 4-6 are manifestations of anxiety, but the percentage of anxious children who have been maltreated is not known. Further research, especially with measures other than parental report, is needed to delineate the relationship between such behaviors and maltreatment.

Section summary

Many behaviors have been discussed as sequelae of maltreatment. The available research confirms a greater prevalence of behavioral disturbance in maltreated than in nonmaltreated children. Maltreated children appear susceptible to a variety of behavioral sequelae, with the specific behaviors exhibited by a particular child being a function of family, developmental, and environmental factors which interact with the maltreatment. The etiological complexity of behavioral sequelae precludes a unilateral association between specific types of maltreatment and consequent behaviors, but as in other characteristics, the presence of a greater number of behavioral indicators warrants increased concern about the prospect of abuse or neglect in the child's environment.

CHAPTER SUMMARY

This chapter has discussed the indicators and sequelae of child maltreatment in several areas of functioning. Maltreated children are most commonly identified by the presence of certain physical characteristics. The sequelae of maltreatment, however, extend far beyond these physical injuries. Maltreated children have been shown to suffer in the cognitive, socioemotional, affective, and behavioral, as well as the physical, domains of functioning.

Although an extraordinary number of dysfunctional characteristics have been associated with maltreatment, the research delineating the specific causes and long-term implications of these characteristics is inadequate. It would be naive, however, to presume that because the long-term implications have not been

INDICATORS/SEQUELAE	RECOMMENDATIONS

I. Physical Characteristics
  A. Injuries or burns
    1. Location
    2. Appearance
    3. Circumstances
  B. Neurological damage
  C. Genital trauma
  D. Other disorder or diseases
  E. Other physical symptoms
    (e.g., symptoms of anxiety)
  F. Failure to Thrive
	I. Further Evaluation/Treatment

II. Cognitive Functioning
  A. Language
  B. Intelligence
  C. Attention/concentration
  D. Motivation
	II. Needs:
	  A. Speech and language therapy
	  B. Academic supports
	  C. Therapy/academic programming
	  D. Therapy/academic programming

III. Socioemotional Functioning
  A. Parent-child attachment
  B. Interpersonal behavior
    1. With adults
    2. With children
  C. Social perceptions
  D. Self-esteem
	III. Needs:
	  A. Parent-child group therapy
	  B. Parenting/classroom
	    management therapy
	
	  C. Parent training/therapy
	  D. Parent training/therapy

IV. Affect
  A. Inappropriate or unusual
  B. Depression
	IV. Therapeutic Needs

V. Behavioral Sequelae	V. Treatment Needs
	  A. Home
	  B. School

Figure 4-13
Assessment summary of characteristics of maltreated children.*

*A comprehensive assessment covering these areas will require a multimethod approach, including interviews, observations, family history, medical examination, and psychological assessment.

delineated they are not significant. Intellectual deficits, language delays, interpersonal problems, and affective and behavioral disturbance all interfere with adaptive functioning in the world, and undoubtedly lead to patterns of coping that are far less than optimal for the individual. Because of the potential long-term effects of the sequelae of maltreatment, these children must be carefully assessed in each domain and provided with the necessary treatment services to improve their functioning where difficulties are noted. For quick reference, Figure 4-13 provides an assessment summary outlining each of the characteristics reviewed in this chapter.

The challenge to expound upon and clarify what we know about child maltreatment is now greater than ever. More must be learned about the specific processes that cause maltreated children to be developmentally at risk, and ways to counteract these forces must be explored. Only by expanding our current knowledge base can we begin to more accurately identify and more effectively help the many children who are currently being abused and neglected in our society.

REFERENCES

Ainsworth, M., Blehar, M., Waters, E., & Wall, S. (1978). Patterns of Attachment. Hillsdale, NJ: Erlbaum.

Allen, R.E., & Oliver, J.M. (1982). "The Effects of Child Maltreatment on Language Development." Child Abuse and Neglect, 6, 299-305.

Appelbaum, A.S. (1977). "Developmental Retardation in Infants as a Concomitant of Physical Child Abuse." Journal of Abnormal Child Psychology, 5, 417-423.

Barahal, R.M., Waterman, J., & Martin, H.P. (1981). "The Social Cognitive Development of Abused Children." Journal of Consulting and Clinical Psychology, 49, 508-516.

Blager, F.B. (1979). "The Effect of Intervention on the Speech and Language of Abused Children." Child Abuse and Neglect, 5, 991-996.

Blager, F., & Martin, H.P. (1976). "Speech and Language of Abused Children." In H.P. Martin (ed.), The Abused Child: A Multidisciplinary Approach to Developmental Issues and Treatment. Cambridge: Ballinger Publishing Co.

Blumberg, M.L. (1981). "Depression in Abused and Neglected Children." American Journal of Psychotherapy, 35, 342-355.

Bradley, R.H., & Caldwell, B.M. (1984).   "The Relation of Infants' Home Environments to Achievement Test Performance in First Grade: A Follow-up Study." Child Development, 55, 803-809.

Caffey, J. (1972). "On the Theory and Practice of Shaking Infants: Its Potential Residual Effects of Permanent Brain Damage and Mental Retardation." American Journal of Diseases of Children, 124, 161-169.

Caffey, J. (1974). "The Whiplash Shaken Infant Syndrome: Manual Shaking by the Extremities with Whiplash-induced Intracranial and Intraocular Bleeding, Linked with Residual Permanent Brain Damage and Mental Retardation." Pediatrics, 54, 396-403.

Call, J.D. (1984). "Child Abuse and Neglect in Infancy: Sources of Hostility Within the Parent-Infant Dyad and Disorders of Attachment in Infancy." Child Abuse and Neglect, 8, 185-202.

Camras, L.A., Grow, J.G., & Ribordy, S.C. (1983). "Recognition of Emotional Expression by Abused Children." Journal of Clinical Child Psychology, 12, 325-328.

Dean, A.L., Malik, M.M., Richards, W., & Stringer, S.A. (1986). "Effects of Parental Maltreatment on Children's Conceptions of Interpersonal Relationships." Developmental Psychology, 22, 617-626.

Dykes, L.J. (1986). "The Whiplash Shaken Infant Syndrome: What Has Been Learned?" Child Abuse and Neglect, 10, 211-221.

Egeland, B., & Sroufe, A. (1981). "Attachment and Early Maltreatment." Child Development, 52, 44-52.

Egeland, B., Sroufe, L.A., & Erickson, M. (1983). "The Developmental Consequence of Different Patterns of Maltreatment." Child Abuse and Neglect, 7, 459-469.

Elmer, E. (1978). "The Effects of Early Neglect and Abuse on Latency Age Children." Journal of Pediatric Psychology, 8, 14-19.

Elmer, E. (1977). "A Follow-up Study of Traumatized Children." Pediatrics, 59, 273-279.

Elmer, E., & Gregg, G.S. (1967). "Developmental Characteristics of Abused Children." Pediatrics, 40, 596-602.

Feldman, K.W. (1987). "Child Abuse by Burning." In R.E. Helfer & R.L. Kempe (eds.), The Battered Child. Chicago: University of Chicago Press.

Friedrich, W.N., Einbender, A.J., & Luecke, W.J. (1983). "Cognitive and Behavioral Characteristics of Physically Abused Children." Journal of Consulting and Clinical Psychology, 51, 313-314.

Friedrich, W.N, Urquiza, A.J., & Beilke, R.L. (1986). "Behavior Problems in Sexually Abused Young Children." Journal of Pediatric Psychology, 11, 47-57.

Galdston, R. (1975). "Preventing the Abuse of Little Children: The Parents' Center Project for the Study and Prevention of Child Abuse." American Journal of Orthopsychiatry, 45, 372-381.

Galdston, R. (1965). "Observations of Children Who Have Been Physically Abused by Their Parents." American Journal of Psychiatry, 122, 440-443.

George, C., & Main, M. (1979). "Social Interactions of Young Abused Children: Approach, Avoidance, and Aggression." Child Development, 50, 306-318.

Gersten, M., Coster, W., Schneider-Rosen, K., Carlson, V., & Cicchetti, D. (1986). "The Socioemotional Bases of Communicative Functioning: Quality of Attachment, Language Development, and Early Maltreatment." In M.E. Lamb & B. Rogoff (eds.), Advances in Developmental Psychology, Vol. 4. Hillsdale, NJ: Erlbaum.

Giblin, P.I., Starr, R.H., & Agronow, S.J. (1984). "Affective Behavior of Abused and Control Children: Comparisons of Parent-Child Interactions and the Influence of Home Environment Variables." The Journal of Genetic Psychology, 144, 69-82.

Green, A.H. (1978). "Self-destructive Behavior in Battered Children." American Journal of Psychiatry, 135, 579-582.

Hoffman-Plotkin, D., & Twentyman, C.T. (1984). "A Multimodel Assessment of Behavioral and Cognitive Deficits in Abused and Neglected Preschoolers." Child Development, 55, 794-802.

Howes, C., & Espinosa, M.P. (1985). "The Consequences of Child Abuse for the Formation of Relationships with Peers." Child Abuse and Neglect, 9, 397-404.

Iverson, T.J., & Segal, M. (1986). "The Behavior Observation Record." Nova University, unpublished manuscript.

Iverson, T.J., Tanner, S.L., & Segal, M. (1987). "Assessing Abused and Neglected Children's Social Interactions with the Behavior Observation Record." Nova University, unpublished manuscript.

Jacobson, R.S., & Straker, G. (1982). "Peer Group Interaction of Physically Abused Children." Child Abuse and Neglect, 6, 321-327.

Johnson, B., & Morse, H.A. (1968). "Injured Children and Their Parents." Children, 15, 147-152.

Kazdin, A.E., Moser, J., Colbus, D., & Bell, R. (1985). "Depressive Symptoms Among Physically Abused and Psychiatrically Disturbed Children." Journal of Abnormal Psychology, 94, 298-307.

Kempe, R.S., Cutler, C., & Dean, J. (1980). "The Infant with Failure to Thrive." In C.H. Kempe & R.E. Helfer (eds.), The Battered Child. Chicago: University of Chicago Press.

Kempe, R.S., & Kempe, C.H. (1978). Child Abuse. Cambridge: Harvard University Press.

Kempe, C.H., Silverman, F.N., Steele, B.F., Droegemueller, W., & Silver, H.K. (1962). "The Battered Child Syndrome." Journal of the American Medical Association, 181, 17-24.

Kinard, E.M. (1982). "Child Abuse and Depression: Cause or Consequence?" Child Welfare, 61, 403-413.

Kinard, E.M. (1980). "Emotional Development in Physically Abused Children." American Journal of Orthopsychiatry, 50, 686-696.

Kristiansson, B. & Fallstrom, S.P. (1987). "Growth at the Age of 4 Years Subsequent to Early Failure to Thrive." Child Abuse and Neglect, 11, 35-40.

Lewis, M. (1980). "Peer Interaction and Maltreated Children: Social Network and Epigenetic Models." Infant Mental Health Journal, 1, 224-231.

Lindberg, F.H. & Distad, L.J. (1985). "Post-traumatic Stress Disorders in Women Who Experienced Childhood Incest." Child Abuse and Neglect, 9, 324-334.

Martin, H. (1972). "The Child and His Development." In C.H. Kempe & R.E. Helfer (eds.), Helping the Battered Child and His Family. Philadelphia: J.B. Lippencott.

Martin, H.P., & Beezley, P. (1977). "Behavioral Observations of Abused Children." Developmental Medicine and Child Neurology, 19, 373-387.

Martin, H.P., Beezley, P., Conway, E.F., & Kempe, C.H. (1974). "The Development of Abused Children." Advances in Pediatrics, 21, 25-73.

Merritt, H.H. (1979). A Textbook of Neurology. Philadelphia: Lea & Febiger.

Money, J., Annecillo, C., & Kelly, J.F. (1983). "Growth of Intelligence: Failure and Catchup Associated Respectively with Abuse and Rescue in the Syndrome of abuse Dwarfism." Psychoneuroendrocrinology, 8, 309-319.

Morgan, S.R. (1979). "Psychoeducational Profile of Emotionally Disturbed Abused Children." Journal of Clinical Child Psychology, 8, 3-6.

Morse, W., Sahler, O.J., & Friedman, S.B. (1970). "A Three-year Follow-up Study of Abused and Neglected Children." American Journal of Diseases of Children, 120, 439-446.

Ney, P.G., Moore, C., McPhee, J., & Trought, P. (1986). "Child Abuse: A Study of the Child's Perspective." Child Abuse and Neglect, 10, 511-518.

Reidy, T.J. (1977). "The Aggressive Characteristics of Abused and Neglected Children." Journal of Clinical Psychology, 33, 1140-1145.

Relich, R., Giblin, P.T., Starr, R.H., & Agronow, S.J. (1980). "Motor and Social Behavior in Abused and Control Children: Observations of Parent-child Interactions." Journal of Psychology, 106, 193-204.

Sandgrund, A., Gaines, R.W., & Green, A.H. (1974). "Child Abuse and Mental Retardation: A Problem of Cause and Effect." American Journal of Mental Deficiency, 79, 327-330.

Schmitt, B.D. (1987). "The Child with Nonaccidental Trauma." In R.E. Helfer & R.S. Kempe (eds.), The Battered Child. Chicago: University of Chicago Press.

Schmitt, B.D. (1980). "The Child with Nonaccidental Trauma." In C.H. Kempe & R.E. Helfer (eds.), The Battered Child. Chicago: University of Chicago Press.

Schneider-Rosen, K., & Cicchetti, D. (1984). "The Relationship Between Affect and Cognition in Maltreated Infants: Quality of Attachment and the Development of Visual Self-recognition." Child Development, 55, 648-658.

Sebold, J. (1987). "Indicators of Child Sexual Abuse in Males." Social Casework: The Journal of Contemporary Social Work, 68, 75-80.

Segal, M., Iverson, T.J., & Layden, P. (1985). "The Identification and Remediation of the Effects of Child Maltreatment in Preschool Age Children." Nova University, unpublished manuscript.

Showers, J.S., & Bandman, R.L. (1986). "Scarring for Life: Abuse with Electric Cords." Child Abuse and Neglect, 10, 25-31.

Slade, B.B., Steward, M.S., Morrison, T.L., & Abramowitz, S.I. (1984). "Locus of Control, Persistence, and Use of Contingency Information in Physically Abused Children." Child Abuse and Neglect, 8, 447-457.

Smetana, J.G., Kelly, M., & Twentyman, C.T. (1984). "Abused, Neglected, and Nonmaltreated Children's Conceptions of Moral and Social Conventional Transgressions." Child Development, 55, 277-287.

Snow, C.E. & Gilbreath, B.J. (1983). "Explaining Transitions." In R.M. Golinkoff (ed.), The Transition from Prelinguistic to Linguistic Communication. Hillsdale, NJ: Laurence Erlbaum Associates.

Terr, L.C. (1970). "A Family Study of Child Abuse." American Journal of Psychiatry, 127, 125-131.

Watkins, H.D., & Bradbard, M.R. (1984). "Young Abused Children's Knowledge of Caregiving Behaviors." The Journal of Genetic Psychology, 144, 145-146.

Yeatman, G.W., Shaw, C., Barlow, M.J., & Bartlett, C. (1976). "Pseudobattering in Vietnamese Children." <u>Pediatrics</u>, <u>58</u>, 616-618.

Chapter 5

Intervention in Child Maltreatment

Actions and Outcomes

Child abuse and neglect is destructive to the victims, perpetrators, and society at large. As discussed in previous chapters, evidence which confirms the detrimental affects of maltreatment, both to the individual and society, is accumulating. The sensationalism surrounding child abuse in the early 1960's spawned a plethora of legislation aimed at protecting children, and subsequently the states have implemented a complex system of interventions for the purpose of ameliorating the problem.

Along with the actions and programs mandated by state legislatures, the private sector has developed a variety of programs to address the problem of child maltreatment. Programs which educate the public, provide treatment for the victims and/or perpetrators, or otherwise augment publicly funded programs have sprung up across the United States. The purpose of the current chapter and the following chapter on prevention is to familiarize the reader with this system of interventions. The current chapter discusses reporting, investigating, and treating abused and neglected children and their families. The goal of this chapter is to provide the reader with sufficient information to effectively work within the system and enhance responsible action on the behalf of maltreated children.

REPORTING

State law mandates the reporting of suspected child maltreatment to the proper authorities for most professionals who come in contact with children and/or families. For example, Florida law, which is fairly representative, mandates reporting by:

Any person, including, but not limited to, any:

(a)   *Physician, osteopath, medical examiner, chiropractor, nurse, or hospital personnel engaged in the admission, examination, care, or treatment of persons;*

(b)   *Health or mental health professional other than one listed in paragraph (a);*

(c)   *Practitioner who relies solely on spiritual means for healing;*

(d)   *School teacher or other school official or personnel;*

(e)   *Social worker, day care center worker, or other professional child care, foster care, residential, or institutional worker; or*

(f)   *Law enforcement officer, who knows, or has reason to suspect, that a child is an abused or neglected child... (F.S. 1985, Chapter 415).*

In addition, failure to report by a mandated reporter is typically considered a misdemeanor criminal act, and individuals who report in good faith are protected from any civil or criminal liability resulting from the report. In other words, there is a strong bias toward overreporting, with protection for those who report and sanctions for those who do not.

Despite the legislative bias toward overreporting, it is generally agreed that maltreatment is significantly underreported in our society. There are several possible reasons for hesitating to report suspected child maltreatment. Concern about the parents' reactions or the possible consequences for the child is common. Similarly, the feeling that reporting suspected maltreatment is an invasion of the families' privacy, a highly regarded value in our society, often leads to anxiety about taking action. Finally, confusion as to what constitutes a reportable case of maltreatment may lead to ambivalence about reporting. This confusion may be in part due to inadequate training in identifying maltreatment but is more often a function of the ambiguous criteria regarding what constitutes child abuse and neglect in our society. Consequently, the first step in cases of suspected maltreatment is determining if a report of abuse or neglect is warranted.

The Decision to Report

State statutes which mandate the reporting of suspected maltreatment also provide definitions of what is considered child abuse and neglect. However, as was discussed in chapter 1, these definitions are generally so broad and open to interpretation that they are of little help except in cases which are fairly straightforward to begin with. Cases which involve the presence of the visible physical indicators discussed in Chapter 4 or cases which involve environmental conditions which pose a clear and immediate threat to normal development, such as inadequate food and clothing, are easy to identify as cases that should be reported. Similarly, incidents of maltreatment which involve a verbal statement by the child or parent that abuse occurred or which have been witnessed by a third party usually raise no question regarding reporting.

On the other hand, cases in which the suspicion is based on subjective behavioral or emotional indicators, vague reports of previous incidents of maltreatment, or evidence of parent-child interactions consistent with maltreatment in the absence of specific and objective indicators are more difficult to decide. These are the cases that tend to go unreported, often to the detriment of the child.

Factors affecting the decision to report

When the decision to report child abuse or neglect is unclear, several factors must be weighed. The nature of the indicators giving rise to the suspicion of maltreatment must be closely examined. In addition, the welfare of the child must be weighed against the cost of possible disruption in families which may already be unstable. In some cases, the family disruption resulting from a report may place the child at greater risk than if no report were made, such as the case when a family has recently committed to counseling or other support services only to find that their efforts to seek help result in allegations of child maltreatment. Finally, the implications of choosing not to report a questionable case must be carefully considered. Current statutes offer no protection to individuals who, in good faith, choose **not** to report a case of possible maltreatment.

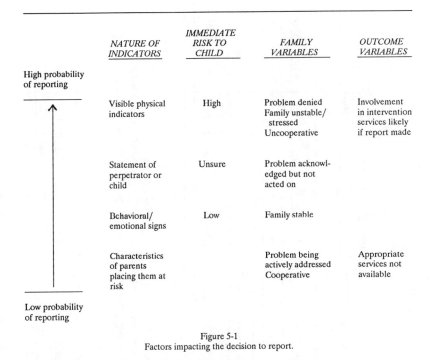

	NATURE OF INDICATORS	IMMEDIATE RISK TO CHILD	FAMILY VARIABLES	OUTCOME VARIABLES
High probability of reporting				
↑	Visible physical indicators	High	Problem denied Family unstable/ stressed Uncooperative	Involvement in intervention services likely if report made
	Statement of perpetrator or child	Unsure	Problem acknowl- edged but not acted on	
	Behavioral/ emotional signs	Low	Family stable	
	Characteristics of parents placing them at risk		Problem being actively addressed Cooperative	Appropriate services not available
Low probability of reporting				

Figure 5-1
Factors impacting the decision to report.

Date _____ Time _____ a.m. _____ p.m. Unit _____

Received by _____

Phone _____
Office _____
Abuse Registry _____

Reporter (confidential) _____ Phone _____ Address _____

Child's last name	First	DOB/POB	Race	Sex	School	Grade	Height	Weight	Distinguishing Features

Parents/Caregivers:

Last name	First	Age	Race	Sex	Address	Phone (Home/Business)	Occupation	SS#

Does the child live with parents? _____ Yes _____ No

Are parents _____ married _____ divorced _____ separated _____ deceased

If child does not live with parents, specify relationship of caregiver. _____

Siblings/Others:

Last name	First	Age	Race	Sex	Relationship	Check if living at home	Address

Alleged Perpetrator:

Last name	First	DOB	Age	Race	Sex	Address	Phone	Occupation	SS#

Circumstances of Report:

Witness:

Last name	First	Relationship to Victim	Age	Address	Phone

Complaint Alleges: ____ PA ____ N ____ SA ____ EA ____ Custody ____ Delinquency ____ Other (specify) ____

Prior Agency Contact:

Agency	Dates	Reason for Contact	Outcome

Is family aware of report? ____ Yes ____ No   Is perpetrator, if not a family member, aware? ____ Yes ____ No

Directions to home
school _____

Other relevant information _____

_____   _____
Signature   Date   Time

Figure 5-2
Intake Report Form

Figure 5-1 shows several of the factors which need to be considered when determining whether a case of suspected maltreatment should be reported. As mentioned above, the presence of certain conditions should lead to an immediate report. These conditions include the presence of **objective physical indicators, a high or moderate degree of immediate risk** to the child, or **a high degree of future risk** to the child. If these conditions are not present, then combinations of factors need to be considered. For example, if the **indicators are vague and/or subjective**, the **immediate risk to the child is low**, and the family is involved with or willing to become involved with **support services** to improve the parent-child relationship, reporting may not be in the child's best interest. In this example, it is assumed that support services will be voluntarily sought by the family. Cases in which reporting is likely to **increase access to treatment or support services**, on the other hand, may be indicated even if the objective indicators are not entirely conclusive. Unfortunately, the programs in most communities are underfunded and inadequately staffed, and cases in which there is not clear and immediate evidence of maltreatment are often closed with no follow up. Reporting a case which leads to an investigation and no further action may actually cause the family to avoid seeking help in future problem situations.

In addition to the nature of the indicators and the most likely outcome of the investigation, one must weigh **concern for the child** with the **impact of reporting on the family** as a whole. If reporting is going to lead to excessive or unnecessary disruption of the family, reporting may not be in the child's best interest. Arne Gray, in an article in the June, 1987 *APA Monitor*, points out that the disruption resulting from an investigation is itself abusive and suggests that some forms of mild maltreatment may be less abusive than the investigation (Denton, 1987).

Similarly, there has been much debate about the advantages and disadvantages of reporting suspected maltreatment when the family has been identified by a professional from whom they are seeking therapeutic services. For example, if a family seeks counseling to learn better ways to manage their child and informs the counselor that some of their current methods of discipline are abusive, it is the counselor's responsibility to report the case. Such action, however, may be perceived by the family as punitive rather than helpful and may serve as an impediment to change through counseling. Similarly, an investigation of suspected maltreatment and the related accusations, perceived or real, may serve as a catalyst for family separation. In cases where family or marital tensions could have been resolved, additional stress leading to a premature separation is clearly not in the child's best interest. In other words, there may be a variety of mitigating circumstances which may affect a decision to report questionable cases of maltreatment.

Unfortunately, there are currently no provisions for such circumstances in the reporting laws, and the counselor can be held liable if no report is made. Consequently, a decision not to report, even if such a decision is clearly in the best interest of the child, is a risky decision. Anyone choosing not to report must have very convincing reasons for such a decision and must realize that if the child is subjected to future harm, the decision not to report could open one up to liability.

In short, responsible reporting requires awareness of several factors, including the risk to the child, the family situation, and the likely outcomes if a report is or is not made. Consequently, individuals working with children and/or families need to be familiar not only with the circumstances of the case but also with the child welfare services in their district.   In addition, an understanding of how the local protective services and/or law enforcement responds to reports will aid both in the decision to report and in preparing the family for what to expect.   Appendix B provides information regarding agencies to contact for information about local child welfare services.   Once again, it should be emphasized that there is no protection for individuals who choose not to report in good faith; consequently, unless there is an extremely good rationale for not reporting, borderline cases should be decided in the direction of making a report.

Making a Report

Once the decision to make a report of suspected child maltreatment is reached, it is useful to know what the report will entail and how it will be handled. The first step is to call the designated reporting agency in your area. Many states have a central registry with a toll-free number to which reports from anywhere in the state may be made. Alternatively, there may be a local number or numbers which allow reporting to be made directly to the office responsible for children's services in that district. In some states, a report can be made to either the local social service or law enforcement agency. Appendix B contains a state by state listing of the agencies to which a report of suspected child maltreatment should be made.

The individual you make the telephone report to will ask you several questions. The answers to these questions are important because they will help assure a successful response to your report.   Figure 5-2 shows a typical intake form with samples of the types of information you will be asked for. It is useful to have the information ready when the call is made, and filling out the sample intake form provided in Figure 5-2 is good preparation.

A telephone report of suspected abuse or neglect may go as follows:

Intake: Abuse Hotline, may I help you?

Reporter: I'd like to report a child who I think was physically abused.

I: Where are you calling from?

R: I'm calling from Northbeach.

I: May I have your name?

R: Mary Neighbor

(Any identifying information will remain entirely confidential. Anonymous reports are also accepted).

I: What are you seeing that concerns you?

R: Well, I take care of several kids after school, and today I noticed that one of the children some marks on his back that looked like he was hit with something. When I asked him what happened he said "nothing," and then later said he fell off his bike.

I: *What's the child's name?*

R: B.H.

I: *Do you know his date of birth?*

R: No, but he's eight years old.

I: *What's his mother's name?*

R: J.H.

I: *Father's name?*

R: I don't know -- there is no father in the home.

I: *Is there anyone else who lives at the residence?*

R: There is one brother, and the mother has a boyfriend who may live there as well.

I: *Do you know the name of the boyfriend?*

R: No, she's never mentioned it.

I: *What is the brother's name and age?*

R: D.H. -- he's in his teens.

I: *Where does the child go to school?*

R: He goes to J.P. Elementary. I think he is in second grade there.

I: *You said the child had some bruises. What did they look like?*

R: They weren't really bruises. They were reddish marks that went across his back, probably about a half inch wide. There were three or four of them. They were on the middle and top of his back.

I: *O.K., can you describe the child briefly.*

R: He's white, has curly light brown hair, and is average height and weight.

I: *Is the child with you now?*

R: No, his mother picked him up about a half hour ago.

I: *What's the child's home address?*

R: It's 311 South Street.

I: *Did you talk to the mother when she picked him up?*

R: I asked her about the marks on his back, but she only said he had had an accident. I didn't push it.

I: *Do you know who might have abused the child?*

R: No, I really don't have any idea.

I: *Is there any other information we should know, about the family situation or who may have caused the injuries?*

R: No, except the mother doesn't seem like the type to be that severe on her child. If anything, she lets him get away with too much. I've never seen her do anything when I tell her he's gotten into trouble.

I: *Okay, thank you for the information. Did you tell the child or mother you were going to call us?*

R: No, I didn't mention anything.

I: *Okay, we will follow up on this as soon as possible. Now, let me make sure I have this information correct....*

All the information in the initial report is important to the investigator, but several issues should be highlighted. First, the reporter's name will be asked, but anonymous reports are accepted. If you do give your name, it will not be released to the alleged perpetrators. Next, complete and accurate descriptive information is essential to assure that the investigator is is able to identify the correct child. For example, a child who is severely bruised may go undetected because the parents let the investigator examine a sibling. Complete information about the family makeup will help assure that the correct child or children are investigated and also facilitate the identification of other family members who may also be victims of abuse or neglect. Finally, information regarding behavior patterns of the child and/or family will help facilitate the investigation. For example, if the investigator knows when the child is in school or daycare and when the parents are or are not at home, he or she will be better able to arrange an appropriate investigation.

The remainder of the report will have to do with the actual maltreatment. The reporting individual will be asked to describe the nature of the alleged maltreatment. Specificity and reference to objective indicators are very useful in this description. For example, rather than saying "the parents don't take care of the child," specific observations should be relied upon. Examples of such observations include, "*the child is left at home during the day with no provisions for food"*, *"the child has a bruise resembling a hand shape on his lower back"*, *"the child appears sluggish and malnourished and the parents are not seeking medical help"*, or *"the child has become extremely withdrawn and nonparticipatory in school, refuses to talk about it, and the parents refuse to come in for a conference."* Statements such as these greatly facilitate an investigation because they provide specifics which can be looked for or asked about thus reducing the likelihood that important information will be missed.

Finally, many states request a written report to follow up the telephone report (see Appendix B for the requirements of specific states). If a written follow up is required, a form such as that in Figure 5-2 can be completed and submitted. Often, one can make the notes on an appropriate form before calling in a report, and then simply mail in the form for the written follow up.

In short, making a report of suspected child abuse or neglect is a simple, straightforward process, provided the reporter is prepared to provide the basic information. Taking a few minutes to compile the information before the call, remaining objective during the call, and providing specific information to the intake worker all help to insure a successful follow up to the call.

Section summary

Most individuals who come in contact with families and/or children in their professions are mandated by state law to report suspected cases of child maltreatment. Although the available statutes typically provide definitions of abuse and neglect, these definitions are typically inadequate for deciding cases in which there is no clear and objective evidence of maltreatment. In questionable cases, several factors need to be considered when determining if a suspicion should be reported. The nature of the indicators, the presumed risk to the child, the current involvement of the family in therapy or other relevant services, the probable outcome of an investigation for the child and family, and the reporter's own legal responsibilities must be carefully weighed. Although reporting is in some cases contrary to the best interests of the child, statutory regulations create a bias toward reporting in questionable cases. Protection from civil and criminal liability is provided, in most states, for individuals who report "in good faith." Failure to report, on the other hand, may lead to liability if any future harm should befall the child even if the decision not to report was similarly made in good faith.

Once a decision to report is made, the designated intake agency should be contacted. Filing a report of suspected maltreatment is a straightforward process, particularly if the basic information has been prepared ahead of time. A reporter should be prepared to provide identifying information about the child and family, information regarding the indicators and circumstances surrounding the suspected maltreatment, and other information that will aid the investigator in appropriately and accurately investigating the case. Completing a form with the information prior to calling in a report will help the report go smoothly and can also serve as a written follow up in states where such a follow up is required.

THE INVESTIGATION

Reporting a case of suspected maltreatment begins with the child protection investigation. After the report of suspected maltreatment, an investigator must follow up with a site visit, usually to the home. In cases of physical and sexual abuse the investigator tries to respond immediately, whereas in cases of neglect and emotional abuse the maximum response time is typically 24 hours. State statutes delineate the maximum response time for child abuse investigators.

The primary investigator in cases of child maltreatment is either a law enforcement officer or a social worker trained in protective services. The trend has been to increasingly utilize social workers rather than police officers and, more recently, to coordinate both disciplines in the investigative process.

Having a law enforcement officer and social worker cooperate in the initial investigation is desirable for several reasons. First of all, reported cases of maltreatment differ greatly. Certain cases, particularly sexual abuse and severe physical assault, often lead to criminal prosecution of the offender. The presence of a law enforcement officer facilitates the collection of evidence in a manner that preserves its admissibility in court. On the other hand, in cases where support and treatment for the family is the primary concern, the presence of a social worker may be less threatening to the family and better elicit cooperation. Finally, safety and decision-making process may be enhanced when two individuals cooperate in the investigative process.

When discussing cooperative efforts in the investigation of maltreatment, the key word is cooperate. Too often in the past tensions have developed because the methods of various professions during the initial investigation have differed, giving the impression of antithetical goals for the investigation. For example, social workers have criticized law enforcement because of the focus on punishment instead of treatment, and social workers have, in turn, been criticized for their lack of investigative training and experience (Maden, 1980). The goals of the investigation, however, are always the same, that is, to protect the child. Different methods or emphases for the investigation should complement rather than contradict each other, with different cases requiring different patterns of intervention.

Preliminary Determination of Risk

As mentioned above, the general goal of the initial investigation is to protect the child. In practice, this means making a preliminary determination as to whether the circumstances of the report are **substantiated** and determining the immediate **risk to the child** if he or she stays in the present environment. A report is considered substantiated if the investigator determines there is basis in fact for the report. For example, if a report alleges that a child has scars on his back that seem to be the result of physical abuse, presence of the scars and the absence of a reasonable explanation, other than abuse, for the scars would warrant preliminary substantiation.

If a report appears substantiated, the question of immediate risk would then be addressed. Given the child was physically abused, how probable is it that he will receive further harm if left in the home? If an investigator learns, for example, that a history of verbal abuse has been escalating into physical abuse, that the abuse is worse when the perpetrator has been drinking, and that the perpetrator is, at the time of the investigation, out drinking, the child will most likely be deemed at immediate risk and removed from the home.

The specific decision-making factors which determine conclusions regarding substantiation and risk are not well-delineated. A small body of research, however, has identified several factors which seem to be most salient to the decision-making process.

Preliminary determinations in cases of physical abuse and neglect

Meddin (1985) identified four classes of criteria which were commonly used in initial decision making. These were 1) criteria related to the victim, 2) criteria related to the caretaker, 3) criteria related to the perpetrator, and 4) criteria related to the incident itself. The severity of the incident was the most commonly used criterion for the assessment of risk.   Other important criteria included the cooperation and functioning of the prime caretaker (which reflects the ability of the caretaker to protect the child), the intent of the perpetrator and his or her access to the child, the age and functioning of the child, and previous contact with child protective services.

Alter (1985) identified a two-stage decision-making process in cases of child neglect.   The first stage, at which 40-50% of the decisions are made,   involves immediate evidence of danger to the child.   Factors at this stage include physical harm, the age of the child, and the frequency of neglect. In gray area cases where the immediate risk is not clear, the stage two factors of intent, quality of parent-child relationship, degree of parental social deviance, and parental willingness to change become important decision-making factors.

Decision making clearly relies heavily on evidence related to the severity of the current incident. A child who has severe injuries or very poor physical condition will usually be considered at greater risk than a child who does not exhibit such injuries. For this reason, emotionally abused children are often treated as if they are at less risk than physically abused or neglected children.

Preliminary determinations in cases of sexual abuse

Decision making in cases of sexual abuse is somewhat different than in other types of maltreatment. In cases where sexual abuse is alleged, medical examinations and formal interviews with the child are integrally related to the initial questions of substantiation and risk. In other forms of maltreatment, initial determinations take place in the home and the child is removed if it is determined that high degree of immediate risk to the child exists. In cases of sexual abuse, the child can be removed from the home as the assessment of risk is taking place. For example, a child may be taken to an agency where the interviews can take place and where a medical exam may be conducted. Further, although there is no research supporting the assumption, it is often assumed that the dynamics of incestuous families render the caretaker (usually the mother) less able to protect the child from further abuse than in other types of maltreatment. Consequently, given similar circumstances, sexually abused children are often treated as being at greater risk than children suffering other forms of maltreatment.

Personal biases in decision making

Although the decision-making criteria discussed above appear to be fairly universal (e.g., Alter, 1985), most authors agree that they are not applied in a systematic and predetermined manner. Rather, the decision-making factors comprise a constellation of criteria which are applied in an ad-hoc manner on a case-by-case basis. The absence of systematically applied criteria for determining whether or not to substantiate a case and the immediate risk to the child creates a situation where significant amount of personal bias can affect the conclusions of the investigator. For example, the severity of the incident is a primary criteria for determining risk, but the measure of severity is left largely to the investigator. Similarly, the degree to which parents and/or perpetrators are judged to be motivated and cooperative may be affected by the biases and experience of the investigators. Consequently, it is difficult for reporters to predict the outcome of the case they reported, especially if the case is one of moderate or mild maltreatment.

Professional biases in decision making

Finally, initial decision making appears to be affected by the professional, as well as personal, biases of the investigator. There is some evidence that outcomes may vary depending upon who investigates the case. Maden (1980) cites statistics which suggest that slightly more out of home placement occurs when law enforcement responds alone or in combination with social service agencies. Further, Maden reported a tendency for the families of victims to be referred for services or be subject to agency action more frequently when social services were involved in the investigation.   These data are interesting in light of the presumption that law enforcement agencies are more punishment oriented and social service agencies are more treatment oriented. One cannot tell, however, the extent to which differences in the nature of the cases investigated led to this pattern of results. Law enforcement officials may have investigated more severe cases in general, which would tend to warrant more out of home placement. Maden (1980) does comment that most of the investigations involving both law enforcement and social services were of sexual abuse cases, which most frequently involve removal of the child from the home.

Outcomes of the Initial Investigation

The disposition of the initial investigation in cases of child maltreatment generally involves one of three outcomes: 1) the investigator may fail to find substantiating evidence and the case will be closed, 2) sufficient evidence to substantiate or continue an investigation may be available and the risk assessment will indicate that the child can safely remain at home, or 3) both sufficient evidence to substantiate the report and a determination of ample risk to the child may be present, warranting temporary separation of the child from the high-risk situation. Each of these possible outcomes leads to further actions.

Unsubstantiated reports

Reports may be judged to be unsubstantiated when there is an adequate alternative explanation for the circumstances prompting the report or when there is insufficient evidence that maltreatment occurred. Adequate explanations may entail accidental injury, physical conditions causing a child to appear neglected (e.g., organic FTT), or, less often, malicious accusations made by a disturbed parent or child. Insufficient evidence to substantiate a case occurs when parents deny any abusive behavior and there is no concrete evidence that maltreatment has occurred.

Most cases which are not substantiated are closed after the initial investigation. Some cases, however, are judged to be unsubstantiated and are still opened for protective services.   According to the American Humane Association (1986), approximately 58% of the reported cases were classified as unsubstantiated, but 16% of these cases were opened for protective services.   In other words, there are a substantial number of cases in which there is insufficient evidence to conclude that maltreatment has occurred, but sufficient evidence to assume that the family could benefit from continued involvement in social services.

When cases are closed after the initial investigation, there are statutory provisions for destroying the records within a certain time period. For example, the records for cases which are unsubstantiated must be purged after one year in Florida if no additional reports have been made.   This provision protects the privacy of families which have been wrongly reported, but in some cases may also interfere with protection in cases where there is intermittent maltreatment of a mild or moderate nature.   For example, if a family is reported several times for emotional abuse, but there are extended periods of time between reports, this history may not be available if the previous reporting records have been destroyed.

When cases are not closed after the initial investigation, they may either be substantiated immediately or remain open to gather additional information before a decision is made. Cases in which there is evidence that the child is in sufficient risk to remove him or her from the environment will be substantiated immediately. Similarly, cases in which there is clear and objective evidence of maltreatment will be substantiated immediately, and the necessary recommendations regarding risk will follow.

Substantiated cases where child is not removed

Cases which remain open and the child remains in the home are of two general types. First, maltreatment is confirmed and the family is referred to or enrolled in services to improve the family situation. For example, it may be determined that a child is being physically abused, but that the abuse is not life threatening. If the investigator believes that a program teaching the parents alternative forms of discipline will be sufficient to eliminate the physical abuse, the child may be left in the home and the parents enrolled in such a program. Cases are sometimes closed after the parents become involved in the necessary programs, but in most cases efforts are made to keep the case open until some sort of follow up addresses the effectiveness of the intervention.

Alternatively, cases may be left open because there is some evidence that the initial report should be substantiated, but further investigation is needed to confirm the investigator's initial impressions. For example, a child may show a variety of behavioral and emotional indicators of maltreatment, but in the absence of overt physical indicators or admissions on the part of the parents and/or perpetrators, additional investigation may be necessary before a decision can be made regarding the validity of the allegations. When cases remain open for additional investigation, efforts are usually made to involve the perpetrator(s) in some form of treatment while the investigation is ongoing.

Substantiated cases where the child is removed

Finally, a number of cases are substantiated on the initial investigation and, in addition, the child is determined to be at sufficient risk to temporarily remove him or her from the threatening environment. The express goal of child welfare programs is to preserve the family, and there must be a high degree of immediate risk before a child is removed from his or her family. Removing the child is most common in cases of sexual abuse, severe physical abuse, and severe physical neglect. When a child must be separated from his or her family, the child is usually removed from the home and placed in temporary shelter or with relatives. Less often, although perhaps more desirable, the child is protected by removing the perpetrator from the home.

When a child is temporarily removed from the home, initial efforts are to place the child with relatives or someone with whom the child is familiar. By placing the child with someone familiar, the disruption and associated fear are minimized. On the other hand, there are drawbacks to placing the child with relatives during the early investigation. Because maltreatment is often associated with more general family dysfunction, there is a risk that relatives may not be much better equipped than the parents to adequately care for the child. Further, particularly in cases of sexual abuse, caution must be exercised that family members do not attempt to influence the child to change his or her story. Particularly risky, although not uncommonly done, is taking a child away from an abusive parent and placing the child with grandparents who have been identified as also having a history of abusive behavior. If relatives with a history of adequate parenting are available, however, they represent the least disruptive placement for the child.

When the child cannot be placed with relatives, temporary crisis shelters are utilized for placing children who are removed from the home in emergency situations. The advantage of crisis shelters is that they usually have staff who are specially trained to deal with children who are in crisis. The disadvantage is that, interpersonally, shelters are relatively unstable environments. Children must acclimate to a variety of staff members, and it is consequently much more difficult for the children to adjust and begin resolving the emotional turmoil they are experiencing.

Section summary

Protective service investigations may be conducted by social workers, law enforcement officials, or both disciplines in a cooperative fashion. The primary goal of the investigation is the protection of the child, with the secondary goal being preservation of the unity of the family. When deciding whether a case should be substantiated and the degree of risk to the child, investigators look at several criteria. Foremost among these criteria is the severity of the current incident, the age of the child, and the willingness and ability of the primary caretaker to protect the child from future harm. Other criteria relevant to decision making include the functioning of the child, the expressed desire of the perpetrator to change his or her behavior, and the past quality of the parent-child relationship. Although these criteria appear to be universally applied, their application is not based on a systematic set of procedures.

Consequently, in cases where the criteria are unclear, the biases and experience of the investigator may play a major role in the case outcome.

Investigations into child maltreatment generally result in one of three outcomes. The case may be judged to be unsubstantiated, which means that maltreatment did not occur or that maltreatment may have occurred but the evidence is inadequate to confirm the report.   Most unsubstantiated cases are closed after the initial investigation, although some may be opened for protective services.   The second possible outcome is that there may be sufficient evidence to leave the case open for further investigation, but the risk to the child is judged insufficient to remove the child from the home.   In these cases, efforts are made to involve the parent and child in the necessary support services to prevent further maltreatment to the child.   Finally, a case may be substantiated and the child removed from the home.   This occurs if there is evidence that the child is at immediate risk for further maltreatment if left in the current environment.   Children who are removed from their home may be placed with relatives or in a temporary shelter.   Removing a child is sometimes necessary for his or her protection, but there is much debate about the effectiveness of current options for placement in meeting the abused or neglected child's needs.

THE ROLE OF THE COURTS

A variety of possible actions may follow the initial investigation.   If the child is removed from the home or if there is conflicting information regarding substantiation, further investigation and possible court action may ensue.   In addition, efforts are begun immediately to involve the family, the perpetrator, and/or the child in treatment or support services and, if resistance is met, court action may be invoked to mandate participation.

Court involvement in cases of maltreatment occurs for the following reasons:

1) to assure due process following the temporary removal of a child from his or her parents (a preliminary hearing),

2) to respond to the filing of a petition of dependency for the protection of a child,

3) to determine if contested allegations should be substantiated (adjudication), or

4) as part of the normal criminal justice process following the filing of formal charges, such as physical or sexual assault, contributing to the delinquency of a minor, etc.

Court involvement occurs in almost one third of all maltreatment cases (American Humane Association, 1986).   The nature of the court involvement varies depending on the particular case, the statutes in the state with jurisdiction, and the biases of the particular judge who deals with the case on that day.

Preliminary or detention hearings

The earliest court involvement in cases of maltreatment occurs when children are deemed sufficiently at risk during the initial investigation to be removed from the home and placed with relatives or in a temporary shelter.   If placement occurs, the case must appear before a judge within a specified time period, usually 48 hours or less. This hearing occurs in juvenile court and is termed a **preliminary or detention hearing.**

The purpose of a detention hearing is to assure that the child is removed from his or her parents only when 1) there is substantial risk for immediate harm to the child, and 2) there are no viable alternatives for reducing that risk. During the detention hearing, information relevant to the determination of **probable cause** and **need for detention** is presented.

Probable cause refers to the presumed validity of the allegation of maltreatment. The determination of probable cause is nonadversarial, that is, it is based upon a sworn affidavit or testimony that the child has been maltreated. The legal "proof" needed to determine probable cause is analogous to the allegation associated with the writing of a traffic ticket; in both cases probable cause follows from the statement of an individual presumed to be acting in a conscientious and educated manner.

The need for detention is based upon the degree of immediate risk to the child and the availability of alternatives to ameliorate this risk. Ways to reduce risk to the child while keeping the child with his or her parents are explored, and only if none of these solutions are feasible is detention continued. In most cases the judge will follow the recommendation of the protective service worker when determining the need for detention, because if there is any doubt about the child's safety, the temporary placement will allow time for a more complete investigation. The need for detention is reviewed periodically, in a similar manner, as long as the child remains out of the home.

Petition for dependency

Whether or not the child is removed from the home, court involvement may be initiated by a petition to the courts, requesting that the child be made a dependent of the state for the purposes of protection from further maltreatment. Such a **petition for dependency** describes the circumstances which warrant dependency and may be filed by the state attorney or by a petitioner acting in "good faith." There are usually statutory time limits within which a petition for dependency must be filed, and special provisions for quick filing apply when the child has been removed from the family. This petition is the vehicle which allows social service caseworkers to intervene with the family on behalf of the child.

After the petition is filed, a court date is set for **arraignment** on the allegations. Several possible courses of action may occur during or prior to this hearing. First, the parents may "admit" to the allegations, in which case a plan of treatment may be implemented or a date for a disposition hearing may be set to allow time for the development of such a plan. Conversely, the perpetrator(s) may "deny" the allegations, in which case an adjudication hearing will be scheduled to present evidence related to the determination of the allegations. Finally, there are sometimes provisions for accepting a proposed plan of action without either admitting to or denying the allegations. In Florida, for example, a parent/perpetrator may "consent" to adjudication of dependency without "admitting to" the allegations. If the treatment plan is subsequently not followed, however, the perpetrator can be brought back before the court for adjudication.

Adjudication

Adjudication hearings involve the presentation of evidence as to whether or not the victim(s) of maltreatment should be adjudicated dependent.   As with other hearings, the time limits for scheduling adjudication hearings are shorter if the child has been removed from the home.   Prior to the hearing, the protective service worker assigned to the case must submit a predispositional study, which is essentially the written results of his or her formal investigation.   Based upon these results and the testimony of others involved in the case the judge will decide if the child should be adjudicated dependent.   In these hearings, the child is often represented by an appointed **guardian ad litem** whose purpose is to represent the best interests of the child. The guardian ad litem, often a community volunteer, can also serve as a friend to the child and as a source of consistency during a time when rapid and uncontrollable changes are taking place around the child.

The adjudication hearing results in one of three outcomes.   If the child is adjudicated nondependent, the case is dismissed with no further action. If the child is adjudicated dependent, the case proceeds to **disposition**, which means a treatment plan is initiated. Such a plan may be implemented at the adjudication hearing or at a separate **disposition hearing**. The third possible outcome of a disposition hearing is that adjudication may be withheld if the relevant adults agree to abide by a set of conditions specified by the courts.   If these terms are not followed, however, an adjudication of dependency can occur at a later date.

Criminal charges

In cases of sexual abuse and severe physical abuse or neglect, there is sometimes also criminal court involvement.   Criminal charges can be initiated by the police if they are involved in the initial investigation or by the State Attorney's office after reviewing a case investigated by the social service agency.   Criminal cases follow the typical procedure for criminal court, which involves an arrest or surrendering of the alleged perpetrator, the filing of formal criminal charges by the state attorney's office, and court appearances for bond, adjudication, and sentencing.

Section summary

An investigation of alleged maltreatment may lead to one of several outcomes. Reports in which the investigation reveals insufficient evidence of maltreatment are closed as unsubstantiated.   Reports which are substantiated usually lead to interventions to prevent further maltreatment and to remediate the precipitating factors and sequelae associated with the maltreatment. Some of the reports which are substantiated are also closed after the initial investigation, while others stay open so that the effectiveness of the interventions can be monitored.

Approximately one third of substantiated cases entail some court involvement. Court involvement occurs when children are removed from their parents, when parents respond to a petition for dependency, for the purposes of determining dependency, and when the courts are involved in the disposition process. Adjudication is sometimes postponed or withheld in lieu of the parent's participation in a court-approved intervention program.

The actions and interventions resulting from the initial investigation are for the purpose of protecting the child from further maltreatment and enhancing the environment to promote healthy child development. Consequently, the efforts of social workers, the courts, and others involved in this process should converge on a specific plan of action which addresses the needs of the child and family. The final section in this chapter explores the disposition process in cases of maltreatment.

DISPOSITIONS

The specific needs of maltreated children and their families are infinitely diverse. When abuse or neglect is identified, there has usually been an accumulation of interacting problems, from an intergenerational history of maltreatment to specific developmental problems in the child victim. Social conditions experienced by the family, personality traits of the parents, and characteristics of the child or children all interact to predispose a family toward maltreatment.

Because of multidimensional natures of maltreatment, the interventions utilized must also be diverse. Goals of various interventions range from the immediate protection of the child, to effecting changes so the child can be reunited with the family, to remediating the precipitating factors and sequelae associated with the maltreatment.

Before specific interventions are discussed, ways in which the interventions are implemented and enforced need to be elaborated upon. The individuals most instrumental in developing an intervention plan are the social service caseworkers involved in the initial investigation and subsequent follow up. The primary caseworker, when possible with the cooperation of the family, develops an intervention plan and aids the family in the implementation of this plan. When necessary, the caseworker presents the plan to the courts for approval and subsequent enforcement. Follow-through of the plan can be monitored by the caseworker, the courts, or both. When there is court involvement, there are often specific consequences for failure to carry through a service plan. When there is not court involvement, however, the effectiveness of the intervention is often dependent on the cooperation of the family. Further, monitoring of treatment outcome, especially when there is no court involvement, is often poorly conducted and remains one of the most significant needs in our current system.

The basis for effective intervention in cases of maltreatment lies in the effective analyses of the factors contributing to an abusive or neglectful family situation. A comprehensive analysis would assess the factors affecting long-term development of the child as well as the short-term risk. Although immediate risk is of the utmost importance in any investigation of maltreatment, the energy expended to reduce this risk is virtually wasted if factors relevant to long-term prevention are not dealt with. For example, if parents tend to lash out physically at their children when under stress, efforts to reduce the immediate stress will temporarily alleviate risk for that child. Nobody, however, is immune to repeated episodes of stress throughout their lifetime, and unless these parents are taught more adaptive ways of coping with stress, the short-term intervention of reducing stress will have to be repeated several times. A comprehensive analyses of the family's problem and interventions to address the needs may prevent repeated referrals for the same or similar circumstances.

A comprehensive analyses of the problems associated with maltreatment include assessing the functioning of the parents/perpetrators, the child(ren), and the stable and transient environmental factors. Interventions in each of these areas then follow from this comprehensive assessment.

Interventions for parents/perpetrators

The primary focus of interventions in cases of maltreatment has traditionally been on the parents/perpetrators. The earliest "treatment" for perpetrators was criminal prosecution and punishment, usually through incarceration. Although incarceration is still a common intervention in cases of sexual abuse and severe physical abuse and neglect, therapeutically oriented interventions now predominate.

As discussed in Chapter 3, parents who abuse or neglect their children may have deficits or needs in three general areas of functioning. They may lack the experience or knowledge necessary to generate adaptive parenting behaviors, they may be unable to maintain adaptive parenting when under stress, and/or there may be intrapersonal characteristics or traits which interfere with adaptive parenting. Interventions typically address one or more of these areas.

The service most commonly provided to protective service cases is **counseling by the caseworker**. National statistics indicate that this service is provided in about 74% of the cases (American Humane Association, 1986). Casework counseling involves providing the family with emotional support, helping the family and perpetrator learn more socially appropriate ways to interact with their children, and helping the family find ways to reduce stress and increase support in their environment. In practice, casework counseling may range from simply defining abuse and telling the perpetrator not to abuse the child any more to more systematic efforts to provide the family with appropriate alternatives to cope with the precipitating conditions. In many cases, casework counseling is all that is provided, and once the caseworker feels that the crisis is over, the case is closed.

Casework counseling most directly addresses the educational or informational needs of the parents. Caseworkers can help the parents find alternative ways of interacting with their children, help the parents find ways to cope with stress, and educate the parents about community services which are available. Caseworkers are also the primary source of information about the family's involvement with protective services and should be able to explain why the involvement is occurring and what is to be expected. The emotional support provided by caseworkers is important to relieve the temporary stress associated with the investigation and/or other immediate adversities but does not necessarily result in long-term improvements in the family's ability to cope with stress in the future.

When the family is in crisis of such severity that the caseworker cannot provide the necessary support, the family is often linked to community **crisis support services**. About 10% of the cases require short-term intervention of this nature (American Humane Association, 1986). Outpatient crisis counseling can be provided as frequently as on a daily basis until the immediate problems are resolved. Many communities also provide crisis shelters, which may accommodate a parent, a parent and children, or in some cases even whole families. Examples include domestic violence shelters which provide respite for battered women or family "time-out" shelters where families in crisis can live for up to several days to become reorganized. The majority of crisis services are associated with community mental health centers, and such centers are the best source of information about the crisis services available in a given community.

The main purpose of crisis support services is to help the client through the immediate crisis with minimal disruption in his or her functioning. Crisis services may include counseling, shelter, aid in the provision of basic needs such as food or financial support, and referral information. Such services, however, typically make no claims of addressing the client's long term needs for improved functioning. Although crisis services are in some cases sufficient to facilitate long-term gains, in most cases there are needs which remain to be addressed after the the immediate crisis is resolved.

For example, if an individual has a sporadic employment history and is referred because he is unable to cope with current financial problems, crisis services will usually provide counseling to help cope with the current emotional stress and aid the client in becoming reestablished in the workplace. The reasons for his prior difficulties in maintaining steady employment will still remain, however, and unless additional therapeutic services address these difficulties, this individual will be no less likely to experience similar crises in the future. Probably the most significant deficit in many current systems of crisis intervention is failure to link the client with subsequent therapeutic services to address the factors in his or her pre-morbid functioning associated with the initial development of the problem.

Extended therapeutic services subsequent to crisis intervention are particularly important when individuals display any intra- or interpersonal dysfunction of a long-standing nature. Examples of problems requiring long-term intervention include cognitive or personality characteristics which interfere with interpersonal relations or similar deficits which impair an individual's ability or willingness to learn new behaviors or alternative ways of coping with stress. In cases such as these, casework counseling or crisis services are often only minimally effective, either because they may be rejected by the client or because the client may become dependent upon the caseworker rather than utilizing the tools to improve his or her independent functioning. It is estimated that long-term follow-up services are used in about 56% of cases (American Humane Association, 1986). Long-term services which address specific deficits in parental functioning include individual, family, or group therapy, support groups, counseling, and in-home services such as home visitors or community outreach.

Individual therapy, group therapy, and **support groups** all attempt to facilitate change by providing stable, supportive relationships and helping the parent identify and overcome barriers to effective relationships. Sources of the parent's frustrations can be discussed in a nonthreatening environment, and the individuals can begin to identify and initiate more adaptive ways of functioning. Conversely, specific problem areas such as substance abuse are best addressed in programs specifically designed for those problems.

There are an increasing number of therapeutic services designed for at-risk parents, such as **Parents Anonymous.** Parents Anonymous provides support groups for parents who feel they are at risk for abusing their children and offers support and education regarding parenting and children. In addition, the child and family components of many social service agencies offer therapeutic programs for the parents which they serve. Because programs such as these require a commitment of time, energy, and sometimes money by the parents, they are often underutilized.

Further, the parents who need long-term intervention the most are often the most resistant, and when attendance is mandated by the courts, these parents may attend but are likely to do so with a negative attitude toward the intervention.

Programs such as **home visitors** or **community outreach** largely overcome problems with compliance. Because the services are provided in the home, they reduce demands on the participants and decrease the anxiety associated with receiving services. Home based programs have other advantages as well. By intervening in the normal day-to-day life of the family, the probability that the interventions will be incorporated by the family is increased. In addition, the visitor can identify and resolve potential problems before they occur, both reducing stress on the family and helping them develop effective ways to prevent future problem situations. Finally, treatment compliance can be directly and consistently monitored, which will often increase the client's motivation for carrying through the intervention.

Because of the many advantages of the home visitation format, it is not surprising that this is one of the few interventions which has been empirically shown to be both cost and outcome effective (e.g., Karniski, Van Buren, & Cupoli, 1986). The potential of home visitation, however, is far from being realized. Most programs are loosely organized and often use minimally trained volunteers as the home visitors. Because of the potential impact of such programs for preventing maltreatment, their development should be a high priority in comprehensive intervention program. Using visitors trained in serving high-risk families, such as medical home visitors in cases of physical neglect or discipline specialists in cases of physical abuse resulting from efforts to punish the child, may prove to be the single most effective intervention in child abuse and neglect.

Interventions which address environmental conditions

Several programs exist which attempt to improve the day-to-day living conditions of parents and children. These programs differ from therapeutic programs in that they do not directly attempt to change an individual's functioning but rather attempt to provide support to ease stressful environmental conditions. Examples of such programs include food stamps, AFDC, unemployment compensation, etc.

Social programs which provide basic necessities or employment assistance are sometimes the best interventions for the immediate reduction of stress and immediate improvements in functioning. They run the same risk, however, of other immediate stress reduction techniques such as crisis counseling. In particular, there is a risk that support for the individual, while improving the immediate situation, may not address the factors which interfered with pre-morbid functioning. Consequently, it is important that social programs which provide direct aid such as food, clothing, shelter, or money also make efforts to identify and address the factors precipitating the environmental problems in the first place.

Interventions for children

Interventions for children have traditionally been the least utilized mode of treatment in cases of child abuse and neglect. Traditional interventions for children focused primarily on protecting the child from immediate harm and consequently involved programs to remove children from risk in the least disruptive way.

Recently, however, there has been a surge of interest in programs to remediate the sequelae of abuse and neglect and facilitate healthy long-term development with maltreated children. Further, efforts to combine protective and remedial programs are emerging, such as using specially trained foster parents to treat maltreated children who have been removed from the home. This section discusses several important types of services for maltreated children, including developmental services, therapeutic daycare, play therapy, and foster care. Because of the variety of sequelae of maltreatment (see Chapter 4), multifaceted interventions are usually needed to address the needs of any given child.

Developmental services

Maltreated children may have developmental deficits in the physical, cognitive, or socioemotional domains of functioning. Programs addressing developmental deficits in these areas are available in many communities in both the public (e.g., school board, community mental health agency) and private sectors, but they often are not adequately integrated with protective service programs. The consequence is that assessments of maltreated children are often inadequate, with only those children with the most dramatic and obvious deficits receiving treatment.

Therapeutic daycare

Therapeutic daycare is a rapidly expanding intervention that involves the provision of special services to children at daycare centers. Therapists or developmental specialists go to the daycare center on a regular basis and conduct individual or group sessions with the goals of remediating developmental deficits and dysfunctional interpersonal behavior. Therapeutic daycare has been shown to facilitate significant improvements in functioning in as little as six months (Segal et al., 1985; Iverson, 1986). Because quality daycare alone is a form of prevention and therapeutic daycare provides cost-effective treatment, the development of such programs should be strongly encouraged.

Play therapy

Play therapy is a psychological intervention for children which involves the use of play as a medium to remediate developmental or interpersonal problems. Through play children can express themselves, resolve emotional conflicts stemming from earlier traumatic experiences, and learn effective ways of interacting with others and their environment. Because play therapy provides a nonthreatening approach to remediating the sequelae of maltreatment, it represents a potentially important component of any comprehensive intervention program for children.

Foster care

Foster families are families in the community who have volunteered to care for children who must be removed from their family. Foster families often receive specific training and support in caring for maltreated children. Foster parent programs are available in many communities, but it is not uncommon for the demand for foster parents to exceed the supply. The traditional goals for foster placement involve providing the child with a stable and supportive respite from a disrupted home environment, while simultaneously working with the parents so family reunification can be achieved.

When children are placed in foster care, either voluntarily by the parents or as the result of the court disposition process, an agreement stating the goals for reunification and methods to achieve these goals is negotiated. If the goals are not met, foster placement is extended. When a child is in foster care, the need for continued placement is reviewed periodically, such as at six-month periods. If it appears that the requirements for family reunification cannot or will not be met, the child may become eligible for permanent placement or adoption.

Whereas placement in a foster family can be a very positive experience for a child, there has been much discussion about placement in foster care as being the beginning of "system abuse" (e.g., Cooper, Peterson, & Meier, 1987). System abuse refers to disruption of maltreated children's lives through repeated placement in different foster care settings. Often the most difficult children are most frequently moved from setting to setting, but it is these children who are most in need of a stable, nurturing environment. Efforts to protect them from abusive or neglectful home situations lead to a series of placements, which in turn interfere with these children's ability to develop the trusting relationships which promote adaptive development. Contributing to the problem are the greater needs of these children when entering foster care, and the consequent financial and emotional demands they place on their foster parents (e.g., Hochstadt, Jaudes, Zimo, & Schachter, 1987). In other words, placement in foster care can be a very positive experience for a child, but only if the placement is stable and the foster parents are adequately equipped to deal with the child.

There has been a recent trend to overcome some of the problems associated with system abuse by utilizing specially trained foster parents for children with specific needs. For example, children with medical problems may be placed with individuals who have received specialized medical training. Despite excellent potential for providing a stable environment specifically geared to a child's needs, there are very few of these programs, and they are often unable to function adequately with the funding received.

Section summary

A variety of therapeutic and remedial programs are available for maltreated children, but such programs are often not utilized in a comprehensive and integrative manner. Pooling a community's resources from both the public and private sectors will lead to better identifying the specific needs of maltreated children and subsequently more effective interventions. Similarly, integrating various developmental and therapeutic interventions with other programs such as daycare or foster care will greatly improve the overall utility of these programs.

CHAPTER SUMMARY

The expanding interest and knowledge base in reference to child abuse and neglect has given rise to a complex system of interventions to identify and remediate the problem.   Most individuals who encounter families and children in their professions are now legislatively mandated to report   any instance of suspected maltreatment.   All fifty states provide specific procedures for reporting and investigating maltreatment.   Once it has been determined that maltreatment has occurred, a variety of interventions are available to protect the child, to provide treatment, to prevent future maltreatment, and to remediate the sequelae of child abuse and neglect.   Such interventions may involve parent counseling and therapy, support services to the parents, and developmental and therapeutic programs for children.   Our current challenge is to further develop, integrate, and research the effectiveness of this system of interventions. Only by continued efforts to improve and integrate these services will we begin to overcome the burgeoning social problem of maltreatment.

REFERENCES

Alter, C.F. (1985).   "Decision-making Factors in Child Neglect." Child Welfare, 64, 99-111.

American Humane Association. (1986).   Highlights of Official Child Neglect and Abuse Reporting, 1984. Denver.

Cooper, C.S., Peterson, N.L., & Meier, J.H. (1987).   "Variables Associated with Disrupted Placement in a Select Sample of Abused and Neglected Children." Child Abuse and Neglect, 11, 75-86.

Denton, L. (1987).   "Child Abuse Reporting Laws: Are They a Barrier to Helping Troubled Families?" The APA Monitor, 18.

Hochstadt, N.J., Jaudes, P.K., Zimo, D.A., & Schachter, J. (1987).   "The Medical and Psychosocial Needs of Children Entering Foster Care." Child Abuse and Neglect, 11, 53-62.

Iverson, T.J. (1986).   ECDA Therapeutic Daycare Program Evaluation.   Report submitted to the Early Child Development Association of Broward County.

Karniski, W., Van Buren, L., & Cupoli, J. M. (1986).   "A Treatment Program for Failure to Thrive: A Cost-effectiveness Analysis." Child Abuse and Neglect, 10, 471-478.

Maden, M.F. (1980).   The Disposition of Reported Child Abuse.   Saratoga, CA: Century Twenty One Publishing.

Meddin, B.J. (1985).   "The Assessment of Risk in Child Abuse and Neglect Case Investigations." Child Abuse and Neglect, 9, 57-62.

Segal, M., Iverson, T.J., & Layden, P. (1985). "The Identification and Remediation of the Effects of Child Maltreatment in Preschool-age Children." Nova University, unpublished manuscript.

Chapter 6

Prevention

"The best way to prevent child abuse is public education. If parents could be taught how to reason with their kids, they could get their kids to mind without beating them up."

"Child abuse is rampant in this country, and giving money to the poor is not the answer. When people turn on the T.V. and see nothing but sex and violence -- what's to stop them from beating up on the kids?"

"You're not going to prevent child abuse until you eliminate poverty. People who are living in subhuman conditions with no idea where their next meal is coming from are simply going to snap from time to time."

Although suggestions for preventing child abuse are easy to elicit, child maltreatment is a complex, multifaceted and ecologically embedded phenomenon that defies a simplistic solution. Preventive strategies are naturally linked to causal attribution. People who see maltreatment as the expected outcome of maladaptive parenting may advocate parent training as a prime preventive strategy. People who see child abuse as the product of a violent society may advocate media controls. People who see child maltreatment as the outcome of poverty and hopelessness equate preventive efforts with social reformation.

Because child abuse prevention covers a wide range of programs, policies and advocacy efforts, this chapter provides an overview rather than a comprehensive picture of child abuse initiatives. The overview is divided into three sections. The first section describes preventive programs that target families and children directly. The second section describes preventive initiatives targeting systems that impact on families and children. The third section focuses on major issues associated with prevention. These include the efficiency of early intervention and the larger question of societal vs. parental responsibility for the custody of the child. Each of the programs described in this chapter are listed in Appendix B under the state in which the program exists.

TABLE 6-1

Organizational Framework for Child Maltreatment Prevention Programs

	Nature of prevention efforts		
	Primary	**Secondary**	**Tertiary**
Families and children	Programs promoting the health and well-being of families in general	Programs providing education and support services to at-risk families or parents	Programs that prevent the recurrence of maltreatment and reduce the negative sequelae
Systems impacting families and children	Legislative, community and program initiatives affecting the nature and quality of services to all families and children	Initiatives affecting the nature and quality of services for families and children defined as "at-risk"	Initiatives affecting the services to and/or treatment of families/children identified as abusive or neglectful
Broader socio-cultural issues	Viewing child abuse prevention within the overall context of social reform	A socio-cultural approach addressing prevention by focusing on aspects of society specifically associated with maltreatment	Approaching child maltreatment as a discreet problem, channeling energies to abused/neglected children and their families

Target of prevention efforts

Child abuse prevention efforts are also described as primary, secondary, and tertiary prevention. Primary prevention is concerned with anticipatory efforts that foster healthy family development and prevent abuse from happening. Secondary prevention is concerned with intervention efforts that target at-risk populations. Tertiary prevention takes place when abuse is impending or has already occurred. The objective of tertiary prevention may be to prevent impending abuse, reduce the incidence of further abuse, or mitigate the deleterious effects of disruptive intervention measures (e.g., removal from home, court hearings, etc.). Table 6-1 shows the organization of prevention programs according to the target and nature of the prevention efforts. The programs summarized below are presented according to this conceptual framework.

PROGRAMS FOR FAMILIES AND CHILDREN
PRIMARY PREVENTION

Because child maltreatment is on a continuum, with severe abuse on one end and exemplary parent practices on the other, all programs that promote the health and well-being of families can be thought of as primary prevention. The dramatic increase in reported incidents of child abuse has, in fact, given impetus to a national surge in educational and support services designed to enhance parenting skills and provide support for families.

Programs to strengthen families include a wide range of initiatives that differ on several dimensions. Programs can be described according to the characteristics of the intervention effort, the target population, the sponsoring agency, and/or the size and complexity of the program. In this section programs will be grouped according to the target population. First, we describe programs within the schools that teach parenting skills to future parents; second, we discuss programs for expectant parents; and third, we describe programs for parents and young children.

School-based programs that target future parents

School-based programs that target future parents have become increasingly popular over the past decade. Several prototypical programs have been developed, including family life curricula for elementary school children, child care courses for middle school students, and school-based clinics for junior and senior high students. Most school-based family life curricula have the double objective of preventing early pregnancy and enhancing the parenting skills of future parents.

Education for Parenting: *Curriculum for Students K-6,*
Philadelphia, Pennsylvania

Education for Parenting, initiated in 1978 at the Germantown Friends School, is a school-based program that focuses on child development, parenting, and the interactions between children and parents. The program has been implemented in several independent and public elementary schools in Philadelphia. A special feature of the program is the participation of expectant parents. Parents are invited into the classroom on a regular basis before and after the baby is born. In 1984 Education for Parenting prepared a curriculum manual entitled *An Idea Book*. The curriculum is designed for children from kindergarten through grade six and includes child development, parenting, and observation skills. Classroom experiences with the parents and babies are combined with discussions, readings, keeping journals, and writing stories. As part of the curriculum, elementary school students are given an opportunity to learn child care and babysitting skills by working with younger schoolmates.

Speak Easy: *Curriculum for Junior and Senior High Students, Middlebury, Vermont*

Speak Easy is a curriculum for junior and senior high school students sponsored by Young Families with Children, a community center in Middlebury, Vermont. *Speak Easy* focuses on value clarification, decision making, pregnancy, birth control and venereal disease. Before the course is presented to the students, their parents are enrolled in a parent seminar that covers the material presented in the *Speak Easy* course and provides parents with strategies for communicating with their children.

School-based clinic, *St. Paul, Minnesota*

St. Paul, Minnesota, in 1973, was one of the first cities in the nation to institute school-based clinics to decrease the pregnancy rate and improve the health of infants. Initially the clinic provided only prenatal and postnatal services, pap smears, contraceptive information and testing for pregnancy and sexually transmitted diseases; teenagers were reluctant to use it. This reluctance disappeared when clinic services were expanded to include athletic, job and college physicals, immunizations, and weight control programs.

The St. Paul clinic is considered to be highly successful. Teen birth rates declined from 79 per thousand in 1973, to 35 per thousand in 1976 to 27 per thousand in 1982-1983. Nearly all youth who did give birth remained in the school following their baby's birth (Tereszkiewicz, 1980).

Programs targeted at expectant parents

Programs targeted at expectant parents can contribute to the healthy development of children and their families in three distinct ways. First they can enhance the health, nutritional status, and well-being of expectant parents, thus reducing the incidence of spontaneous abortion and low birth weight. Second the program can prepare the mother for childbirth, thus minimizing the need for medical intervention. Third, the program can prepare new parents with knowledge of child development and skills in baby care. While many of the programs for expectant parents are initiated by hospitals, clinics, obstetricians, and childbirth organizations, some communitywide and even statewide prenatal programs have been initiated.

EPIC: *Program for Expectant Parents,*
Delaware

EPIC is a statewide initiative designed to reduce the incidence of low birth weight in the State of Delaware. The elements of the *EPIC* program include the identification and monitoring of high-risk pregnancies, the targeting of nutrition, social work and nursery services to women in need and the sharing of current information on high-risk pregnancy management. A special feature of the *EPIC* program is the distribution of a statewide screening questionnaire to be completed at the time of pregnancy testing.

Ounce of Prevention, *Illinois*

The *Ounce of Prevention* established in 1982 is a public/private partnership which promotes the well-being of children by working with families and communities to foster healthy child development. *Ounce of Prevention* administers more than 40 community-based prevention programs in churches, social service agencies, health clinics, schools, and other community agencies in Illinois. Over 6,000 adults and teenagers are being served by *Ounce of Prevention* in areas where there is a high risk for abuse and neglect. The *Ounce of Prevention* programs include prenatal and postpartum home visits, peer support groups for teen parents, developmental day care for infants and toddlers, and community drop-in centers for parents and children.

An important thrust of *Ounce of Prevention* is a reduction in the incidence of teenage pregnancy. *Ounce of Prevention* established a series of school-based clinics throughout the state that have had a dramatic impact on reducing the incidence of teenage pregnancy.

COPE: *Coping with the Overall Pregnancy/Parenting Experience,*
Boston, Massachusetts

COPE is a counseling, education, and resource center that is designed to help mothers and fathers resolve the conflicts that arise during pregnancy and throughout their parenting lives. *COPE* provides counseling and education services and initiates discussion groups focusing primarily on pregnancy and parenting issues.

A special feature of *COPE* is its work and family management program for working parents. This program includes four components: 1) a Parent Fair held at the work place with resource information on integrating family and work life, 2) a series of employer-sponsored workshops on work and family management, 3) conference services for businesses on the changing needs of employees, and 4) information and referral services that employers can purchase for employees.

Programs for parents of new babies

Programs for parents of new babies are readily available in communities throughout the country. While these programs hold in common a belief in the importance of a good beginning, the ways in which they achieve their objective are diverse and oftentimes unique.

Programs for parents with new babies differ in several ways including the objectives of the program, the type of delivery system (home based vs. center based), the scope of the services offered, and the characteristics of the target population.

A major development on the national scene is the burgeoning of family support centers that offer a broad range of family support services to parents with new babies. Whereas some of these support programs include a home-based delivery system, the typical family support program is center based with parent education as one aspect of its program offerings. According to a recently published volume, *America's Family Support Programs* (Kagan, 1987), the surge in family support programs reflects a general acceptance of Bronfenbrenner's ecological view of human development (see Chapter 1).

From the ecological perspective, families are seen as systems operating within the context of the community. Family members are interdependent, each influencing the behaviors of other family members, and all being dependent on social support from people outside the community. Families are affected in powerful ways by wider environmental factors, such as low socioeconomic status (Bronfenbrenner, 1979).

The vitality of the family support movement is underscored by the growing membership of the Family Resource Coalition. The Family Resource Coalition is a national federation of more than 2,000 individuals and organizations promoting the development of prevention oriented, community-based programs to strengthen families. Its goals are to provide technical assistance to family support programs, to increase public awareness and support for the needs of families, and to help family programs become better advocates for children and their families.

Family Focus, *Evanston, Illinois*

Family Focus is an association of drop-in centers for parents with young children from birth to age three. Six *Family Focus* centers and one affiliate are currently in operation in the Chicago area. *Family Focus* centers have as their primary mission the promotion of optimal development of children during the first three years by enhancing parental confidence.   Drop-in centers provide a range of formal and informal services planned by staff and parents to reflect the ethnic, racial, and economic characteristics of the community.

Founded in 1976, *Family Focus* is considered to be the prototype of family resource centers.   *Family Focus* assumed sponsorship of the Family Resource Coalition as a way of networking with other family and resource programs.   The *Family Focus* program has been replicated in Illinois, Indiana, New York, Ohio, and Washington, D.C.

Family Center of Nova University, *Fort Lauderdale, Florida*

The Family Center in Fort Lauderdale is a service oriented unit of Nova University.   It provides a spectrum of community services designed to enhance the well-being of families and promote the healthy development of children.   A major function of *The Family Center* is the sponsorship of parent-child classes designed to promote positive interactions between parents and their children.   The parent-child classes are housed in a special campus building with creative indoor and outdoor environments designed for infants, toddlers, and preschool children.   Approximately 600 families participate in parent-child classes in the course of a week.

County Parent/Child Center, *Middlebury, Vermont*

The Addison County *Parent/Child Center* is a community-based family support and education program begun in 1980 by a group of parents, professionals, and concerned community members.   The mission of the *Parent/Child Center* is to provide support and education to families with young children.   The *Parent/Child Center* has three major service modes:

1.   Center-based which include developmental and therapeutic infant care courses, support groups, vocational training, and parenting education.

2.   Outreach services provided in the families' homes or in play groups located in the smaller surrounding towns.   Play groups are open to everyone, while home visits are limited to priority families.

3.   Network services are provided through cooperative agreement with other agencies and schools.

PSP: *Parent Service Programs,*
      California, Florida

Parent Service Programs are public/private partnerships that transform child care centers into family care centers, nurturing the parents as well as the children. Where *PSP* programs are established, parents of young children receive a variety of support services including parent education, practical skills, respite services, and mental health services. Parents are also given opportunities to participate in a variety of social and recreational events.

Parent education

In addition to the surge of family support programs that provide a range of services to families with children, there has been an increase in programs and materials that focus on parent education. Parent education is a broad term that covers a wide range of programs designed to help parents raise physically, mentally, and emotionally healthy children. It may be offered by universities, colleges, employers, child care centers, community centers, or private practitioners. Parent education may be delivered by a structured curriculum, an informal discussion format, books, magazines, pamphlets, videotapes or television programs. Although research demonstrating a direct connection between parent education and maltreatment reduction is not available, parent education presents a nondeficit model that builds on strengths and encourages positive family interactions.

MELD: *Parent Education,*
       Minneapolis, Minnesota

MELD is a parent education program designed to strengthen families at critical transitions in the parenting process. *MELD* brings together populations of parents with similar needs and provides them with the information and technical assistance to develop supportive peer groups. *MELD* programs include MNP (MELD for New Parents, the Adult Program), MYM (MELD for Young Moms), LaFamilia (MELD for Hispanic and Anglo/Hispanic families), and HIPP/MELD (a special MELD program for hearing impaired parents.

A special feature of *MELD* is its professionally designed training and curriculum materials. *MELD's* core curriculum covers topics in five areas: health, child development, child guidance, consumer behavior, and parental growth. This core curriculum is designed in four six-month phases beginning in the seventh month of pregnancy and continuing for two years. Parents are given a detailed handbook called *Parent Part*, conveying the curriculum in each of the four phases. *MELD* groups are led by Parent Group Facilitators who are supervised by *MELD* site coordinators.

Facilitators receive a Parent Group Facilitator Handbook that describes group process and mechanics, and a curriculum book that expands on the curriculum and issues presented in *Parent Part*.

Parents as Teachers, *State of Missouri*

Parents as Teachers (PAT) is a free and voluntary program sponsored by the school system in the State of Missouri. The PAT program is designed as a home-school partnership to help parents give their children the best possible start in life and to lay the foundation for later school success. Offered in all 543 Missouri school districts, the PAT program delivers early childhood screening and parent education to over 35,000 families.

A National *Parents as Teachers* Center was established early in 1987 by the Missouri Department of elementary and secondary schools. The purpose of the Center is to provide training, technical assistance, and research opportunities for professionals interested in parent education in accordance with the PAT model.

Primary prevention -- A summary

Whether a primary prevention program targets future parents, expectant parents or parents of young children, all primary prevention programs hold two characteristics in common. First, primary prevention programs are broad in scope, encompassing many families where the risk factor is minimal. Second, primary prevention programs are built on a wellness model. Their objective is to enhance positive growth in families and strengthen the family unit. While primary prevention is lauded for being a nondeficit model, it is also criticized on a cost/benefit basis because it services many families who do not have at-risk children and who are not at risk for maltreatment.

PROGRAMS FOR FAMILIES AND CHILDREN
SECONDARY PREVENTION

In contrast to primary prevention programs which are designed to promote parent-child positive interactions in the general population, secondary prevention targets families at risk for abuse and neglect. Because secondary prevention programs service families under stress, the per capita cost of secondary prevention is higher than the per capita cost of primary prevention.

Like primary prevention programs, secondary prevention programs can be classified according to their target audience. Some programs focus on future parents, some on expectant parents, and some on parents with children. A second, and perhaps more useful classification of secondary prevention programs is according to the source of the risk. Families may be at risk of maltreating a child because of demographic variables, parent characteristics, or characteristics of the child that effect family dynamics. Many families are considered as having multiple risks because they fall into more than one risk category.

Demographics

Demographic variables that increase the risk of maltreatment include being a teenage parent, extreme poverty or isolation, being a single parent without a support system, or being a member of an undervalued or immigrant population.

Teenage pregnancy

Teenagers are at risk for becoming maltreating parents for several reasons. As discussed in chapter 3, many teenagers are physically and emotionally unprepared to bear children, increasing the risk of spontaneous abortion, low birth weight, and handicapping conditions. In addition, many teenagers lack the support system, the maturity, the stability, and the economic security to parent a child successfully. Finally, teenage populations are at risk for poor nutrition substance abuse.

In response to this triple jeopardy, many public and private programs have focused on this age group. Programs designed to reduce the incidence of teen pregnancy are variously sponsored by schools, church groups, service clubs, neighborhood centers, colleges and universities, parents groups, and adolescent self-help groups.

While some programs targeted at teenagers have as their primary focus the prevention of pregnancy, other programs focus on the provision of prenatal care and instruction in infant care and development for the already pregnant teenager. Model programs for pregnant teenagers differ in terms of the ethnic mix of the population they serve, the accommodations that they make to take into account these ethnic differences, and the professional vs. volunteer status of their program staff.

The Door: *The Center for Alternatives,*
New York, New York

The Door is a community service center that offers a spectrum of health, educational, and cultural programs for lower SES and minority youths in New York City. Since 1983, *The Door* has sponsored the Younger People's Program designed to provide specialized services for adolescents under 16 who are considered to be at risk for school failure, pregnancy, substance abuse, and delinquency.

First Friends, *Sponsored by the Family Place, Washington, D.C.*

The *First Friends* program is an outreach program for low-income minority pregnant women. The program was initiated by the Family Place, a drop-in center for parents and children in Washington, D.C. The purpose of *First Friends* is to help expectant parents maintain a healthy pregnancy and give birth to healthy infants.

First Friends is primarily a volunteer program. Neighborhood volunteer mothers are recruited as Amigos or First Friends for pregnant teenagers in need of support. The goals of the outreach program are the prevention of pregnancy complications, a decrease in incidence of low birth weight babies, and the promotion of healthy development in the postnatal period.

Building Blocks, *Belle Glade, Florida*

Building Blocks is an outreach program for teenage mothers sponsored by a grassroots organization, Neighbors Organized for Adequate Housing (NOAH, Inc.) in Belle Glade, Florida. Using experienced mothers who volunteer as "first friends," the program provides health and nutritional information, child development education, and emotional support to disadvantaged pregnant teenagers ranging from twelve to nineteen years of age.

Families at risk because of poverty and/or isolation

A second demographic variable that increases the risk of becoming a maltreating parent is extreme poverty and/or isolation. Women in rural areas who lack the support of parents and peers and where access to community resources is limited are a known at-risk population. Single parents and/or very poor parents whose day-to-day life is stressful and even dangerous are also at risk for maltreatment.

Listening Partners: *The Lamoille Family Center,*
Morrisville, Vermont

Listening Partners is a prevention program aimed at strengthening the families of poor rural women with young children. The model is built on the premise that there is a relationship between the parents' level of cognitive and moral development and their childrearing practices. With the use of tape recorders, isolated parents are provided with an opportunity to talk about their concerns and frustrations and to receive constructive feedback from supportive peers and professionals.

The Family Place, *Washington, D.C.*

The *Family Place*, Inc. is a nonprofit community drop-in center for low-income parents and parents-to-be. The *Family Place* provides a range of services including emergency assistance, counseling, developmental assessments of infants and children, group discussions, play groups, and skill-building workshops. The workshops involve prenatal care, home-life skills, handicrafts, and parenting special-needs children. All services rendered by The Family Place are free. A unique feature of The *Family Place* is that all staff members speak both English and Spanish.

Families at risk because of minority or immigrant status

Immigrant and minority status when paired with poverty, uprootedness, and isolation increases the risk of giving birth to a premature or handicapped child and of dysfunctional parenting. Programs focusing on immigrant and migrant populations may target expectant parents or parents with infants and young children.

Un Comienzo Sano: A Healthy Beginning, *University of Arizona,*
Yuma County, Arizona

Un Comienzo Sano: A Healthy Beginning is a prenatal education pilot project in the Hispanic farm-worker communities of Yuma County, Arizona. The program includes three elements: 1) a delivery system utilizing indigenous leaders as "Health Protectors," 2) a Spanish-language prenatal education guide, *Un Comienzo Sano,* developed by the Arizona Health Education Centers Program, and 3) a network of local health professionals who serve as program resources. The primary purpose of the program is to improve the health status and increase the utilization of community resources in a rural population of Mexican-American pregnant women.

Avance: *Educational Programs for Parents and Children,*
San Antonio, Texas

The *Avance* Education Program for parents and children is a private nonprofit community-based organization in San Antonio, Texas. *Avance* serves predominately low-income Mexican-American families, primarily mothers and children. Services are provided in three centers located in or adjacent to a federally funded housing project. A 1980 survey of the *Avance* catchment area indicated that 85% of the respondents reported having no occupation, while the remaining 15% held unskilled or semiskilled positions. Many of the parents in the *Avance* program were abused as children, were under economic and social pressure, had ineffective support systems, and have little knowledge of child growth and development. Seventy-seven percent of the parents were high school dropouts.

Avance services are comprehensive in scope and include six separate programs focusing on different populations. These include a two-parent Child Education Program, an educational opportunities and economic development program, a homebound child abuse project, two parent/teen projects, and exercise and arts and crafts classes for parents.

Parents at risk because of intrapersonal characteristics

While poverty and isolation increase the risk factors associated with abuse and neglect, potentially maltreating parents are not found exclusively in demographically targeted populations, and all members of demographically targeted populations do not abuse their children.   In light of this fact, investigators have also focused their attention on nondemographic risk factors that are associated with child maltreatment. Identified risk factors include a history of being abused, parental depression, a history of substance abuse, psychopathology and associated disorders in infant attachment behavior, and having a low birth weight or handicapped infant.

Having a low birth weight or handicapped infant is a particularly important nondemographic risk factor because the infant is in double jeopardy.   On the one hand, the infant is at risk for future problems on the basis of his medical status.   On the other hand, the infant is at risk of parental maltreatment.

A transactional model of parenting suggests that the infant influences parental behavior just as the parents influence the behavior of the infant.   A baby who is unresponsive because of low birth weight or handicapping conditions may be unresponsive to the caregiving overtures.   The parent may feel inadequate and neglected, and in some instances, the stage for maltreatment is set.   Below is a sampling of the many excellent programs available in the area of prevention.   A comprehensive description of these programs is beyond the scope of this chapter because all programs aimed at reducing the incidence or sequelae of low birth weight, and/or handicapping conditions can be considered as secondary prevention.

Newborn Follow-up Project, *California State University*

The *Newborn Follow-up Project*, funded by the California State Department of Health Services, Maternal/Child Health Branch, is an in-home intervention program for high-risk infants who had been in a neonatal intensive care unit.   The *Project* provides assessment, evaluation, monitoring, support and direct nursing intervention to infants and their families who have been identified as having multiple risk factors at the time of delivery.

Home visits are made over a two-year period by an Infant Development Specialist.   Home visits are supplemented by parent support groups targeting adolescents, substance-abusing families, families who experienced the previous loss of a child, and families with special ethnic and cultural needs.

PPSP: *Postpartum Support Project, Presbyterian Hospital and the New York City Department of the Aging*

The *Postpartum Support Project* (PPSP) is a research demonstration project supported by the National Center on Child Abuse and Neglect for new parents identified as at-risk on the basis of relational failure. The project includes regular home visits, foster grandparents, a mothers support group, and social work services in a comprehensive short-term preventive intervention program.

The first component of the *PPSP* program is a home visit by the project social worker and research psychologist to check on the safety of the neighborhood. Following the visit parents are paired with trained foster grandparents. Criteria used in pairing mothers and foster grandparents include ethnic group, personality, accessibility by public transportation, and family activity level. Foster grandparents are expected to visit two different homes for four hours on a twice a week basis. The purpose of these visits is to provide the mother company as well as assistance in managing the demands of children and household. The second component of *PPSP* is a weekly mothers' support group. Support meetings are led by the project social worker. Infants are included in the meeting, and parents are encouraged to discuss their concerns and express their frustration. The third component of the program consists of individual social work counseling and aid in the utilization of social support.

PCC: *The Parent-Child Center, St. Luke's Hospital Center,*
   New York, New York

The *Parent-Child Center* (PCC) provides supportive counseling to parents, and help in establishing a good parent/infant relationship. The *PCC* services families with children from birth to three years who have one or more of the following characteristics:

   Inner-city high-risk infant
   Premature infant
   Infant with chronic illnesses
   Parent-child dyads with disturbed interactions
   Mothers with emotional conflicts about their pregnancy or parenting
   Mothers under 17 years of age

Because the *PCC* services a bilingual population, services are provided in both English and Spanish.

Family Outreach, *Corpus Christi, Texas*

Family Outreach is a network of nonprofit organizations in Corpus Christi, Texas, that trains volunteers to work supportively with families at risk for neglect or abuse. The volunteers are trained to develop one-to-one relationships with potentially maltreating parents and help families access community resources. Volunteers are used to administer the *Family Outreach* programs which keep the program costs low.

Project Help, *Yakima, Washington*

Project Help is a home visitation program, sponsored by a family medical practice, for families identified as at-risk because of parent characteristics.   In addition to home visits from a "helper," expectant mothers are encouraged to attend prenatal classes and are provided with transportation for prenatal clinic visits. "Helper" services continue until the baby is one year old. A unique feature of the program is the sensitizing of medical residents to the importance of parent-infant bonding.

Multirisk families

We have categorized programs in this section in accordance with the risk factor most commonly associated with the population they serve. Unfortunately, risk factors are likely to exist in clusters. The immigrant family is likely to be poor, the teenage parent is likely to be single and to have a low birth weight infant. Regardless of the predominant population they are designed to serve, most preventive programs are designed to serve families where there are multiple sources of risk.

Family Support Center, *Upper Darby, Pennsylvania*

The *Family Support Center* is a community-sponsored agency designed to reduce the risk of neglect and abuse, avoid foster care placement, and prevent developmental delays. Participating families are selected on the basis of having a handicapped or developmentally delayed child or of having five or more stress factors identified by the project as correlated with abuse and neglect. These factors include past incidence of abuse of either the child or parent, physical or mental illness, marital stress, and environmental stress including poverty, isolation, unemployment, or criminal prosecution.

The *Family Support Center* includes three sequential components: home-based services, a Family School, and peer support groups. Home-based services include visits by a social worker or pediatric nurse. The home visitor provides the family with support and nurturance, helps the family set concrete goals, and links the family with other needed support services. Following three months of home visits the family attends the Family School which provides activities for children as well as parents. After 140 hours of Family School parents join a peer support group which provides speakers, play groups, and social functions.

The Beethoven Project, *Chicago, Illinois*

The *Beethoven Project* is an Ounce of Prevention program that is designed to prevent negative outcomes in children from multirisk families. *Beethoven* is a housing complex in Chicago for low-income, primarily welfare, tenants. The *Beethoven Project* is designed to provide a full range of services to families within the project including prenatal classes, family support services, recreation, self-help opportunities, and nursery and preschool programs. The *Beethoven Project* is considered to be an experimental program. If it is successful in achieving its objectives, the *Beethoven Project* will testify that with a full scale effort prevention can work with seemingly hopeless families.

Secondary prevention -- A summary

Secondary prevention has been defined in this chapter as programmatic initiatives designed to target families at risk for child maltreatment. This at-risk status may be associated with demographic variables, parental characteristics, or characteristics within the infant that interfere with the development of healthy parent-child interactions. Programs that target at risk populations are more costly than primary prevention programs because the intervention efforts are more intense. At the same time, secondary prevention programs are more efficient in reducing the incidence of abuse because they focus exclusively on at-risk families.

In addition to the nature of the risk factor, programs targeting families at risk differ on the basis of program variables. These differences include the type of agency sponsorship, the nature of program delivery (homebased vs. centerbased), the qualifications and professional status of the staff, the point in time when intervention is introduced (before, during, or after birth), utilization of community resources, and the length and intensity of the intervention effort. A subtle dimension of difference is the degree to which the program focuses on the factor that places the family at risk, such as substance abuse or depression, and the degree to which the program focuses on building up family resources and teaching parenting skills.

PROGRAMS FOR FAMILIES AND CHILDREN
TERTIARY PREVENTION

While primary and secondary prevention programs seek to prevent the occurrence of child maltreatment, tertiary preventive programs are concerned with preventing the reoccurrence of maltreatment and reducing negative sequelae. Tertiary prevention includes measures taken to remove a child from imminent danger (e.g., foster home placement, institutionalization, youth shelters), measures taken to protect a child from the negative sequelae of abuse, and programs designed to rehabilitate families where abuse has already occurred. It also includes preventive measures designed to reduce the negative sequelae of actions taken in response to abusive incidents.

Tertiary prevention for children

Tertiary prevention programs targeted at the child include a wide range of therapies and therapeutic programs, crisis intervention programs including crisis centers, foster care placement, therapeutic interventions, and provision of designated supporters such as foster grandparents or guardians ad litem. Therapeutic programs for maltreated children have several purposes: to mitigate the effects of the maltreatment experience, to break the generational cycle of abuse, to ease the child's pain, and to reduce the potential of provocative behavior that could lead to the reoccurrence of abuse.

Play therapy is the treatment of choice for counteracting the sequelae of abuse in young children. Play therapy provides the child with opportunities to replay negative experiences in a safe environment and to play out feelings of anger, rejection, anxiety, and repressed hostility. Art therapy and dance therapy can be incorporated successfully into a play therapy session. Play therapy can take place on an individual or a group basis.

Therapeutic Child Care, *Early Childhood Development Association, Broward County, Florida*

Theraplay is a group play therapy program in Broward County, Florida for preschool children under protective services based on adjudicated maltreatment. Theraplay group play sessions take place twice a week in Title XX child care settings administered by a community-based nonprofit organization, Early Child Development Association. Parent group meetings, held in the evenings, include training in stress management, child development, and child management techniques. Once a month parents and children meet together providing the program staff an opportunity to facilitate parent-child interactions.

Tertiary prevention for parents

Tertiary prevention/intervention programs for parents are programs that are initiated after the maltreatment has occurred. In some cases parents are separated from their children because the safety and well-being of the child are considered to be at stake. In other situations, particularly when the problem is neglect rather than abuse, parents and children remain together.

Tertiary prevention/intervention models include family therapy, substance abuse programs, and stress management programs. Intervention agents include visiting nurses or social workers, foster grandparents, center-based and institution-based therapists. Additional support services for families at risk for repeated maltreatment include hotlines, respite care, emergency babysitting programs, and Parents Anonymous.

Home Builders Program, *Behavioral Sciences Institute,*
Pierce, Spokane and Snohomish
Counties, State of Washington

The *Home Builders Program* provides intensive in-home intervention for abusing families.   The purpose of the program is to provide intensive intervention to dysfunctional families as an alternative to removing children from the home. Social workers assigned to families are on call 24 hours a day. The *Home Builders Program* is currently being replicated in the South Bronx, New York.

Tertiary prevention -- A summary

Tertiary prevention initiatives are high cost programs designed to prevent the reoccurrence of abuse or mitigate its sequelae. From one point of view, tertiary prevention efforts could be looked upon as treatment. From a different point of view, tertiary prevention could be thought of as long-range primary prevention potentially reducing the incidence of abuse in future generations.

Section summary

In this section we have focused on programmatic initiatives designed to prevent the occurrence of neglect and abuse by strengthening the resources of the family. In actuality programs designed to prevent abuse are not very different from programs designed to prevent other negative developmental outcomes, including school delay. Factors that place a family at risk for abuse and neglect such as poverty, isolation, minority status, and lack of a support system are the same factors that increase the risk of school failure, developmental delay, and conduct disorder. On the positive side, programs that focus on strengthening families, whether or not their prime purpose is the prevention of abuse, can produce many positive outcomes, including a reduction in the incidence and severity of child maltreatment.

PREVENTIVE EFFORTS TARGETING SYSTEMS
THAT IMPACT DIRECTLY OR INDIRECTLY
ON FAMILIES AT RISK FOR ABUSE

Programs designed to prevent abuse and neglect through direct intervention with families have as their primary goal the facilitation of positive parent-child interactions and the strengthening of family resources. Prevention efforts that target systems outside of the family take two quite different approaches to maltreatment prevention. While some programs are designed to increase the responsiveness of the system to the needs of families and thereby buffer families against stress that leads to abuse, other initiatives focus on systems are designed to protect children from potentially abusing adults. Garbarino (1987) describes these two thrusts as the juxtaposition of social control and social nurturance.

In this section we look at six systems that impact on families; the child care system, the schools, the work place, the medical system, the court system, and the media. As we describe preventive initiatives we will identify ways in which different systems assume the dual function of nurturing families and protecting children against parental maltreatment. The nature of prevention efforts targeting systems, just as with programs affecting families and children, can be thought of primary, secondary, or tertiary.

Primary prevention involves those initiatives that affect the system's responses to all children and families, such as efforts to provide quality day care for all parents in the work place. Secondary prevention targets programs impacting on high-risk populations, such as the passage of legislation making the public school system responsible for meeting the needs of infants and toddlers classified as high-risk children. Tertiary prevention involves initiatives addressing treatment or intervention programs and may focus on either training or legislative issues. Depending on the specific objectives, initiatives involving any of the systems discussed below can represent primary, secondary, or tertiary prevention.

Child care

Child care is associated with the prevention of child abuse in two distinct ways. First, as adults interacting with children, child care workers are potential abusers of children and laws have been enacted to protect children in child care settings. Second, child care is a critical resource for families. Families who do not have access to quality and affordable child care may be forced to place their children in inadequate facilities or leave their children unattended. Furthermore, the unavailability of adequate options can increase family tensions with abuse as a possible outcome.

Concerns with protecting children from the possibility of abuse in child care has led to a proliferation of child care laws and ordinances. For example, many states require background checks on child care staff and mandatory courses in child abuse prevention for child care workers. Training courses are designed to make child care workers aware of unacceptable disciplinary practices, alert child care workers to the signs and symptoms of abuse, and inform child care workers of mandatory reporting procedures. Whereas training components focusing on improving child care skills represent primary prevention, those aspects of training involving recognition and reporting of maltreatment are tertiary in nature.

Schools

Programs have been implemented within primary, elementary, and high schools to sensitize school personnel to the problems of abuse. Workshops, manuals for teachers, and media presentations have been used to educate teachers to identify early signs of abuse and neglect, to be good listeners when children disclose abuse, and to follow appropriate reporting procedures.

School systems are involved in primary and secondary, as well as tertiary, child abuse prevention. Schools that are responsive to the needs of individual students, provide opportunities in decision making and value clarification, help young people recognize their own potential, and that explore career opportunities are engaging in primary prevention.

Work place

With an estimated 52 percent of mothers with children under six in the work force, pressures associated with the work place have had a disruptive effect on family life. In a series of studies sponsored by the Bank Street College of Education, Ellen Galinsky (1980) interviewed working families and identified major stressors that working families experienced. The stressors described by parents include problems associated with work hours, inflexible schedules, time spent in transit, and problems associated with providing child care and care of aging parents.

Corporate policies identified by Galinsky that reduce parental stress include flexible work hours, job-sharing opportunities, more liberal overtime and personal days, variable maternity/paternity leave procedures, dependent care assistance, preventive health benefits, employee assistance and counseling services, and child care support.   Although most corporations have not adopted the kinds of reforms advocated by the Bank Street study, corporate child care is becoming increasingly popular. Employers who have instituted child care on their premises point to several advantages. Employee morale is better, absenteeism is reduced, and corporations are able to attract and maintain higher quality employees.

Historically, the first and probably the best known employer sponsored child care centers were sponsored by the Kaiser Corporation in Portland, Oregon, during the Second World War. In order to accommodate working mothers, Kaiser centers were open 24 hours on a year-round basis (Child Care Initiatives, AMA Survey Report, 1983).

The legal system

The legal system has the ultimate responsibility for enforcing child abuse laws. In some instances child abuse laws are unequivocal, and guilt and innocence are easy to establish. In most cases, however, decisions related to child maltreatment are a matter of judgment, and judges and jurists are left wrestling with questions revolving around parental rights, the best interests of children, and the ability of the family to respond to treatment.

The Bridge Family Center, *Atlanta, Georgia*

The *Bridge Family Center* in Atlanta, Georgia, provides services for families in crisis. In addition to sexual abuse treatment programs that provide assistance to the child victims and parent abusers, the *Bridge* also offers training to family and juvenile court judges as well as district attorneys. A major goal of the training is to help professionals understand the dynamics of sexual abuse and minimize damage to victims and families as they go through the court system and post-jail adjustment period.   The training program was developed by *Bridge* in conjunction with the Council of Juvenile Court Judges, the Judicial Council, the District Attorney's associate, and the Georgia Police Academy.

The medical system

Historically, the medical profession has taken a lead role in recognizing and publicizing the problem of child abuse.   Because nurses, doctors, and hospital personnel are in a prime position to identify signs and symptoms of abuse and neglect, medical professionals play a central role in maltreatment prevention.

Prevention programs that target the medical profession include:

1)   Educational programs to sensitize professionals to the importance of preparing expectant parents for parenthood, and of teaching parenting skills (primary prevention).

2)   Educational programs for medical personnel working in maternity wards, ICU's, and nurseries.   These programs, which represent secondary prevention, alert doctors and nurses to early signs of parenting disorders, including maternal depression, substance abuse, and difficulties with bonding.

3)   Educational programs alerting all medical personnel to the indicators of maltreatment and informing personnel of required reporting procedures (tertiary prevention).

The media

Because violence on television has been associated with increased aggression, child abuse is often blamed on television watching.   The argument is given that people who watch violent television shows develop a distorted set of values in which violence is permissible and even justified.   Controlling the amount of violence on television particularly during prime time is frequently suggested as a measure to prevent abuse.

While the media has been implicated in the spread of child abuse, it also plays a critical role in child abuse prevention.   Several excellent documentaries on child abuse have received national coverage.   Popular magazines and newspaper articles made the public aware of and sensitive to physical and sexual abuse.   The book, *Death from Child Abuse, No One Heard* (the true story of the last week of a child's life), has sparked a grassroots effort to heighten public awareness of child abuse.   Ironically, child neglect has received relatively little attention in the media, even though it is more frequently reported than all other forms of maltreatment.

Section summary

In this section the focus has been on systems that play a role in the prevention of child abuse by impacting the social spheres in which children and families are involved.   In many instances, the systems we describe play a dual role, providing supports to the family on the one hand and on the other hand imposing sanctions when the well-being of the child is in jeopardy.   Inevitably, the balance between family nurturance and social control is delicate and precarious.   A system that is nurturant to families protects their rights to privacy and allows the family to make decisions related to child rearing.   At the same time a system that is protective of children must reserve the right to intervene when the actions of a family have the potential of harming their child.

BROADER SOCIOCULTURAL ISSUES
OF PREVENTION

In the previous sections, two different approaches to child abuse prevention were described.   In the first approach, intervention initiatives are focused on families and children directly.   In the second approach, intervention initiatives are focused on systems within the community that impact on families and children.   In this final section, we consider the effectiveness of child abuse efforts to date and frame our current efforts in the broader context of national policy and cultural priorities.

Efficacy of child abuse prevention

In seeking to evaluate the efficacy of child abuse prevention two different questions can be asked.   The first question relates to the success of child abuse prevention efforts.   To what degree are programs successful in reducing the incidence and severity of child abuse?   The second question relates to the cost/benefit ratio. Can abuse prevention programs be justified from an economic as well as a humanitarian viewpoint?   In order to answer the second questions we will look at estimates of the cost/benefit ratio of child abuse prevention, comparing the cost of preventive programs to the cost to society when a child is the victim of abuse.

Program evaluations

Because evaluations of program outcomes are costly and difficult, relatively few summative and/or longitudinal evaluations have been undertaken of the programs described in this chapter.   Where evaluations have been undertaken, they often measure intermediate objectives, such as program attendance, reduction of the incidence of infants with low birth weight, or an increase in the percentage of infants demonstrating secure attachment behavior, rather than demonstrating a change in abuse statistics.

The Family Support Center in Upper Darby, Pennsylvania, is one of very few programs that has implemented an evaluation designed to measure the effect of the program on the incidence of child abuse. The outcome evaluation compared the incidence of abuse in program families with a sample of at-risk families with comparable risk factors. In the untreated sample, nine out of 49 infants were maltreated over a 12-month period. Of the 74 children receiving home-based services through the Family Support Center, only four were maltreated over a 10-month period. Based on this data the incidence of abuse was reduced from one in nine families to one in eighteen.

Cost/benefit ratio of child abuse

Estimating the cost benefit ratio of child abuse is not an easy task. In order to derive a relatively accurate cost/benefit ratio we would have to answer the following questions. How successful are preventive programs in reducing the incidence of abuse? What is the average cost of an effective preventive program? What is the average cost to society of a child who is abused and who, as the result of abuse, becomes a societal failure?

Irving Harris, president of The Ounce of Prevention Fund, in an address published by the Child Study Center, Yale University (1987), makes the following estimates. Six hundred thousand children are born each year at high risk of societal failure. Without intervention at least half of these children would become societal failures. The cost to society of a failed individual is $300,000. Using Harris' figure and assuming that the cost of intervention is $10,000 per child, a national intervention program would cost $6 billion. This would result in a savings of $45 billion (150,000 x $300,000) with a cost/benefit ratio of slightly better than 7-1. These figures are impressive and argue favorably for increased efforts toward a national initiative.

The broader context of abuse

Despite the dearth of outcome studies, there is a general consensus that well-designed preventive programs reduce the incidence of child abuse in at-risk populations by at least 50%. There is also a general consensus that prevention makes sense from an economic as well as a humanitarian point of view. The unresolved issue, however, for many child advocates is not whether or not prevention works but if it works well enough. Is a 50% reduction in child abuse a satisfactory outcome? Is it good enough to have as our objective the protection of children from harm, or should we look toward a society that provides all children with the opportunity to reach their full potential?

In a discussion of the principles of child abuse prevention Garbarino (1980) points to two approaches to intervention. One approach targets "discrete pieces of the problem of child abuse in isolation from the broader socioeconomic, cultural and political context." The other approach views child abuse in the context of social reform. Because the highest correlate of child abuse is low socioeconomic status, many child advocates take the position that an all-out effort to combat the maltreatment of children must begin with social reform. Such social reform, reflecting true primary prevention, can only come about if there is a national shift in priorities and a rededication to the welfare of children and their families.

responsibility of the family. A society concerned with its own survival must assume joint custody of its children, providing each child with the maximum opportunity to grow and thrive in a fully functioning and nurturant family. As we provide buffers and supports for families, the immediate benefactors are the children in the family and the ultimate benefactors are the children and society of the future.

CHAPTER SUMMARY

This chapter has presented programs and issues relating to the prevention of child maltreatment. Prevention can be viewed 1) involving the target of the prevention effort (families/children, systems affecting families/children, or broader sociocultural issues), and 2) whether the effort represents primary, secondary, or tertiary prevention. Primary prevention involves broad-based efforts aimed at improving conditions for all children and families, whereas secondary prevention targets children and families who are considered to be at risk for maltreatment. Tertiary prevention involves efforts to respond to maltreatment in way which minimize the negative consequences and decrease the probability that maltreatment will recur in the future. While prevention initiatives targeting children and families or the systems that impact on children and families contribute greatly to improving the quality of life for the individuals involved, the greatest social benefit will ultimately result from fundamental reforms leading to a set of social conditions in which all children are assured the opportunity to fully develop into healthy, productive adults.

REFERENCES

A.L. Mailman Family Foundation, Inc. Annual Report, 1985-1986. White Plains.

Bronfenbrenner, U. (1979). Ecology of Human Development. Cambridge: Harvard University Press.

Cicchetti, D., Bush, M., Toth, S., & Gillespie, J.F. (1987). "Stage-salient Issues in Infancy and Toddlerhood: Implications for a Transactional Model of Intervention and Cognitive Development Theory, Psychology, and Intervention." In E. Names & P. Cowan (eds.), New Directions in Developmental Psychology. San Francisco: Jossey Bass.

---- (1987). Children in Need: Investment Strategies for the Educationally Disadvantaged. New York, Committee for Economic Development.

Galinsky, E. (1986). "Family Life and Corporate Policies." In M. Yogman & T.B. Brazelton (eds.), Support of Families. Boston: Harvard University Press.

Garbarino, J., & Sherman, D. (1980). "High Risk Neighborhoods and High Risk Families: The Human Ecology of Child Maltreatment." Child Development, 51, 188-198.

Harris, I.B. (1987). "What Can We Do to Prevent the Cycle of Poverty?" Yale University, Clifford Beers Lecture.

Kagan, S.L., Powell, D.R., Weissbourd, B., & Zigler, E.F. (1987). America's Family Support Programs. New Haven: Yale University Press.

Krupinski, E., & Westel, D. (1987). Death from Child Abuse and No One Heard. Winter Park, FL: Currier-Davis Publishing.

Maged, R.Y. (1983). Child Care Initiatives for Working Parents. The AMA Survey Report. New York.

Tereszkiewicz, L. & Brindis, C. (1986). "School-based Clinics Offer Health Care to Teens." Youth Law Review, 7, August.

APPENDIX A

National Resources

REPORTING

National Child Abuse Hotline
800-422-4453

Handles crisis calls and provides information and referrals to every county in the United States.   The hotline is manned by professionals holding master's or Ph.D. degrees in psychology.   The hotline also provides literature about child abuse prevention.   Referrals include the telephone numbers for reporting child abuse, shelters, legal aid, mental health, sexual abuse treatment programs, advocacy, and various national organizations.

The National Center for Missing and Exploited Children
1835 K Street, N.W., Suite. 700
Washington, DC 20006
202-634-9821

The center has a toll-free telephone number (800-843-5678) for reporting information that could lead to the location and recovery of a missing child.   The center assists families, citizens' groups, law enforcement agencies, and governmental institutions.

TRAINING AND INFORMATION

American Humane Association (AHA)
American Association for Protecting Children
9725 E. Hampton Avenue
Denver, CO 80231

The American Humane Association is a national center for creating and promoting child protective services in every community.   It provides training, education, program planning, community planning, and consultation.

American Medical Association (AMA)
Department of Human Behavior
535 N. Dearborn Street
Chicago, IL 60610

The American Medical Association provides referrals related to child abuse and family violence; a copy of the *AMA Diagnostic and Treatment Guidelines Concerning Child Abuse and Neglect* is available free upon written request.

C. Henry Kempe National Center for the Prevention and Treatment of Child Abuse and Neglect
1205 Oneida Street
Denver, CO 80220
303-321-3963

The center conducts training programs, offers technical assistance and emphasizes the development of treatment programs for abused children. A catalog of materials and services is available upon request.

Child Welfare League of America (CWLA)
67 Irving Place
New York, New York 10003
212-254-7410

The Child Welfare League of America is an organization composed of direct-service agencies throughout The United States and Canada. Members include both public and private agencies. This organization sets standards for its members to assist them in providing quality social services for children and their families. A catalog of audio-visual materials and publications is available free upon request.

Coalition for Child Advocacy
P.O. Box 159
Bellingham, WA 98227

Presentations to service clubs, church groups and middle and high schools on child abuse and neglect issues. Volunteers demonstrate through theater to parents and teachers how to provide children with the the skills to prevent sexual abuse. Players also teach parenting skills through theater. The Family Support Team is a parent-aide program made up of trained volunteers working with families in which child abuse, neglect, or sexual abuse has occurred. Multidisciplinary teams meet monthly to review child abuse and neglect and sexual abuse cases. A resource center loans films and articles on child abuse and neglect and related issues. A crisis nursery in Island County provides parents respite from the demands of parenting. There is also a research project called "Child Watch: Looking Out for America's Children" which investigates the effects of reductions in services to children and families.

Family Service America
44 E. 23rd Street, 10th Floor
New York, New York 10010

A membership organization of agencies that deals with family problems, serving more than a thousand communities throughout the United States and Canada. Sponsors conferences, offers technical assistance, and provides library services to FSA agencies to help them improve the quality of services offered. Member agencies serve families and individuals through counseling, advocacy, and family life education. Agencies also deal with adolescent single parents.

International Society for the Prevention of Child Abuse and Neglect
1205 Oneida Street
Denver, CO 80220
303-321-3963

The society provides a forum for the exchange of information on child abuse and neglect by publishing *Child Abuse and Neglect: The International Journal* and by sponsoring an international congress on child abuse and and neglect every two years.

National Committee for Prevention of Child Abuse
Box 2866E
Chicago, IL 60690
312-663-3520

A volunteer-based organization of concerned citizens working with community, state, and national groups to increase and convey knowledge about child abuse prevention and to render that knowledge into community action through sound policies and prevention programs.

National Directory of Children and Youth Services
P.O. Box 1837
Longman, Colorado 80502-1837
303-776-7539

A regularly updated National Directory which includes a comprehensive county by county listing of health and social service agencies serving children in each of the 50 states. Also includes national resource information and a "Who's Who in Federal Children and Youth Services."

Youth Services Clearinghouse, Contact Center, Inc.
P.O. Box 81826
Lincoln, NE 68501
800-228-8813

Provides information on youth-serving programs and materials for youth service providers and policymakers on such topics as juvenile corrections and alternatives, delinquency prevention, runaways, alcohol and drug abuse, youth employment, status offenders, sexuality, schools, youth victims, funding, and legal perspectives and legislation.

TREATMENT AND PREVENTION

Adults Molested as Children United
P.O. Box 952
San Jose, CA 95108
408-280-5055

A self-help program for adults who were sexually abused as children and may be now suffering the low self-esteem, anger, and guilt often experienced by the victims of child sexual abuse. Members are involved in weekly therapy groups to resolve the conflicts and problems that the sexual abuse has caused in their lives.

American Family Society
Washington, DC 20088
301-460-4455

An independent, nonprofit organization designed to help improve the quality of family life. Helps parents by providing ideas that support family unity. Publishes the Family Time Calendar, which gives many ideas on family activities, and Family Matters, a monthly newsletter.

Big Brothers/Big Sisters of America
230 N. 13th Street
Philadelphia, PA 19107
215-567-2748

Single parents and families under stress can find extra support and occasional respite from parenting responsibilities through this program. Under the direction of a professionally trained staff, volunteers support families by working with children in need of additional attention and friendship.

Parents Anonymous
800-421-0353 (Toll free outside California)
800-352-0386 (Inside California)

Self help groups serve parents under stress and parents with abused children. Group members support and encourage each other in searching out positive alternatives to abusive behavior. One of the members is selected as the leader and becomes the group's chairperson. The chairperson is aided and backed up by a sponsor who is a professional in one of the mental health fields. There are no fees, and no one is required to disclose his or her name.

Parents United/Daughters and Sons United
P.O. Box 952
San Jose, CA 95108
408-280-5055

A national self-help organization with many local chapters throughout the United States. Assistance to families involved in child sexual abuse and also sponsors self-help groups for adults who were sexually abused as children. Daughters and Sons United gives help to child victims of sexual abuse whose parents are involved with Parents United.

Saint Joseph Center for Abused Handicapped Children
555 North 30th Street
Omaha, NE 68131
402-449-6511

Purpose of the center is to identify, evaluate, treat, and prevent the abuse and neglect of handicapped children in the United States. Consulting services also available.

LEGAL

National Association of Counsel for Children
1205 Oneida Street
Denver, CO 80220
303-321-3963

A national membership organization of attorneys and others involved in juvenile court proceedings. Members specialize in child abuse and neglect and other cases in which children's legal interests need to be protected. This organization sponsors training and educational conferences for attorneys, child advocates, and guardians ad litum. Legal fees are negotiated on an individual basis.

APPENDIX B

State Reporting and Program Information

The following is a state-by-state reference which presents information on child abuse reporting and agencies to contact for additional information on local programs for children and families. Reporting information includes the agencies to which suspected abuse or neglect should be reported, the services provided by these agencies, and a list of professions legally mandated to report suspected maltreatment. The "usual group" of professions mandated to report include physicians, law enforcement agents, educators, health care workers, psychologists, and other mental health providers. Deviations from this list are noted on a state by state basis.

The programs noted for each state can provide information regarding services available locally as well as current updates regarding local treatment and prevention initiatives. While every effort has been made to assure the information below is accurate, many programs rely on annual funding and/or private donations for their operations, and the information may change quickly in accord with changes in funding. The authors apologize for cases in which the information below may have changed or became obsolete.

ALABAMA

Report To: County Department of Human Resources

Written follow-up report should follow immediately. Reporters may remain anonymous.

Mandated Reporters: Usual group, including coroners

Services Provided: Homemaker and parent aid services as preventive measures are provided, as well as foster, day, and adoptive care services, in addition to public awareness programs implemented by the Department of Education.

Other Programs Available:

Alabama Children's Trust Fund
P.O. Box 4251
Montgomery, AL 36103
205-261-5710

Children's Center
Funded by Exchange Club
205-833-6221

Sunshine Center
A private agency of Montgomery Family Violence Center
205-263-2300

Parent's Anonymous
205-265-7838

For Information
Concerning Other
Programs Contact: State Department of Human Resources
Bureau of Family & Children's Services
Office of Child Safety
64 North Union Street
Montgomery, AL 36130-1801
205-261-3409

ALASKA

Report To: (statewide)
1-800-478-4444

Written follow-up report not required.

Mandated Reporters: Usual group including audiologists, hearing aid dealers, religious healing practitioners and surgeons.

Services Provided: Adult and child protection services; foster care; day care; adoption services; homemaker program; emergency shelter; case work and case management services; youth corrections services; domestic violence programs; some public awareness; parent aid in Juneau and Sitka; programs similar to parent aid in other communities.

Other Programs
Available: Parents United (Anchorage area only)

For Information
Concerning Other
Programs Contact: Department of Health and Social Services
Division of Family and Youth Services
P.O. Box H-05
Juneau, AK 99811-0630
907-586-1861

ARIZONA

Report To: Administration for Children, Youth & Families
602-542-3981

Written follow-up report required from mandated reporters

Mandated Reporters: Usual group

Services Provided: Child Protection Services (CPS) clients may be subsidized
for day care services.   CPS also provides parent aide
services, shelter care, counseling and day support programs,
foster care and adoption services, community education,
and case management for open cases with treatment
referrals.

Other Programs
Available: Parent Support Center
2415 East Fillmore Street
Phoenix, AZ 85008
602-273-6961

Parents Anonymous
2509 East Fillmore Street
Phoenix, AZ 85008
602-275-0555
HELPLINE HOTLINE: 1-800-352-0528

Prehab of Arizona
P.O. Box 5860
Mesa, AZ 85211-5860
602-969-6955

Child Sexual Abuse Treatment Center
4653 South Lakeshore Drive, Suite 2
Tempe, AZ 85282
602-820-2208

Victim Witness Program
5850 West Glendale Avenue
Glendale, AZ 85301
602-435-4063

Un Comienzo Sano: A Healthy Beginning
University of Arizona, Rural Health Office
3131 East 2nd Street
Tucson, Arizona 85716
602-626-7946

For Information
Concerning Other
Programs Contact: Community Information and Referral
                             1515 East Osborn Road
                             Phoenix, AZ 85014
                             602-263-8856

ARKANSAS

Report To: Division of Children and Family Services
                             Child Protective Service Unit
                             P.O. Box 1437
                             Little Rock, AR 72203
                             501-682-8545 or 1-800-482-5964

                             Written follow-up reports not required.

Mandated Reporters: Usual group

Services Provided: Casework; homemaker services; and family services

For Information
Concerning Other
Programs Contact: Above mentioned address

CALIFORNIA

Report To: May contact police or local Social Services Agency.

                             Written follow-up report required within 36 hours.

Mandated Reporters: Usual group

Services Provided: Emergency response system and shelters available in
                             addition to counseling and parent training programs.
                             Protective, foster, and day care services are provided at the
                             county level.

Other Programs
Available: California Children's Trust Fund
                             Office of Child Abuse Prevention
                             California State Dept. of Social Services
                             744 P Street
                             MS 9-100
                             Sacramento, CA 95814
                             916-323-2888

Newborn Follow-Up Project
California State University
5151 State University Drive
Los Angeles, CA 90032
213-343-4413

Parent Service Project (PSP)
199 Porteous Avenue
Fairfax, CA 94930
415-454-1811

For Information
Concerning Other
Programs Contact: Department of Social Services
Adult & Family Services Division
744 P Street
MS 17-18
Sacramento, CA 95814
916-445-6410

COLORADO

Report To: County Department of Social Services

Written follow-up report required although no time limit is imposed.

Mandated Reporters: Health care professionals, educators, and mental health professionals.

Services Provided: Services are provided at county level with state supervision. Placement programs (foster, day and adoptive care) in addition to alternative measures (counseling, group and day treatment programs). Licensing and supervision of day care and residential programs is performed through the state.

Other Programs
Available: C. Henry Kempe National Resource Center
303-321-3963

For Information
Concerning Other
Programs Contact: Department of Social Services
Division of Family and Children's Services
Child Protection Services
2200 West Alameda Street
Denver, CO 80223
HOTLINE: 303-893-6111

CONNECTICUT

Report To:
(statewide)

(statewide emergency services hotline - 24 hrs)
"Careline" and Central Registry
1-800-842-2288, 1-800-842-7352, 203-344-2599

(locally)

Regional office of Dept. of Children & Youth Services
(8:30-4:30)

Written follow-up report not required.

Mandated Reporters: Usual group. Reporters must provide identification.

Services Provided:

The department operates four services through four levels of continuum of care. They include preventive services, support services, supplementary services, and substitute services. The care of each child is individually guided with a treatment plan that is goal oriented, time limited, and family focused. Emergency services systems available in addition to foster and adoptive care services. The agency is also responsible for the licensing of child care facilities, foster and adoptive patents, and provisions of mental health and delinquency services.

Other Programs
Available:

Write to:
Department of Children and Youth Services
170 Sigourney Street
Hartford, CT 06105
203-566-3661

For Information
Concerning Other
Programs Contact:

Above mentioned agency

DELAWARE

Report To: Statewide HOTLINE 1-800-292-9582 (24 hrs.)

Written follow-up report not required.

Mandated Reporters: Anyone suspecting maltreatment with special emphasis on the usual group, including medical examiners.

Services Provided: Protective Services investigations;   direct or contracted services for counseling, parent aides, day care, support and educational information. Also provides foster and adoptive care in addition to protective services.

Other Programs
Available: Parents Anonymous of Delaware
124 D. Senatorial Drive
Wilmington, DE 19807
302-654-1102

EPIC (Effective Pregnancy and Infant Care)
Division of Public Health
Robbins Building
P.O. Box 637
Dover, Delaware 19903
302-736-4744

For Information
Concerning Other
Programs Contact: Division of Child Protective Services
Administration Offices
330 E. 30th Street
Wilmington, DE 19802
302-571-6410

DISTRICT OF COLUMBIA

Report To: Child and Family Services Division, DHS
202-727-0995 (24 hr. number)
or
Metropolitan Police Department
202-727-4326

(The Child and Family Services Division within the Family Services Administration of DHS is charged with investigating reports of neglected children.   The Metropolitan Police Department is responsible for investigating cases of abused children.)

Written follow-up report may be requested.

Mandated Reporters: Usual group, including medical examiners

Services Provided: Emergency care;   diagnostic and treatment services; casework services such as family counselor, foster home care, vocation rehabilitation, homemaker or caretaker services, day care services, visiting nurse, alcohol or drug counseling, classes on bringing up and caring for children, and psychological services.

Other Programs
Available:

The Family Place, Inc.
3309 16th Street N.W.
Washington, DC 20010
202-265-0149

The Clearinghouse on Child Abuse and Neglect
P.O. Box 1182
Washington, DC 20013
703-821-2086

For Information
Concerning Other
Programs Contact:

Write to: Department of Human Services
Child and Family Services Division
500 First Street, NW, Rm 8000
Washington, DC 20002
202-475-0257

FLORIDA

Report To:

State Abuse Registry
Human Resources HOTLINE
1-800-96-ABUSE

Written follow-up due within 48 hrs.

Mandated Reporters:

Anyone suspecting maltreatment is mandated to report, but written follow-up is required by usual group only.

Services Provided:

Emergency shelters, crisis counseling in addition to pre-protective counseling measures. Community training of HRS staff and other child care workers within the district. Adoption, foster and day care services provided. Specialized family services are available through Dept. of HRS.

Other Programs
Available:

Building Blocks
141 N.W. 2nd Street
Belle Glade, FL 33430
407-996-3889

Child Care Connection
4740 North State Road 7
Building C, Suite 200
Fort Lauderdale, Florida 33319
305-486-3900

Kids in Distress
305-565-1601
(Crisis Line - 565-4886)

The Family Center
Nova University
3301 College Avenue
Fort Lauderdale, FL 33314
305-475-7670

Women in Distress
305-761-1133

Child Protection Team
(Broward General Medical Center)
305-355-5760

Sexual Assault Treatment Center
305-761-7273

For Information
Concerning Other
Programs Contact: Children, Youth & Family Services Program
                          Dept. of Human Resource Services
                          1317 Winewood Blvd.
                          Building 8, Room 317
                          Tallahassee, FL 32399-0700
                          904-488-5881

GEORGIA

Report To: County Department of Family & Children Services (24 hrs)
                          or
                          Contact law enforcement officials, who in turn will contact
                          county authorities.

                          Written follow-up report not required.

Mandated Reporters: Licensed health care professionals, social workers,
                          educators, child-care personnel, and law enforcement
                          agents.

Services Provided: Interstate Compact is in effect. Some counties have multidisciplinary teams for the handling of sexual abuse cases. Protective, foster care, and adoption services are provided. Also, family preservation and reunification program in some counties. In addition, "It's O.K. to Tell" campaign is an ongoing statewide public awareness project.

Other Programs
Available: The Bridge Family Center of Atlanta
                            77 Peachtree Place, N.W.
                            Atlanta, GA 30309
                            404-881-8344

                            Georgia Council for Child Abuse
                            404-653-7260
                            1-800-532-3208

For Information
Concerning Other
Programs Contact: Division of Family & Children Services
                            878 Peachtree St. N.E., Room 502
                            Atlanta, GA 30309
                            404-894-5301

HAWAII

Report To:
(OAHU Branch)   24 hr. Protective Services Intake
                            808-942-5877

(HAWAII, MAUI and
KAUAI Branches)   These three branches rely on police departments for after hours coverage.   Workers are available on emergency standby basis to assist with foster care placements as necessary.

                            All mandated reporters except the police must provide a written report following their verbal referral to CPS.

Mandated Reporters: Usual group including medical examiners and coroners.

Services Provided:
(OAHU Branch)   Child protective services; day care services; emergency shelter homes (ESH); child abuse and neglect multidisciplinary team; family services; foster care services; homemaker services; treatment services (through purchase of services; Oahu CPS advisory committee.

(HAWAII Branch)	Child protective services; child abuse/neglect multidisciplinary team (Hilo and Kona); day care services; foster care services; and homemaker services.
(KAUAI Branch)	Social services unit; day care services; emergency shelter homes; foster care; homemaker services; child abuse/neglect multidisciplinary teams; Kauai child abuse and neglect advisory committee.
(MAUI Branch)	Same as Oahu

For Information
Concerning Other
Programs Contact: Department of Human Services
P.O. Box 339
Honolulu, HA 96809
808-548-2211

IDAHO

Report To: Local Department of Health & Welfare

Written follow-up report not required.

Mandated Reporters: Usual group

Services Provided: "Nurturing" program for parents and child, as well as maternity and infant care and parenting classes through school districts.   The department also provides child development centers and licensing of child care staff. Therapeutic day care, foster care, and adoption services are also offered.   In addition, reunification programs remain widespread throughout the state.

Other Programs   *Family Advocate Program*
Available: 208-345-3344

Parent's United (sexual abuse self-help group)
208-334-6800
Tough Love (self-help for parents of teens)
208-344-6870

Victim's Assistance Programs (counseling, preparation for testifying in cases of child abuse)

Guardian Ad Litum Program
208-345-3344

For Information
Concerning Other
Programs Contact: Department of Health & Welfare
                             Division of Family & Children's Services
                             State House
                             Boise, ID 83720
                             208-334-5700

ILLINOIS

Report To: Statewide 24 hr. HOTLINE
                             1-800-25-ABUSE

                             Written follow-up report required within 48 hrs. from
                             mandated reporter.

Mandated Reporters: Usual group

Services Provided: Licensing of child care facilities, family counseling services,
                             and homemaker services are provided. Residential, foster
                             and day care services available in addition to adoptions. An
                             array of youth and community preventive projects are
                             ongoing, as well as prevention programs which are carried
                             out in the school system.

Other Programs
Available: The National Committee for Prevention of Child Abuse
                             Publishing Dept.
                             P.O. Box 94283
                             Chicago, IL 60690
                             312-663-3520
                             (Handles pamphlet publications)

                             National Committee for Prevention of Child Abuse and
                             Neglect
                             332 South Michigan Avenue, Suite 950
                             Chicago, IL 60604-4357
                             312-663-3520

                             Beethoven Project
                             c/o Ounce of Prevention
                             188 West Randolph, Suite 2200
                             Chicago, IL 60601
                             312-853-6080

Family Focus
2300 Green Bay Road
Evanston, IL 60201
312-869-4700

Illinois Child Abuse Prevention Fund
Children & Family Services
406 E. Monroe Street
Springfield, IL 62701-1498
217-785-2459

Ounce of Prevention
188 West Randolph, Suite 2200
Chicago, IL 60601
312-853-6080

*For Information
Concerning Other
Programs Contact:*   Department of Children's & Family Services
406 E. Monroe Street
Springfield, IL 62701-1498
217-785-2459

INDIANA

Report To: County Child Abuse and Neglect
HOT-LINE (24 hrs.)

HOTLINE numbers can be obtained from County
Departments of Public Welfare or the State Department of
Public Welfare/Child Welfare Social Services Division.

May also report cases to local police department or Child
Protection Services Agencies (located in county
departments of public welfare).

State Department of Public Welfare
Institutional Abuse Hotline (in state):
1-800-562-2407

For suspected cases of institutional abuse/ neglect.
Written follow-up report not required.

Mandated Reporters: Anyone suspecting maltreatment

Services Provided:
(state agencies)   Investigates alleged institutional abuse situations; consults with counties regarding the provision of CPS Services including the investigation of sexual abuse situations; licenses day care, residential, and foster care facilities; and provides comprehensive training program for Child Welfare Staff, including supervisors. The state also provides input into community awareness programs regarding child abuse and neglect and provides reimbursement for the cost of many county child welfare programs.

(county agencies)   Investigate all individual family situations; involving alleged child abuse and neglect including sexual abuse; provide ongoing services to foster homes and day care homes (including licensing); provide adoption services; and provide ongoing services and placement services to families and children when appropriate.

Other Programs
Available: Indiana Chapter for Child Abuse & Neglect
310 North Alabama Street
Indianapolis, Indiana 46204
317-634-9282

For Information
Concerning Other
Programs Contact: Division of Child Welfare Social Services
141 South Meridian St.
Indianapolis, IN 46225
317-232-4420

Field Services (child-abuse)
317-232-4431

IOWA

Report To: Central Child Abuse Registry:

In state   1-800-362-2178
Out of state   515-281-5581

Written follow-up report required within 48 hrs.

Mandated Reporters: Usual group

Services Provided: Family centered and home-based services available, in addition to foster and protective day care programs. Various support groups (i.e., Parent's United) and other preventative programs are available to heighten public awareness.

Other Programs
Available: Iowa Chapter of the National Committee for the Prevention of Child Abuse
515-281-6327

Child Protective Services
515-281-5583

Iowa Children's Trust Fund
1200 University Avenue
City View Plaza, Suite G
Des Moines, IA 50314
515-281-6327

Parents Anonymous
Des Moines, IA
515-244-8646

For Information
Concerning Other
Programs Contact: Department of Human Services
Division of Social Services
Hoover State Office Building
Des Moines, IA 50319
515-281-5758

KANSAS

Report To: Area office of The Department of Social and Rehabilitation Services, Division of Children in Need of Care
or
Local Law enforcement

Written follow-up report not required.

Mandated Reporters: Usual group

Services Provided: Family services (i.e., subsidizing of low income families, paraprofessional family support agents and direct case work services), parental education programs, and in-home family-centered therapy projects are available. Residential, foster, and day care services are provided in addition to counseling and supportive self-help groups.

Other Programs
Available: Kansas Children's Trust Fund
Youth Services
Smith-Wilson Building
300 Southwest Oakley
Topeka, KS 66606
913-296-4656

For Information
Concerning Other
Programs Contact: Department of Social & Rehabilitation Services
Division of Children in Need of Care
Smith-Wilson Building
300 Southwest Oakley
Topeka, KS 66606
913-296-3282

KENTUCKY

Report To: Statewide HOTLINE
1-800-752-6200

Parents Anonymous Counseling
1-800-432-9251

Mandated Reporters: Usual group, including dental health care professionals, medical examiners, and coroners.

Services Provided: Day, foster, and protective care available in addition to city and county prevention programs. Adoption placement provided. Marriage, individual, and family counseling available through social services.

Other Programs
Available: Child Abuse HOTLINE
502-588-4550
(In Louisville, Jefferson Counties)

Parent's Anonymous HELPLINE
(Lexington) 502-588-4550

For Information
Concerning Other
Programs Contact: Dept. of Social Services
                            275 E. Main Street
                            Frankfort, KY 40621
                            502-564-4650 or 502-564-2136

LOUISIANA

Report To: Division of Children, Youth & Family Services in the parish
                            where child resides

                            Hotline Numbers - Parish offices:

Caddo-Bossier	318-226-7622
Calcasieu	318-491-2417
E. Baton Rouge	504-925-4571
Jefferson	504-361-6008
East Bank	504-838-5345
West Bank	504-361-6083
Lafayette	318-265-5958
Orleans	504-483-4911
Ouachita	318-362-5311
Rapids, Grant & Lasalle	318-487-5116
Terrebonne	504-876-1741
Vernon (Ft Polk)	318-238-3098

                                   or

                            Report may be made to local police

Mandated Reporters: Usual group, including coroners

Services Provided: Foster care, day care, and adoptive care services are
                            provided, in addition to protective and family services.

Other Programs
Available: Louisiana Children's Trust Fund
                            Earl K. Long Hospital
                            1525 Airline Highway
                            Baton Rouge, LA 70805
                            504-358-1063

                            Louisiana Council on Child Abuse
                            333 Laurel Street, Suite 875
                            Baton Rouge, LA 70801
                            504-346-0222

For Information
Concerning Other
Programs Contact: Office of Human Development
P.O. Box 44367
Baton Rouge, LA 70804

MAINE

Report To: Adult & Children's Emergency Services

In state 1-800-452-1999
Outside of state 207-289-2983
or
Maine Department of Human Services

Written follow-up report required within 48 hrs.

Mandated Reporters: Usual group, including dental health care professionals, state fire inspector, Christian Science practitioners, and homemakers.

Services Provided: Offers child protective services including investigation, family counseling, child placement, and intervention projects with police and hospitals. Foster care services also available.

For Information
Concerning Other
Programs Contact: Department of Human Services
State House, Station 11
221 State Street
Augusta, ME 04333
207-289-3707

MARYLAND

Report To: Local Department of Social Services

Write to office of Child Protective Services in Baltimore for individual telephone numbers:

Child Protective Services
Division of Child Welfare Services
312 East Oliver Street
Baltimore, MD 21201
301-361-2235

Written follow-up report required within 48 hrs.

Mandated Reporters: Usual group

Services Provided: Emergency assistance programs are provided, in addition to individual and group therapy for parents and child.   Each county   provides intake and treatment services.   Protective, foster,   and   day   care   available   in   addition   to   adoptive services.

Other Programs
Available: Maryland Action for Prevention of Child Abuse
Parent's Anonymous
301-728-7021

Exchange Club Center for Prevention of Child Abuse
301-576-2414

(The center handles referrals from Department of Social Services and provides a home-based lay therapist program)

For Information
Concerning Other
Programs Contact: Social Services Administration
Program Management
311 West Saratoga Street, 5th Floor
Baltimore, MD 21201
301-333-0221

MASSACHUSETTS

Report To:

(Mandated Reporters)   Regional Dept. of Social Services
(between 9:00-5:00 weekdays)
(after 5:00 & on weekends)

(Non mandated)   Statewide Hotline 1-800-792-5200

Written follow-up required within 48 hrs.

Mandated Reporters: Usual group in addition to probation officers,   foster parents, firefighters, and magistrates of district courts.

Services Provided: Comprehensive emergency services; family planning and homemaker chore projects available.   Parent aides, substitute care, and sexual abuse prevention/ treatment. Intensive Family Support program in addition to services provided for women in transition including pregnant and parenting adolescents.   Extensive counseling services are available.

Other Programs Available:

American Humane Association
303-695-0811
TOLL FREE: 1-800-227-5242

Child Welfare League of America
202-638-2952

COPE (Coping with the Overall Pregnancy/Parenting Experience)
530 Tremont Street
Boston, MA 02116
617-357-5594

Judge Baker Guidance Center
617-232-8390

National Center on Child Abuse & Neglect
202-245-2856

For Information Concerning Other Programs Contact:

Dept. of Social Services
150 Causeway Street
Boston, MA 02114
617-727-0900

MICHIGAN

Report To: County offices of the Michigan Department of Social Services, Children's Protective Services Units (24 hrs)

Written follow-up report required within 72 hours from mandated reporters.

Mandated Reporters: Usual group

Services Provided: Domestic violence program, day care, foster care, adoptive care, and prevention and protection services provided in concordance with other family assistance programs. Counseling, homemakers, parent aides, parent nurturing, and parent education services are also provided. In addition, public education measures, in the way of pamphlets, videos, and media are also available.

Other Programs
Available: Michigan Children's Trust Fund
P.O. Box 30026
Lansing, MI 48909
517-373-4320

Michigan State University
(currently evaluating multidisciplinary teams for Dept. of Social Services)

Michigan Foster Care Review Board Program
1000 Long Boulevard, Suite 3
Lansing, MI 48911
517-334-6403

For Information
Concerning Other
Programs Contact: Department of Social Services
Office of Children & Youth Services
300 South Capital Avenue
P.O. Box 30037
Lansing, MI 48909
517-373-0093

MINNESOTA

Report To: Local Social Services
or
County law enforcement for non-familiar abuse

Written follow-up within 72 hrs.

Mandated Reporters: Usual group

Services Provided: Task force for child abuse, individual plans of services which could include removal of the child, protection, counseling, foster care, and adoption. Supportive/preventative services for high risk families in addition to pre- post-natal primary abuse prevention projects for high risk pregnant women, as a means of enhancing self-esteem and fostering healthy interpersonal relations.

Other Programs
Available: Minnesota Children's Trust Fund
612-296-5437 (KIDS)

Crime Victim's Witness program
612-642-0396

MELD
123 North Third Street, Suite 804
Minneapolis, MN 55401
612-332-7563

School-Based Clinics
St. Paul, MN

For Information
Concerning Other
Programs Contact: Department of Human Services
Child Protection Services
160 East Kellogg Boulevard
St. Paul, MN 55101
612-298-5655

MISSISSIPPI

Report To: Child Abuse HOTLINE (statewide)
1-800-227-8000

Mandated Reporters: Usual group, including clergy or any person having reasonable cause to suspect

Services Provided: Training of foster parents; protective, foster, and adoption services and various public awareness programs. Referral and direct treatment services also provided by the agency.

Other Programs
Available: Write to County Dept. of Public Welfare

For Information
Concerning Other
Programs Contact: Dept. of Public Welfare
                        Division of Social Services
                        P.O. Box 352
                        Jackson, MS 39205
                        601-354-0341

MISSOURI

Report To: Missouri Child Abuse and Neglect
                        HOTLINE 1-800-392-3738

                        (outside Missouri)
                        314-751-3448

                        Written follow-up NOT required.

Mandated Reporters: Usual group

Services Provided: Statewide technical assistance team comprised of
                        physicians, educators, and mental health workers to provide
                        public awareness.   Annual statewide Child Abuse
                        Conference and community based child abuse councils.
                        Protective, foster, and adoptive care provided in addition to
                        day care for families at risk. Contract services also include
                        counseling, in-home treatment, and respite care.   Family
                        therapy and parent-aide projects are also available.

Other Programs
Available: Parental Stress Helpline
                        1-800-367-2543

                        (services provided for those feeling overwhelmed due to
                        parental pressures)

                        Parent's Anonymous (local chapters)

                        Parents as Teachers: The National Center
                        8001 Natural Bridge Road
                        St. Louis, MO 63121
                        314-553-5738

*For Information
Concerning Other
Programs Contact:*   Dept. of Social Services/Division of Family Services
Children's Services Section
Broadway State Office Building
221 West High
P.O. Box 88
Jefferson City, MO 65103
314-751-3221

MONTANA

Report To: Child Abuse HOTLINE
1-800-332-6100 (in state only)
406-443-5398 (out of state)

or

Department of Family Services
P.O. Box 8005
Helena, MT 59604
406-444-3865

Written follow-up report is required.

Mandated Reporters: Usual group

Services Provided: Full service child protective services agency. Community
size will dictate the the range of services available beyond
the required CPS services.

*For Information
Concerning Other
Programs Contact:*   Department of Family Services
P.O. Box 8005
Helena, MT 59604
406-444-3865

NEBRASKA

Report To: Statewide HOTLINE 1-800-652-1999 (24 hrs.)

Written follow-up NOT required.

Mandated Reporters: Anyone suspecting maltreatment

Services Provided: Reunification strongly urged.   Crisis intervention.   Day, foster, and adoption services available.   Family therapy and community teams assist families in crisis in addition to allotting funds for family support.   The agency is responsible for the licensing and training of foster parents, along with the subsidizing of guardianships.

Other Programs
Available: Parent's Anonymous - Omaha
Children's Trust Fund
Parent's United - Omaha

For Information
Concerning Other
Programs Contact: Dept. of Social Services
Division of Family & Child Welfare
Nebraska Center for Children's Youth
2320 North 57th Street
Box 4585
Lincoln, NE 68504
402-471-3305

NEVADA

Report To: Local Welfare Division of the Dept. of Human Resources
or
Local law enforcement agency
or

(Northern part of state)   Suicide Prevention & Crisis
702-323-4533 (Hotline)

(Balance of states)   1-800-992-5757 (Hotline)

(Southern part of state)   Clark County Juvenile Court Services
702-455-5200

Written follow-up report within 72 hrs.

Mandated Reporters: Usual group, including clergy and coroners.

Services Provided: Emergency shelter care in addition to adoptive, day, and foster care services are available.   Family counseling, homemaker programs, and other family reunification projects are in operation throughout the state.

*Other Programs
Available:*   Nevada Children's Trust Fund
                              (Prevention programs)

*For Information
Concerning Other
Programs Contact:*   Dept. of Human Resources
                              Welfare Division
                              2527 North Carson Street
                              Carson City, Nevada 89710
                              702-885-4128

NEW HAMPSHIRE

Report To: Division for Children & Youth Services
                              6 Hazen Drive
                              Concord, NH 03301-6522
                              603-271-4455 or 1-800-852-3345

Mandated Reporters: Usual group, including clergy and coroners.

Services Provided: Receives and investigates reports of abuse and neglect;
                              recruits, licenses, and trains foster and adoptive families;
                              and provides child placement and family services through 12
                              offices and a centralized adoption unit.

*Other Programs
Available:*   Multidisciplinary Teams (Contact local DCYS offices for
                              contact information)

                              Home and Community Health Care
                              Parent's Anonymous
                              Commerce Building
                              Lebanon, NH 03766
                              603-448-1597

                              New Hampshire Task Force on Child Abuse and Neglect
                              P.O. Box 607
                              Concord, NH 03302
                              603-225-5441

                              Children at Risk Program
                              Dept. of Maternal & Child Health
                              Dartmouth Hitchcock Medical Center
                              Hanover, NH 03756
                              603-646-5473

For Information
Concerning Other
Programs Contact:

Dept. of Health & Welfare
Division for Child & Youth Services
6 Hazen Drive
Concord, NH 03301-6522
603-271-4455 or 1-800-852-3345

NEW JERSEY

Report To:

Office of Child Abuse Control (OCAC)

State HOTLINE 1-800-792-8610

or

Family Helpline 1-800-THE KIDS or 1-800-843-5437

OCAC will then contact a Special Response Unit worker in the perspective county to initiate a response.

Mandated Reporters:

Anyone suspecting maltreatment

Services Provided:

"Safe, Strong and Free" -- statewide child self-defense campaign. Training of foster parents at local levels and recruitment of foster parents at state levels. Protective, foster, adoptive, and day care services available. Funding for homemaker services also provided. Parental education programs and numerous services for expectant mothers are available.   Group home and residential placements available.

Other Programs
Available:

Parent's Anonymous
1-800-843-5437

Public Advocate Program

For Information
Concerning Other
Programs Contact:

Dept. of Human Services
Division of Youth & Family Services
Community Education
CN 717
1 South Montgomery Street
Trenton, NJ 08625
609-292-8318

NEW MEXICO

Report To:

Social Services County Office
(no HOTLINE)

Mandated Reporters:

Anyone suspecting maltreatment with special emphasis on professionals

Services Provided:

Substitute care; public awareness campaign and adoption services provided. Intake and treatment handled within department.

*Other Programs
Available:*

Contact: Dept. of Human Services
Social Services Division
P.O. Box 2348
Santa Fe, NM 87504-2348
505-827-4372

*For Information
Concerning Other
Programs Contact:*

Above mentioned agency

NEW YORK

Report To:

Statewide Reporting HOTLINE
(NYS Register of Child Abuse and Maltreatment)
1-800-342-3720 (24 hrs.)

Domestic Violence HOTLINE
1-800-942-6906

Written follow-up within 48 hrs. for mandated reporters.

Mandated Reporters:

Usual group, including attorneys

Services Provided:

State-supervised, county-administered child protection, foster and day care available, in addition to preventive services (i.e., child & family trust fund, community preventive services programs, and community public awareness programs). Crisis nurseries, respite care, and multidisciplinary review teams are provided.

Other Programs
Available:

New York State Children and Family
  Trust Fund Advisory Board
40 N. Pearl St., 11th Floor
Albany, NY 12243
518-474-9516

The Door: A Center for Alternatives
International Center for Integrative Studies
121 Avenue of the Americas
New York, NY 10013
212-941-9090

The Parent-Child Center
(for children 0 to 3 1/2 years)
St. Luke's Hospital
411 West 114th Street, 5C
New York, NY 10025
212-523-3089

Post-Partum Support Project
Department of the Aging
Columbia Presbyterian Hospital
622 West 168th Street
Room VB69
New York, NY 10032
212-305-7702

SCAN - N.Y. Parent-Aides Assoc., Inc.
207-215 East 27th Street
Lower Level
New York, NY 10016
212-683-2522

New York State Federation on Child Abuse and Neglect
134 South Swan Street
Albany, NY 12210
518-445-1273

For Information
Concerning Other
Programs Contact:

Dept. of Social Services
Public Information
40 North Pearl Street
Albany, NY 12243
518-474-9516

NORTH CAROLINA

Report To: Local Dept. of Social Services

Mandated Reporters: Anyone suspecting maltreatment

Services Provided: Each county department of social services provides the following child welfare services: adoption, day care, and foster care services, in addition to protective and chore/homemaker services. Health support and individual/ family adjustment services also provided.

Other Programs
Available: Child Protective Services
                                325 North Salisbury Street
                                Albemarle Building
                                Raleigh, NC 27611
                                919-733-2580

                                Child Abuse Prevention Program
                                Dept. of Public Instruction
                                116 West Edenton Street
                                Raleigh, NC 27603-1712
                                919-733-0100

For Information
Concerning Other
Programs Contact: North Carolina Dept. of Human Resources
                                Division of Social Services
                                325 North Salisbury Street
                                Raleigh, NC 27611
                                919-733-3055

NORTH DAKOTA

Report To: County Dept. of Social Services

                                Written follow-up required within 48 hrs.

Mandated Reporters: Usual group

Services Provided: Foster, adoptive, and protective care available, in addition to homemaker assistance programs and group/individual counseling services. The agency also handles licensing and regulation of child care facilities, in addition to maintaining a public awareness campaign through the North Dakota Children's Trust Fund.

Other Programs
Available:

North Dakota Children's Trust Fund
701-224-4806

Parent's Anonymous
c/o Mental Health Association
P.O. Box 160
Bismarck, ND 58502
701-255-3692

For Information
Concerning Other
Programs Contact:

Dept. of Human Services
Office of Human Services
Children & Family Services
State Capitol
Bismarck, ND 58505
701-224-4806

OHIO

Report To: Local Children's Services Agency (24 hrs., 7 days a week)

Mandated Reporters: Usual group including speech pathologists, audiologists, and
                          coroners

Services Provided: Protective services, case management services, emergency
                          shelter, information and referral services, unmarried parent
                          services, substitute care, homemaker/home health aide
                          services, protective day care, community education, crisis
                          services, employment services, environmental management
                          services, parent aide, parent education, crisis nursery
                          services, adoption services, emergency caretaker services,
                          day treatment, and volunteer services.

For Information
Concerning Other
Programs Contact:

Family, Children, and Adult Services
Bureau Program Policy
30 East Broad Street, 30th Floor
Columbus, OH 43266-0423
614-466-9274

OKLAHOMA

Report To:

Statewide Child Abuse
HOTLINE 1-800-522-3511

or

Child Welfare Services
Local Dept. of Human Resources

Mandated Reporters: Anyone suspecting maltreatment

Services Provided: Preventative, foster, and day care provided, in addition to protective services and the licensing of child care workers and foster parents. Public awareness campaign also active throughout the state, in addition to extensive adoption services and unintended pregnancy counseling projects.

Other Programs
Available:

Office of Child Abuse Prevention Health Dept.
(not part of DHS)
405-271-4477

Parent's Assistance Center
Parent's Anonymous
405-232-8226

For Information
Concerning Other
Programs Contact:

Department of Human Services
Division of Children & Youth Services
P.O. Box 25352
Oklahoma City, OK 73125
405-521-3777

OREGON

Report To: Children Services Division - State Branch Offices

or

Local law enforcement

Written follow-up NOT required.

Mandated Reporters: Usual group

Services Provided: Family therapy, child protective services, family sexual abuse treatment program, and foster, day, and group care provided; training for foster parents available in some regions, permanent planning and adoption services, education classes, homemaker services, and juvenile parole.

Other Programs Available: Write to: Dept. of Human Resources
Children's Services Division
198 Commercial Street S.E.
Salem, OR 97310
503-378-4374

For Information Concerning Other Programs Contact: Above mentioned agency

PENNSYLVANIA

Report To:
(Mandated Reporters)   "CHILDLINE" 1-800-932-0313

(Non-mandated Reporters)   Contact: Local County Children & Youth Agency

Or call 1-800-932-0313

Written follow-up report within 48 hrs. from mandated reporters only.

Mandated Reporters: Any person who, in the course of their employment, occupation, or practice of their profession come in contact with children.

Services Provided: Child protection, foster and day care available in addition to emergency shelters; counseling services and life skills education programs. Adoption placement provided.

Other Programs Available: The Joseph J. Peters Institute of Sexual Abuse for Victims and Perpetrators

"SCAN"

Children's Hospital in Philadelphia

Children's Hospital in Pittsburgh

Parent's Anonymous

Education for Parenting
31 West Coulter Street
Philadelphia, PA 19144
215-438-1255

Family Support Center
201 South 69th Street
Upper Darby, PA 19082
215-352-7610

For Information
Concerning Other
Programs Contact:

Dept. of Public Welfare
Children, Youth, and Families
P.O. Box 2675
Harrisburg, PA 17105-2675
717-787-3984

RHODE ISLAND

Report To:

Statewide HOTLINE
1-800-742-4453

(CANTS) Child Abuse & Neglect Tracking System

Central registry for reporting
1-800-RI-CHILD (1-800-742-4453)

Mandated Reporters: Usual group

Services Provided:

Emergency shelters, child abuse prevention services, and juvenile probation and correctional programs, in addition to foster, adoptive, and day care services available. The agency also handles group and foster home licensing and certification.

Other Programs
Available:

Rhode Island Children's Trust Fund

Preventative programs including:

Parent aides program for children at risk (contracted)

Comprehensive Emergency Services - CES (contracted)

For Information
Concerning Other
Programs Contact: Dept. for Children and Their Families
610 Mount Pleasant Avenue
Providence, RI 02908
401-457-4708

SOUTH CAROLINA

Report To: County Dept. of Social Services
(each of own 24 hr. HOTLINE)

Written follow-up NOT required.

Mandated Reporters: All those in contact with the public are mandated.

Services Provided: Protective, foster, and day care services available. Family
counseling and homemaker programs provided, in addition
to foster parent training sessions and public awareness
campaigns.

Other Programs
Available: Columbia Mental Health Center
1618 Sunset Drive
Columbia, SC 29203
803-737-5550

Council on Child Abuse and Neglect
1800 Main Street, Suite 3A
Columbia, SC 29201
803-733-5430

Palmetto Place, Inc.
(Community center for abused and neglected children)
P.O. Box 3395
Columbia, SC 29230

SISTER-CARE Inc.
(Agency for abused women and their children; 24 hr. shelter
contact)
P.O. Box 1029
Columbia, SC 29202
803-765-9428

For Information
Concerning Other
Programs Contact: Dept. of Social Services
                        Child, Family, and Adult Services
                        P.O. Box 1520
                        Columbia, SC 29202
                        803-734-5670
                        (State Office - not 24 hr.)

SOUTH DAKOTA

Report To:
(Day)   County Dept. of Social Services
                                or
                        Local law enforcement
                                or
                        State Attorney's office

(After 5:00 p.m.)   Local law enforcement

                        Written follow-up required within 48 hrs.

Mandated Reporters: Usual group

Services Provided: Protective and rehabilitative services, foster and adoptive
                        care provided, in addition to the licensing and regulating of
                        group and residential homes, foster homes, and day care
                        programs.   An interstate compact, dealing with child
                        placement is in place.

Other Programs
Available: Child protection multidisciplinary teams to aid in
                        education-prevention, case management, and family
                        intervention

                        South Dakota Children's Trust Fund

                        Federal Child Abuse and Neglect

                        Prevention/Treatment Grants

                        Private treatment community groups and agencies.

For Information
Concerning Other
Programs Contact:

Dept. of Social Services
Child Protective Services
700 Governor's Drive
Pierre, SD 57501
605-773-3227

TENNESSEE

Report To:

County Social Services
        or
Law enforcement
        or
Juvenile court judge

Written follow-up report not required.

Mandated Reporters: Anyone suspecting maltreatment

Services Provided: Counseling and homemaker services available, in addition to foster, adoption, and day care programs.   Child protection plans are designed through the agency, along with educational and informational services.

Other Programs
Available:

Children in Crisis Program
LeBonheur Hospital
901-327-4766

Columbus Home Abuse Prevention
119 Dameron Avenue
Knoxville, TN 37917
615-524-3832
(Agency provides: crisis intervention up to 14 respite care foster parents - volunteers)

Memphis City School Mental Health Center
2597 Avery Avenue
Memphis, TN 38112
901-454-5200
(Agency provides: intensive therapy for sexual, as well as prevention education)

Statewide Child Sexual Abuse Task Force

Parents Anonymous

For Information
Concerning Other
Programs Contact: Department of Human Services - Social Services
Citizens Plaza Building
400 Deaderick Street
Nashville, TN 37219
615-741-5927

TEXAS

Report To: Statewide HOTLINE
1-800-252-5400

(during work hours)   Local Department of Human Services

Written follow-up report not required.

Mandated Reporters: Anyone suspecting maltreatment

Services Provided: Protective, foster, and adoptive care for children in
protective services caseloads, in addition to recruitment and
training of foster parents.   Currently, the agency is also
conducting an educational public awareness campaign.

For Information
Concerning Other
Programs Contact: Department of Human Services
P.O. Box 2960
Austin, TX 78769
512-450-3011

AVANCE
301 South Fril
San Antonio, TX 78207
512-270-4630

Family Outreach
1329 7th Street
Corpus Christi, TX 78404
512-888-6041

UTAH

Report To: Local Department of Social Services

Mandated Reporters: Anyone suspecting maltreatment

Services Provided: Prevention effort in which the community and schools aim to teach the children to recognize signs of abuse and neglect; follow-up in-house intervention is provided in addition to family and individual therapy. Substitute care, foster parent training, and crisis nurseries are available.

Other Programs
Available: Utah Children's Trust Fund

Parent's Anonymous
(Weber & Davis counties)
801-773-5770

Center for Family Development
(Salt Lake county)
801-466-8353

Parents United of Utah Valley
801-374-9952

For Information
Concerning Other
Programs Contact: Department of Social Services
Division of Family Services
120 North 200 West
Salt Lake City, UT 84103
801-538-4080

VERMONT

Report To: District Office of Dept. of Social Services
or
Central office 802-241-2131

Written follow-up within 72 hrs.

Mandated Reporters: Usual group and librarians

Services Provided: Intensive home based services and in-home parenting education programs available, in addition to therapeutic and preventative day care services. Foster and adoptive care programs active throughout the state. Mental health counseling services available. Educational public awareness projects sponsored by the agency for professional and lay persons.

Other Programs
Available: Statewide Parent's Assistance Hotline
                                1-800-PARENTS or 1-800-727-3687

                                Vermont's Parent's Anonymous

                                Speak Easy
                                Parent/Child Center of Addison County
                                11 Monroe Street
                                P.O. Box 646
                                Middlebury, VT 05753
                                802-388-3171

                                Addison County Parent/Child Center
                                11 Monroe Street
                                Middlebury, VT 05753
                                802-388-3171

                                Listening Partners
                                Psychology Department
                                University of Vermont
                                Burlington, VT 05405
                                802-656-4058

For Information
Concerning Other
Programs Contact: Agency of Human Services
                                Dept. of Social and Rehabilitation Services
                                103 South Main Street
                                Waterbury, VT 05676
                                802-241-2101

VIRGINIA

Report To: Statewide HOTLINE
                                1-800-552-7096

                                Written follow-up not required.

Mandated Reporters: Usual group including probation officers

Services Provided: Foster, protective, and adoptive care, in addition to
                                educational public awareness programs throughout the
                                state.

Other Programs
Available: Parents Anonymous

SCAN

For Information
Concerning Other
Programs Contact:

Department of Social Services
Bureau of Child Welfare Services
8007 Discovery Drive
Richmond, VA 23229-8699
804-662-9081

WASHINGTON

Report To:

Statewide HOTLINE
1-800-562-5682 (adoption support)

or

Local State Department of Social and Health Services
Division of Family & Children's Services

Written follow-up required from mandated reporters.

Mandated Reporters:

Usual group

Services Provided:

Intake and investigation of reports of child abuse and
neglect. Information and referral services for victims and
families are offered.   "Homebuilders" program, crisis
intervention service intervention service aimed at
maintaining the children in the home and "street kids"
program, a temporary shelter for children until family
reconciliation. The agency provides adoptive, foster, and
therapeutic day care, in addition to parent skills training and
a family reconciliation program. An interstate compact on
the placement of abused or neglected children also is in
operation as is an active Victims of Domestic Violence
program.

Other Programs
Available:

Write to: Dept. of Social & Health Services
Division of Children and Family Services
State Office Building, 2
Mailstop 41
Olympia, WA 98504
206-753-0419

Family Medicine of Yakima Valley
421 South 47th Avenue
Yakima, WA 98902
509-965-1776

Homebuilders Program
Behavioral Sciences Institute
34004 9th Avenue South, Suite 8
Federal Way, WA 98003
206-927-1550

For Information
Concerning Other
Programs Contact: Dept. of Social and Health Services
Division of Children & Family Services
State Office Building, 2
Mailstop 41
Olympia, WA 98504
206-753-0419

WEST VIRGINIA

Report To: Statewide HOTLINE 1-800-352-6513

or

Local Dept. of Human Services Office

Written follow-up MAY be asked of a mandated reporter within 48 hrs.

Mandated Reporters: Usual group

Services Provided: Emergency shelters, homemaker services, and child protection and day care services available. The agency is also responsible for the training of foster parents and adoption programs. Education projects designed primarily for mandated reporters.

For Information
Concerning Other
Programs Contact: Write to: Dept. of Human Services
Bureau of Social Services
Building 6, Room 850,
Capitol Complex
Charleston, WV 25305
304-348-7980

WISCONSIN

Report To: County Dept. of Social Services

Written follow-up not usually required.

Mandated Reporters: Usual group

Services Provided: Foster, adoptive, and protective services available in addition to therapeutic day care for children at risk. The agency is responsible for training foster parents and the licensing/regulation of child care facilities. Both state and county levels participate in public awareness campaigns.

*Other Programs
Available:*   Wisconsin Committee for Prevention of Child Abuse
608-256-3374

Wisconsin Children's Trust Fund
608-266-6871

*For Information
Concerning Other
Programs Contact:*   Dept. of Health and Social Services
Office for Children, Youth, and Families
State Office Building, 1W
Wilson Street
P.O. Box 7851
Madison, WI 53707
608-267-2245

WYOMING

Report To: County Dept. of Social Services
or
State Attorney's Office

Written follow-up report not required.

Mandated Reporters: Anyone suspecting maltreatment

Services Provided: Protective services are provided including legal assistance and Guardian Ad Litum, in addition to foster, adoptive, and day care programs. The agency also provides homemaker services, counseling, and runaway/independent living programs for older juveniles.

For Information
Concerning Other
Programs Contact: Department of Health & Social Services Child Support
Hathaway Building
Cheyenne, WY 82002
307-777-6098

SUBJECT INDEX